W9-DEJ-762

The Resilient Practitioner

"This visionary work is essential reading for practitioners and students in the helping fields. With poetic wisdom and academic clarity, Tom Skovholt addresses the issues involved in sustaining professional vitality."
—SALLY HAGE, Ph.D.
UNIVERSITY OF WISCONSIN

"In The Resilient Practitioner, *Tom Skovholt demonstrates a compassionate appreciation for the complexities of the helping fields. Clearly, he has experienced these developmental challenges, and has listened and guided well as others have navigated these challenging tasks. Now, in this book, his wisdom can be shared with many other 'high-touch' professionals."*
—KATE F. HAYS, Ph.D.
SPORT PSYCHOLOGIST
DIRECTOR, THE PERFORMING EDGE
TORONTO, CANADA

"Tom Skovholt has identified precisely the difficult career issues for practitioners in the helping professions. He specifies particular steps in balancing care for others and self, sustaining the professional and personal selves, and preventing burnout. Skovholt stimulated me to consider self-care in a whole new way—not as a narcissistic withdrawal from responsibility, but as a means to sustain intellectual excitement and emotional commitment to those with whom I work."
—SUSAN NEUFELDT, Ph.D.
CLINICAL SUPERVISOR
UNIVERSITY OF CALIFORNIA,
SANTA BARBARA

The Resilient Practitioner

*Burnout Prevention
and Self-Care Strategies for
Counselors, Therapists, Teachers,
and Health Professionals*

Thomas M. Skovholt
University of Minnesota

Allyn and Bacon
Boston • London • Toronto • Sydney • Tokyo • Singapore

To

my daughter Rachel
whose birth was a beautiful moment
and whose continual presence is a pleasure

and to

counselors, therapists, teachers, and health professionals everywhere
whose professional caring for others
makes this a better world.

Executive Editor: Virginia Lanigan
Series Editorial Assistant: Erin Liedel
Marketing Managers: Brad Parkins and Kathleen Morgan
Production Editor: Annette Pagliaro
Editorial Production Service: Nesbitt Graphics, Inc.
Composition Buyer: Linda Cox
Manufacturing Buyer: Suzanne Lareau
Cover Administrator: Kristina Mose-Libon
Electronic Composition: Omegatype Typography, Inc.

Copyright © 2001 by Allyn & Bacon
A Pearson Education Company
160 Gould Street
Needham Heights, MA 02494

Internet: www.ablongman.com

All rights reserved. No part of the material protected by this copyright notice may be reproduced or utilized in any form or by any means, electronic or mechanical, including photocopying, recording, or by any information storage and retrieval system, without written permission from the copyright owner.

Library of Congress Cataloging-in-Publication Data

Skovholt, Thomas M.
    The resilient practitioner: burnout prevention and self-care strategies for
    counselors, therapists, teachers, and health professionals/Thomas Skovholt.
        p.   cm.
    Includes bibliographical references and index.
    ISBN 0-205-30611-X
    1. Medical personnel—Mental health.   2. Psychotherapists—Mental health.
3. Teachers—Mental health.   4. Counselors—Mental health.   5. Medical
personnel—Job stress.   6. Psychotherapists—Job stress.   7. Teachers—Job
stress.   8. Counselors—Job stress.   9. Burn-out (Psychology)—Prevention.
I. Title.

    RC451.4.M44 S57 2000
    610.69—dc21

                                                                00-044755

Printed in the United States of America
10 9 8   07 08 09

Contents

Preface

How does the opera singer take care of the voice?

The baseball pitcher, the arm?

The carpenter, the tools?

The professor, the mind?

The photographer, the eyes?

The ballerina, the legs?

The counselor, therapist, teacher, or health professional, the self?

In this book, I address people in the "high touch" (Naisbitt, 1984) career fields—the helping professions, the caring professions, or human service, education, and health occupations. Some readers may not identify with this broad occupational group (counselors, therapists, teachers, professors, social workers, nurses, doctors, physical therapists, and other health professionals) because they seem so different. For example, a public school teacher may think that her work is very different from that of a nurse or a counselor. My own experience in all three of these arenas has helped me to see that there are great commonalities among counseling, teaching, and healing. I have worked as a psychological counselor, career counselor, and psychotherapist in many settings, with a wide variety of other counselors and therapists as colleagues. Earlier, I spent two years as a nurse's aide, working in a hospital on a team with doctors, nurses, occupational therapists, physical therapists, recreational therapists, and paraprofessional workers like myself. I felt that there were many work concerns that we all shared. Since then, I have spent many years as a teacher of college students, providing instruction from the most basic developmental courses in a junior college and at a prison to the most advanced level with doctoral students. I have also taught in community education and have given workshops and presentations to professional audiences. I view all of these as high touch professions and as caring professions because of common work ingredients.

A leading career development inventory, the Campbell Interest and Skill Survey combines "helping others through teaching, healing and counseling" into one of seven work orientations (Campbell, 1994, p. 2), providing evidence for similarity among these fields. When reading this material, I invite you to consider the commonalties rather than the differences in the careers. If the commonalties can be understood, then this material may be of use to a variety of individuals working in different high touch fields. The questions to be asked by all are: How do those in the caring professions, who use their own self as a method of change, prevent burnout and maintain professional vitality? How does one establish balance between other-care and self-care? What are the keys to practitioner resiliency?

Acknowledgments

It took part of nine years for me to write this book. Imagine how much help I had in formal and informal ways from so many people while traveling through this task. I received helpful feedback on the content from many people including Lynda Borchers, Dan Detzner, Sally Hage, Len Jennings, Fran LaFave, Susan Lee, Mary Mullenbach, John Romano, Helge Rønnestad, and L. P. Smith.

I appreciate the sustaining love from my family: my mother and father, Jane and Annie, Glen and Anna, David, Rachel, Hanna, and Cathy. I also appreciate the friendship of Shirley, Rachel, and David.

Elisabeth Nealy and Carla Hill were able and patient with word processing through many drafts. Thanks to them. I also appreciate editors Ray Short and Virginia Lanigan at Allyn & Bacon for their support and guidance.

Thomas M. Skovholt

Caring for Others versus Self-Preservation

The Great Human Drama

I tend to give my time away to others before I take it for myself.
JUNIOR HIGH SCHOOL TEACHER, 1996

I have always been better at caring for and looking after others than I have been at caring for myself. But in these later years, I have made progress.
—CARL ROGERS at age 75 (Rogers, 1995, p. 80)

There is a continual pull, constant strain, a tautness. It may not be intense. The common form is subtle, felt as body tension. Usually it doesn't knock one over. It is more like a small wave rippling through—maybe a wave going in two directions or waves pulling in three directions. Or is it four? Sometimes it is a skirmish that quickly becomes war.

Exhausted when saying yes, guilty when saying no—it is between giving and taking, between other-care and self-care. This is a universal dilemma in the human drama. It is just more intense for those in the high touch fields. It gets highly illuminated when intense human interaction—helping, teaching, or healing—is the occupational core. Here, giving of oneself is the constant requirement for success. Caring for others is the precious commodity.

The best ones struggle the most and figure it out or leave or burn, from the inside to the outside, while hope dies. It is not natural to put the other before the self. The human senses—smell, sight, taste, touch, hearing—are there to protect the me, to promote the me. To know the world through the senses of the other is like swimming upstream, naturally hard and easy to resist. How much should one work for the other—this moment, this hour, this day? When there is another day and another day and more demands and more demands.

To be successful in the high touch professions, we must continually maintain professional vitality and avoid depleted caring. For counselors, therapists, teachers, and health professionals, this can be a very difficult task. Since Freudenberger (1974) first used the term *burnout*, many authors have discussed the difficulty of professional vitality in the helping and related fields (Berry, 1988; Cherniss, 1995; Corey & Corey, 1989; Grosch & Olsen, 1994; Guy, 1987; Larson, 1993; Maslach, 1982; Pohl, Kay, & Toft, 1990; Robinson, 1992; Samples, 1991; Sussman, 1995).

A central occupational strength in the caring professions—perspective taking—makes the boundary regulation between the needs of others and the needs of self a difficult task. Occupationally, we are trained to see life from the perspective of the other, and by personality, perhaps we do this naturally. L. King (personal communication, February 1996) suggests that we often have a personal history of active caring for others: "We are often the great friend who listens, the 'fixer' in a relationship, the diplomatic person in a disagreement, and/or the 'helper' within the family of origin." In another place, I wrote:

> *One of the most distinguished characteristics of our profession is our intense focusing on highly skilled perspective taking: a combination of empathy, perceptual flexibility, tolerance for ambiguity and affective sensitivity. When successful, all of this translates into a profound ability to understand the world as other people understand it. This well-honed ability, one of our occupational strengths, is not possessed by many people in other occupations. (Skovholt, 1988, p. 283)*

In the theater of life, the other becomes the illuminated part of the stage; our I is outside the illumination. The lives of others—their hopes, ideas, goals, aspirations, pains, fears, despair, anger—are in focus. Like a leaf under a microscope, we see all of this in highly illuminated detail. As a counseling, therapy, teaching, or health practitioner, the other gets our attention. Out of the illuminated microscope, we easily lose sight of our own needs, like the need to not respond to all needs.

Settings of intense human need can be very unsettling for those in the caring professions. This occurs because we are taught to assess, experience, and respond to human need at a much more intense level than the public. That is the goal of training. Nursing homes are an example of a difficult arena. With a honed ability to do perspective taking, one can easily feel the loneliness, fear, and despair of the residents. One practitioner struggled mightily to visit her client in such a place without being overwhelmed by all the other human need. She was caught in the option of exhaustion versus guilt while searching for boundaries of when to reach out and when to pull back. Here, the "shoemaker has no shoes" problem of low self-care can easily occur. Sussman (1995) comments:

> *Many therapists, for example, grew up playing the role of caretaker, go-between, parentified child or burden-bearer within their families of origin. Having learned at an early age to attune themselves to others, therapists often have great difficulty attending to their own emotional needs. (p. 4)*

Where in the practitioner's life is self-preservation held and nurtured? Perhaps the answer can be found in the struggle between altruism and self-preservation within the bigger human drama. As a species, we have been remarkably able to increase our numbers. In recent years, it has been at an astonishing rate, from 2.5 billion in 1950 to 5.5 billion in 1993 (*Demographic Yearbook*, 1993, p. 129). We have accomplished this growth and domination of all other living species with an acute sense of species self-preservation.

Biologically, each of us is wired to preserve the self. The senses continually warn us of danger. The physical defense system fights disease and threat with white blood cells, energy pouring from the adrenal glands, and other miraculous processes. The desire to have children is often thought of as a biological self-preservation. The psychological defenses keep us from harm through the use of denial, rationalization, and projection.

Just as self-preservation seems to be such an urgent human drive, we can find evidence for altruism and self-sacrifice as central. How about the altruism and self-sacrifice of winners of the Medal of Honor, the nation's highest award for bravery? One citation reads:

First Lieut. John R. Fox, Cincinnati

> *An organized attack by uniformed German formations was launched [near Sommocolonia, Italy] around 0400 hours, 26 December 1944.... Although most of the U.S. infantry forces withdrew from the town, Lieutenant Fox reported at 0800 hours that the Germans were in the streets and attacking in strength. He called for artillery fire increasingly close to his own position.... His commander protested that...the bombardment would be too close.... The Germans continued to press forward in large numbers, surrounding the position. Lieutenant Fox again called for artillery fire with the commander protesting again... "Fox, that will be on you!" The last communication from Lieutenant Fox was: "Fire it! There's more of them than there are of us. Give them hell!" The bodies of Lieutenant Fox and his party were found in the vicinity of his position when his position was taken.... [His action] inflicted heavy casualties, causing the deaths of ap-*

proximately 100 German soldiers, thereby delaying the advance of the en-
emy. (cited by Bennet, 1997, p. E7)

Books such as *The Courage to Care* by Rittner and Myers (1986) and *Res-*
cuers: Portraits of Moral Courage in the Holocaust by Block and Drucker (1992)
tell of ordinary people who made extraordinary sacrifices of the self. Kohlberg
(1979), a leading scholar in moral development, measures morality with the
famous case of Heinz, a boy caught in the dilemma of either stealing medi-
cations to keep his mother alive or not stealing—caring for others versus
self-preservation.

The dilemma of Heinz is a sample of the larger human drama of altruism
versus self-preservation. Within this larger human pull of altruism versus
self-preservation, counselors, therapists, teachers, and health professionals
do their work, attempting to live on the balance beam between too much
other-care and too much self-care. For example, how much sleep deprivation
should the practitioner endure to adequately prepare to help the client, student, or patient the next day? This is just one example of many dilemmas
continually faced by practitioners in the high touch fields.

Exploration of the practitioner's world begins in the next chapter. There,
the deep satisfaction of high touch work is explored.

2

Joys, Rewards, and Gifts of Practice

What do we live for, if it is not to make life less difficult to each other?
—MARY ANN EVANS (Eliot, 1956, p. 537)

This is the true joy in life, the being used for a purpose recognized by yourself as a mighty one; the being thoroughly worn out before you are thrown on the scrap heap; the being a force of Nature instead of a feverish selfish little clod of ailments and grievances complaining that the world will not devote itself to making you happy.
—GEORGE BERNARD SHAW (Larson, 1993, p. 2)

When we do not care, we lose our being, and care is the way back to being.
—R. MAY (1969, p. 286)

A teacher affects eternity; he can never tell where his influence stops.
—H. ADAMS (1918, p. 300)

A person who saves one life, is as if he saved a whole world.
—THE TALMUD (translated by Danby, 1933, p. 388)

The reward of teaching is knowing that your life made a difference.
—W. AYERS (1993, p. 24)

An intimacy with suffering is the beginning of heightened psychological and spiritual awareness.
—C. GARFIELD (1995, p. 195)

I am a teacher at heart, and there are moments in the classroom when I can hardly hold the joy. When my students and I discover uncharted territory to explore, when the pathway out of a thicket opens up before us, when our experience is illuminated by the lightning—life of the mind—then teaching is the finest work I know.
P.J. PALMER (1998, p. 1)

Occupationally, we nurture human development. This can be very reward-ing! Making a positive difference in human life and being there for others are central career interests for counselors, therapists, teachers, and health professionals. The close connection to others and the opportunity to help people bring the joys, rewards, and gifts of practice. Being successful in high touch work can produce a profound sense of satisfaction.

People have asked why I did not choose a research career in a lab or a technical field such as software design. My answer is always the same—why work with things when you can work with people? Interacting closely with the most complex of all species is a great deal. The opportunity to try to make human life better is an even better deal. And to get some money for the effort is even a better deal!

What are some of the specific joys, rewards, and gifts of practice?

Joys of Practice

The focus of the work is on positively affecting human need. This goal can be elusive and difficult to achieve, a reality quite familiar to veteran practi-tioners. Consequently, when the practitioner hits a bulls-eye of success, there is a joy-of-practice reaction. Witness these joy-of-practice reactions.

Larson (1993) asked nurses to describe "the most positive moment he or she ever had as a helper." Three of them said:

> *When a wife of a patient whose case I just opened called the office after I left their home and told my supervisor, "Thank you for sending us such a wonderful nurse."*

> *When a patient said to me, "I'm so glad you're my nurse today—because I wanted you to be the one to be with me on the day I die." She died at the end of my shift that day.*

> *A mother of a child with leukemia once said, "We come to this clinic every week and know that you care for many, many children, but when you come to see us, I feel like we are the only people you have seen that day." (pp. 6–7)*

A senior psychologist at a Southern university described to me a joy in his practice:

> *I had a very nice phone message when I checked in yesterday (on my birth-day); a client who I worked with about four years ago had called to tell me that she is doing very well, is about to be married, and feels that the only*

reason she is alive and living so happily now is because of the work we did together. She had been clinically depressed and suicidal for months, and I had worked my butt off with her; such a nice result!

For a member of the clergy, the pleasure of helping came in this way:

One day he went to visit a woman who was very ill. As he started to leave the room, the woman spoke to him: "You have been such an important person in my life. I want you to know that I have great love for you." These kind words sailed straight into the minister's heart. (Rupp, 1994, p. 17)

An elementary school teacher experienced a similar "practitioner joy":

This past fall I received in the mail two letters from two former students, then beginning fifth grade. They were asked by their teacher to write a letter to their favorite elementary teacher. These two girls each wrote to me, telling me that I had been their favorite, and they each had their reasons why.... The letters brought tears to my eyes, and I know I will save them forever. I kept them at my desk this whole past year, as a reminder that I'm a good teacher and that I am positively influencing children's lives. Receiving those letters was one of the happiest moments during my teaching career. (Sheila McNeill, personal communication, 1996)

Can you think of anything better than to have a ringside seat in the human drama and, at times, assist in making the drama turn out well? I am fortunate to be in the helping professions, and I acknowledge this with happy memories of past practitioner experiences, enjoyable present work, and positive anticipation of the future in this field.

Rewards of Practice

I do not try to help the other grow in order to actualize myself, but by helping the other grow I do actualize myself.
                                        —M. MAYEROFF (1990, p. 40)

There is richness to the experience of relating on an intimate level with many people.
                                        —P. P. HEPPNER (1989, p. 74)

As described in the Mayeroff and Heppner quotations, the high touch fields can provide many "psychic income" rewards. Radeke and Mahoney (2000) describe some of the rewards in the high touch field of psychotherapy (see Table 2.1 on page 8). In comparing the experience of research psychologists

TABLE 2.1

| | Percentage agreement | |
| | Psychological Researchers | Psycho-therapists |
Dimensions		
Made me a better person	78	94**
Made me a wiser person	81	92**
Increased my self-awareness	69	92**
Appreciation for human relationships	56	90**
Accelerated psychological development	69	89**
Increased tolerance for ambiguity	58	81**
Increased capacity to enjoy life	51	75**
Felt like a form of spiritual service	25	74**
Resulted in changes in my value system	38	61**

**p<.001.
Items taken from Radeke, J. T., & Mahoney, M. J. (2000). Comparing the personal lives of psychotherapists and research psychologists. *Professional Psychology: Research and Practice, 31,* 82–84.

and psychotherapists, the therapists were significantly higher on important dimensions.

Some rewards are related to the "helper therapy principle," an idea first described by Reissman in an important 1965 article. Essentially, the idea is that the giver in a human exchange gets a lot from giving. An example is the sponsor role in Alcoholics Anonymous (AA). In an article, I elaborated on Reissman's idea by suggesting four ways that giving is rewarding (Skovholt, 1974). These means are:

1. *Identity development.* The idea here is that the giving role gives the practitioner a sense of identity. Also, the need for effectance motivation (the joy of being a cause) and competence motivation (the innate desire to be competent) is met through the practitioner's work. Lastly, a close connection with others reduces a sense of loneliness. In recent years, much professional literature in health and psychology has documented the importance of social connections for wellness. For example, in *The Broken Heart*, Lynch (1979) describes how disconnection from others through fight or flight responses correlates with heart disease.
2. *Social exchange theory.* Theories of social exchange attempt to explain the human rules used in resource exchange. Foa (1971) developed a six-resource model: love, status, information, money, goods, and services. In essence, by giving one or more professional resources—information and services—the practitioner receives versions of love, status, and money. People, including practitioners, treasure receiving these resources.

3. *Modeling.* The modeling literature is rich with examples of how we learn by observation. Examples are learning to teach by watching one's teacher and learning to parent by watching one's parent. This is a powerful human development method. Practitioners closely observe those they work with when attempting to make positive changes in an emotional, intellectual, or physical area. Much of the interaction and observation occurs in private space, although some is public (i.e., the classroom). Like a cultural anthropologist in these encounters, the high touch practitioner is able to closely observe human behavior and learn from it. Of course, this must be done in an ethical way in which the needs of the other are primary. Yet, these encounters do provide rich opportunities to learn via modeling. Often the learning is about deeper human themes, such as the impact of motivation on change, the ingredients of success, ways to encounter pain, and how friends and family affect goals. If done in an ethical way, this modeling can be instructive for the practitioner.

4. *Direct reenforcement.* The practitioner's work can lead to direct social reenforcement, such as forms described by Skinner (1953) of attention, approval, and affection. Certainly, getting reactions like these can help make practitioners' work satisfying.

Gifts of Practice

I suggest that the great gift of practice is *species immortality.* This is a term that I use to describe the connection that we, as practitioners, have to the ongoing evolution of our species, *Homo sapiens.* Through helping, teaching, and health care, practitioners are connected to the great human life chain that stretches from the far past into the far future. Like sharing one's DNA with others in a biological chain, practitioners, through their acts of empowering human growth, are connected in a positive way to the ongoing human story.

Connecting oneself to the growth and development of the species can provide enormous meaning, sometimes clearly felt and sometimes unconscious, for the practitioner. When the search for meaning is elusive for so many in contemporary society, finding a source of meaning is a great gift to the high touch practitioner. Conversely, meaning burnout, a concept explored in Chapter 7, can be very distressing for the practitioner because the gift of meaning seems to be gone.

Mayeroff (1990) expresses this sentiment about the value of meaningful work in his book *On Caring:*

> *The specific need certain others have for me, if they are to grow, makes it possible for me to live the meaning of my life.... Simplification takes place*

in my life through recreating it around caring. Much that is incompatible and irrelevant to my caring is eliminated, and I achieve a fundamental clarity as to who I am and what I am about. (pp. 77, 87)

In summary, there can be great joys, rewards, and gifts for the practitioner. They can combine in unique forms at different times during a practitioner's life. They can vary in form and intensity across different practitioners and different high touch fields. Yet, although differences exist, the positive quality of the work—the joys, rewards, and gifts—are real and sustaining.

3

The Caring Cycle as the Practice Essential

Positive memories of teachers are reserved for particular and special people: the teacher who touched your heart, the teacher who cared about you as a person, the teacher whose passion for something—music, math, Latin, kites—was infectious and energizing.... Good teaching requires most of all a thoughtful, caring teacher committed to the lives of students.

—W. AYERS (1993, pp. 5, 18)

Care is a state composed of the recognition of another, a fellow human being like one's self: identification of one's self with the pain or joy of the other; of guilt, pity and the awareness that we all stand on the base of a common humanity from which we all stem.

—R. MAY (1969, p. 284)

The essential ingredient that makes psychotherapy effective and successful...is human involvement and struggle. It is the willingness of the therapist to extend himself or herself.

—M. S. PECK (1978, p. 173)

The central factor in the success of high-risk youth is the presence of a caring, competent adult in the child's life.

—A. MASTON (personal communication, 1998)

Caring as Central in Counseling, Therapy, Teaching, and Health Careers

In a world where technological innovation is illuminated in splendor and applause, it seems much too simple to say that something more basic is more important. Yet, in the counseling, therapy, teaching, and health fields, the research evidence overwhelmingly points to the power of human caring as the essential among essentials.

Recently, a colleague and I asked people to describe in two words a teacher they *most liked* in their experience as students. Others were asked to describe their *best* teacher (Skovholt & D'Rozario, 2000). In this study, we asked people to recall their own lives as students and then describe the teacher competence at the highest level. Each person in this sample of 171 individuals gave us two words for a total of 342 words. The favorite word chosen did not describe how brilliant or well-educated the teacher was, the prestige of the teacher's university training, the methods of teacher education that the teacher learned or practiced, or the teacher's physical attractiveness. The most popular word described whether the person felt cherished by the teacher in a personal way because, overwhelmingly, the most popular word used to describe the most-liked or best teacher was *caring*. Themes were created from the words in this study, with the strongest theme being *caring and understanding*. For this theme, the following words—*caring, understanding, kind, patient, concerned, helpful,* and *loving*—were stitched together to highlight the importance of the connection that the teacher makes with a student.

Examining factors in student achievement, Wentzel (1997) found that the teacher's caring was central to the success of students and concluded that "perceptions of supportive and caring relationships with teachers are important" (p. 417). Mayeroff (1990) describes the benefits of caring this way: "Perhaps few things are more encouraging to another than to realize that his growth evokes admiration, a spontaneous delight or joy, in the one who cares for him" (p. 56). The process seems to work as described by psychiatrist Scott Peck (1978) when illuminating the crucial importance of parental love for the child. He wrote: "For when children know that they are valued, when they truly feel valued in the deepest parts of themselves, then they feel valuable. The feeling of being valuable—'I am a valuable person'—is essential to mental health and is a cornerstone of self-discipline" (p. 24). Here, this idea of the capacity for self-discipline, an essential skill for student success, may help us understand why teacher caring is valued so highly by students. As additional evidence, let me mention how caring, defined as love, is the bedrock, central element in the parent–child bond. And think of popular songs on the radio. No matter what song, singer, country, year, or decade, they often speak of one kind of caring—romantic love—usually found or broken.

My premise is that caring is the essential quality that must be *maintained* in the high touch careers and that the inability to care is the most dangerous signal of burnout, ineffectiveness, and incompetence. The inability to care, therefore, must be strongly guarded against during one's career in this field.

The Caring Cycle

Let us now turn to the three parts of the caring cycle: empathic attachment, active involvement, and felt separation. In many ways, in counseling, therapy, teaching, and healing, we constantly must first feel for the other, be involved, then separate—being able to feel for, be involved with, and then separate from person after person in a highly effective, competent, useful way. One essence of practice for counselors, therapists, teachers, and health professionals is to be a highly skilled relationship maker who constantly attaches, is involved, and separates well. In a major contribution in understanding human development, Bowlby described these processes in the classic books *Attachment* (1969), *Separation* (1973), and *Loss* (1980). This practitioner's work mirrors the larger human drama of connection and disconnection between people.

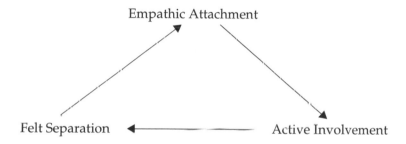

This process continues over and over in interaction with those we try to counsel, teach, or heal: **Empathic Attachment → Active Involvement → Felt Separation → Empathic Attachment**... Making positive attachments, being involved, and making positive separations with others in need of counseling, therapy, learning, and healing is, it seems, the core professional skill for practitioners in the caring professions.

How many helping contacts does the average parole officer have each day? How many therapy clients does the average psychologist see each week? How many patients does the average physical therapist work with each month? How many students does the average grade school teacher instruct per year? How many suddenly fired clients does the average outplacement counselor have per decade? How does one do this over and over again? How is this done well? Person after person—attach, be involved, then separate, attach, be involved, then separate—week after week, month after month, year after year. Long-term counselors, therapists, teachers, and health professionals work 30 to 40 years. They make attachments, involvements, and separations over and over again.

It is the endless caring cycle, with distinct phases, that makes up the life of the practitioner. Each of the phases—attachment, involvement, and separation—is important in itself, and each will be discussed separately. However, it is also important to focus on the cycle as a whole and the need for competent practitioners to be skilled at all phases of the cycle. It is not easy to be skilled at each phase because they are distinct and call for different practitioner attributes. Attachment demands an emotional connection and openness to the experience of the other. Involvement demands the content skills of the practitioner and the energy to do the work. Separation paradoxically demands the opposite of attachment. To remove oneself is the opposite of connecting oneself. It reminds me of the saying about the tasks of parenting—"roots and wings." Parents who make roots often find it hard to give wings because of the emotional connection to their sons and daughters. Giving wings is easy for the parent who never develops deep roots, although the child usually suffers in such a situation. The same dilemma confronts the practitioner, yet, as with good parenting, the challenge is to be good at both attachment (roots) and separation (wings).

Some individuals are extremely good at involvement but less skilled at attachment or separation. Teachers who focus on specialized content (e.g., high school mathematics) may have this orientation. The specialized content or skills may be the focus for the individual's work (e.g., teaching high school mathematics, critical care nursing, psychological assessment), and the emotional connection–disconnection may be less a focus. The emotional dimension at the involvement phase, however, is also important for ideal results in the counseling, therapy, teaching, and health professions. Now, for a discussion of each phase.

Empathic Attachment

The therapeutic value of empathy continues to receive strong support.
                        —A. BACHELOR & A. HORVATH (1999, p. 142)

Attaching, connecting, bonding—these are key terms that describe the emotional oxygen-giving link between the counselor, therapist, teacher, or health professional and the other. Attachment theory, described by Bowlby (1988), is considered the most important conceptual work in understanding how a child becomes emotionally secure and able to be close to others. The 1996 National Teacher of the Year, Mary Beth Blegen, a history teacher from rural Minnesota, says that "good teaching today is a conversation with kids" (Monsour, 1996, p. 1A). To me, she is talking about the importance of the attachment, connection, or bond between the teacher and the student. Pistole (1999) has provided a rich review of attachment theory in the caring professions.

The literature in the counseling and psychotherapy field supports the power of the human relationship dimensions in this work. In a 72-page literature review on the counseling relationship, Sexton and Whiston (1994) state in the *first* line of their abstract: "The quality of the counseling relationship has consistently been found to have the most significant impact on successful client outcome" (p. 6). They go on to say:

> *The success of any therapeutic endeavor depends on the participants establishing an open, trusting, collaborative relationship or alliance.... Research has shown that failure to form such an alliance is strongly associated with client noncompliance with treatment plans...premature termination...as well as poor outcome. (p. 7)*

In an exhaustive book about the history of psychotherapy written for the 100th anniversary of the American Psychological Association, Norcross and Freedheim (1992) state:

> *There is virtual unanimity among the contributors and among reviews of the outcome research that the therapist–patient relationship is central to positive change. Moreover, strong consensus is arising that a facilitative therapeutic alliance is a common, transtheoretical feature. (p. 892)*

When Bergin and Garfield (1994) concluded, in their research review, that "there is massive evidence that psychotherapeutic techniques do not have specific effects" (p. 822), they too were supporting the importance of the human relationship as central to client growth. As part of the Pennsylvania Psychotherapy Project, Luborsky, Crits-Christoph, Mintz, and Auerbach (1988) reviewed 378 outcome studies completed between 1946 and 1986. In the vast majority of the studies, success depended on the client's experience of a positive, helpful relationship with the practitioner. This research illuminates the power of the professional relationship within counseling, therapy, teaching, and healing. In a new review of the literature, Bachelor and Horvath (1999) make the same conclusion: "The quality of the therapeutic relationship has been shown to be a significant determinant of beneficial outcomes across diverse therapy approaches" (p. 133).

Attaching with Our "Underside of the Turtle" Side

What is the nature of this attachment process? How is this important but difficult task done well? To do this well, we often need to attach with our caring side; I call it the underside of the turtle versus the hard shell. With the hard shell, we cannot get hurt, but we cannot attach very well either. So we must continually present our soft side and attach with it. And we must do this with individuals who are often struggling with emotional, intellectual, or physical needs.

Often, the job of the counselor, therapist, teacher, or health professional is to establish a good relationship with individuals who cannot relate well or are highly distressed. Children who are socially rejected often believe that others with good intentions actually want to harm them (Dodge & Feldman, 1990). The helper must often relate to people who have psychological or physical complaints and want things to be figured out for them *or* want answers to their questions *or* are confused or lacking in confidence *or* are hostile or depressed. Often the person is highly distressed, in pain, or feels unsuccessful. There may be a loss or struggle of some kind. For example, Kokotovic and Tracey (1990) found that hostile clients with poor personal relationships often were not able to contribute positively to the counselor–client working relationship. Mallinckrodt (1991) wrote, "For a significant number of clients, early childhood experiences may have severely limited their capacity to form intimate adult relationships" (p. 407). In a related article, Mallinckrodt (1992) said, "Early relations with parents have far-reaching consequences for healthy adult functioning.... Counselors must provide an especially responsive interpersonal environment to compensate for the effects of others' earlier failure to respond" (p. 459). To be effective, other-care givers are expected to be able to attach successfully with these highly distressed individuals. Being highly skilled at creating positive human relationships is, as shown by Mallinckrodt's research, an essential occupational trait for counselors, therapists, teachers, and health professionals.

The responsibility for competent, ethical, professional relationship-making is with the practitioner, not the client, student, or patient. The client may be very depressed or angry; the student may feel very stupid and ashamed about academic challenges; the patient may have a serious physical illness. The practitioner must step forward and create a positive human connection so that counseling, therapy, teaching, or healing can occur. To do the job well, the practitioner must absorb so much from the other, especially in the more emotionally demanding fields within the caring professions, such as psychotherapy.

Learning how to attach with the caring side—the underside of the turtle versus the hard shell—is a part of all degree training programs in the counseling, therapy, teaching, and health fields. For example, school counselors, social workers, elementary teachers, nurses, physicians, and physical therapists are all taught professional relationship skills and how to be empathetic with their clients, students, and patients. Practitioners spend hours trying to learn the attachment skills of attending, intense listening, emotional sensitivity, and nonverbal understanding. Accurately absorbing the reality of the other, caring about the other, and feeling the feelings of the other are essential in this skill of empathic attachment. They learn metaphors for helping, such as "the ocean," a visual way of thinking about immersing oneself in the world of the other, an empathic immersion. For some individuals in the caring professions, learning to be empathic is difficult. These individuals often leave this work while in training, voluntarily or upon request, because of an inadequate ability to connect.

Optimal Attachment

Although the focus in the caring professions is on caring enough, in reality the problem for many in the helping fields is caring too much—excessively feeling the distress emotions of the other, such as sadness, fear, shame, anxiety, and despair, and replaying the "movie" of the other's life over and over again in their own minds. The practitioner can be engulfed by the other's pain and even experience vicarious traumatization, a process described in Chapter 6. Learning an optimal level of attachment, in which the practitioner experiences the world of the other but is not overwhelmed, takes years of training, practice, and supervision. It is an essential professional skill and a complex one. Learning how to regulate and modulate the level of emotional attachment takes time. It is a paradoxical skill—learning how to be emotionally involved yet emotionally distant, united but separate.

Novices in the caring professions are especially vulnerable to being overwhelmed by the realities of others. I describe this problem under the term *emotional boundaries* in Chapter 5 about stress experienced by novices. Learning physical boundaries, such as with touching between practitioner and client or student or patient is important. Learning the skills involving emotional boundaries can be even more difficult. For example, a school social worker asked, "When a student or family is really upset and there are no easy answers, I keep trying, and then I take it home with me. How can I leave it at the office?" (I. Smith, personal communication, February 21, 1996). Is this optimal attachment? Being able to know an optimal level and artfully perform the sequence of attach-involve-separate is a characteristic of a skilled practitioner.

Larson (1993), writing about emotional demands in the helping fields, describes "the helper's pit" where the practitioner becomes overinvolved emotionally and then experiences the pain in a way that puts him or her in a pit of distress feelings. Reflecting an earlier idea by Lief and Fox (1963) about detached concern as ideal for physicians, Larson suggests "detached concern" as an optimal style of involvement and writes that it is "the state of being emotionally involved while simultaneously maintaining a certain emotional distance" (p. 38). Writing about family functioning, Olson (2000) describe the optimal level of family functioning as a midpoint between enmeshed and disengaged on one dimension and chaotic and rigid on another dimension (Figure 3.1). Perhaps this can also be a guide to practitioner attachment.

Difficulty in Attaching

The task of attaching to the other is especially hard when the client, for example, does not have the skills for positive attachment. Forming optimal, positive professional attachments over and over is often especially difficult for practitioners or those in training who have had serious attachment distress in their personal lives. If the practitioner had intense stress in his or her primary attachments in childhood or adolescence, such as a very distressed relationship with the oppostie-sex parent, then forming consistent, optimal professional attachments in later life can be difficult. To paraphrase Freud, sometimes the child is the parent of the adult, which means that childhood events can profoundly affect adult life. Other attachment distress examples include losses such as a major geographic move and its effects such as culture shock.

In *Fear of Intimacy*, Firestone and Catlett (1999) make a compelling case for the impact of early life experiences on later life capacity for intimacy. For example, the authors argue that the child can be strongly affected by the same sex parent's modeling of intimacy/non-intimacy behavior. Unless the child, when an adult, consciously addresses the fear of closeness, the internalized early life messages can overwhelm any other reality and produce an extreme reaction of fear and avoidance.

As an extension, personal life attachment behavior can have a direct bearing on the practitioner's professional attachment style. The effect on professional attachment may mean that the practitioner either attaches too deeply, is unable to attach sufficiently to understand clients, students, or patients or make them feel cared about, or expresses an inconsistent attachment style with one person or across a number of clients, students, or patients. The inconsis-

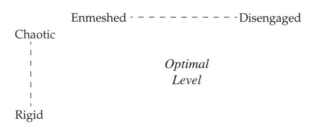

FIGURE 3.1   Levels of Family Functioning

Source: Olson, D. H. (2000). Circumplex model of marital and family functioning. *Journal of Family Therapy, 22*(2), 144–167.

tency can seriously affect the quality of the professional relationship and, therefore, the possible benefits for the other.

The skill of professional attachment is complex. It is more than just trying to help. For optimal effectiveness, there must be a profound understanding of the other. The helper-healer in the following short story was aiming for skilled professional attachment but missed a key element.

Some Other Day

Preserve me from the occupational therapist, God.
She means well, but I'm too busy to make baskets.
I want to relive a day in July when Sam and I went berrying.
I was eighteen,
> My hair was long and thick
> And I braided it and wound it round my head so it wouldn't get
> caught on the briars.
But when we sat in the shade to rest I unpinned it and it came tumbling
down.
And Sam proposed.
I suppose it wasn't fair to use my hair to make him fall in love with me,
But it turned out to be a good marriage.
Oh, here she comes, the therapist with scissors and paste.
Would I like to try decoupage?
"No," I say, "I haven't got time."
"Nonsense," she says, "you're going to live a long, long time."
That's not what I mean,
> I mean that all my life I've been doing things
> For people, with people. I have to catch up
> On my thinking and feeling.
About Sam's death, for one thing.
Close to the end, I asked if there was anything I could do....
He said, "Yes, unpin your hair."
I said, "Oh, Sam, it's so thin now and gray."
"Please," he said, "unpin it anyway."
I did and he reached out his hand—the skin transparent, I could see the
blue veins—
> And stroked my hair.
If I close my eyes, I can feel it. Sam
"Please open your eyes," the therapist says;
"You don't want to sleep the day away."
She wants to know what I used to do.
Knit? Crochet?
Yes, I did those things,

And cooked and cleaned
And raised five children
And had things happen to me.
Beautiful things, terrible things.
I need to think about them,
       Arrange them on the shelves of my mind.
The therapist is showing me glittery beads.
She asks if I like to make jewelry.
She's a dear child and means well.
So I tell her I might
Some other day.

E. MACLAY (Greenwinter, 1977, pp. 46–48)

Active Involvement

In every class I teach, my ability to connect with my students, and to connect them with the subject, depends less on the methods I use than on the degree to which I know and trust my selfhood—and am willing to make it available and vulnerable in the service of learning.

—P. J. PALMER (1998, p. 10)

By far the most common and important way in which we can exercise our attention is by listening.... How difficult it is to listen well. Listening well is an exercise of attention and by necessity hard work.... There are times when I shudder at the enormity of what I am doing when I accept another patient.

—M. S. PECK (1978, pp. 121, 141)

Trust in the other to grow and in my own ability to care gives me courage to go into the unknown.... And clearly, the greater the sense of going into the unknown, the more courage is called for in caring.

—M. MAYEROFF (1990, pp. 34–35)

This is the work phase for the practitioner. One's content area expertise—counseling with adolescents, teaching adults to read, or helping physical therapy patients with strength and flexibility—rises up as a dominant part of this phase. A central question becomes: Does the practitioner know how to assess the problem and make things better? However, the focus of this book is not about the content areas of the caring professions. These fields vary greatly (e.g., from psychotherapy to physical therapy), and covering all the specific content skills here would remove us from the focus of this book—the wear and tear of emotional giving in one's professional work.

The active involvement of self-phase demands the continuous attachment of the practitioner to the client, student, or patient. The consistent, sustained work for the other makes the active involvement of self-phase of the cycle. An analogy is with the work of parenting, in which the long phase of active involvement follows the early days of birthing and attachment. The consistent caring for one's child over the days, weeks, months, and decades is one indicator of positive parenting. In a shortened time period, therefore, the practitioner's consistent emotional caring works the involvement phase. This time period may be the mental health counselor's health maintenance organization (HMO) contract for 10 sessions, the teacher's rhythm of an academic year, or the physician's following of an elderly patient's long, slow decline. The involvement phase can also be the majority minutes of a one-session meeting, the time between attachment and separation. This could be, for example, a one-time advising appointment, tutoring session, or home nurse visit.

Separating Well

With every hello there is a goodbye. —*S. HOLM, junior high school teacher*

Parting is such sweet sorrow.
  —*W. SHAKESPEARE* (Romeo and Juliet, Act 2, Scene 2)

All counseling relationships must eventually end. —*R. GOODYEAR (1981, p. 347)*

We know almost nothing about professional separations. The literature does not address this topic. In personal life, attachments and separations are connected, as in the accepted thesis that the quality of previous attachments and separations predicts future attachments and separations. If so, do professional separations take on as much importance as professional attachments? Perhaps the ability to separate well, to be energized paradoxically by the professional loss process, may be a key attribute for the relationship-building elements of long-term professional vitality in the helping professions.

How then do highly competent practitioners separate? Teachers of children give hints of their attachment when they speak of their students as "my kids." Are there, in fact, elements of loss and grief in this professional separation process? Are there elements of a grief process that operate positively and enable the practitioner to attach again to another client, student, or patient? Some examples of the dynamics of professional attachment and separation follow.

When I taught undergraduate courses more than I do now, they were one academic quarter of 10 weeks. I would often have a group of 30 students— living, feeling, thinking, acting human beings with names, faces, hopes, fears, and dreams. I would struggle to learn their names, and they may have thought that I was indifferent to them for one reason or another. I realized in time that, each quarter, I was still struggling with the loss of the classes that I had the quarter before and that I was still possessed by those classes. It was a kind of emotional, retroactive inhibition. A class can, after all, be a living group, a living organism that, all of a sudden with the final test, disappears and dies forever. It would usually take until the sixth or seventh week of the new quarter for my grief (Is that the right word for this loss? Do we even have language to describe the loss of professional attachments?) to wane and my embarrassment at not knowing names to grow. Then I would learn the names, only to have the whole process repeat itself the following quarter. I did not understand this attachment, involvement, and separation process for a number of years. I am sure most of the undergraduates knew nothing of it. They just hoped to be treated well, learn something, get a good grade, and move on.

A colleague working as a residence hall director in the past spoke of a similar loss reaction. For years, he experienced a three-week depression in June when the resident assistants and students left the dorm. The dormitory, teeming with people to whom he was professionally attached, suddenly was empty. He expected to be relieved and elated. Instead, he felt lost. For years, he did not really understand his reaction.

A doctoral student in the helping professions (S. Renninger, personal communication, February 1995) described her struggles with professional separation:

> *The more clients that I see, and the more clients that I terminate with, the more I am aware that this is a process of loss. I believe it is currently affecting my professional work as I am increasingly having difficulty getting close to my clients. I find myself hardening and retreating behind my "expertise." ... I believe that this year I feel the losses more than ever before, and I think it is connected to the brief therapy I am providing. I saw most of my clients at my past therapy site for the entire year. We had time to connect and time to terminate over a period of several sessions.*

Do highly experienced, highly competent practitioners—experts in attachment, involvement, and separation—experience the separation process in a way that permits them to attach again? Is there a way to do this that distinguishes positive professional separations from negative professional separations in terms of the ability to attach again? Is there a pattern of attachment, involvement, and separation that continues, cycle after cycle, and produces good, ongoing professional attachments, involvements, and separations for proficient practitioners? My suggestion is that an optimal level of other-care vs. self-care correlates highly with proficient professional attachments for counselors, therapists, teachers, and health professionals.

The concepts of "anticipating grief" and "honoring the loss" can facilitate the separation. Anticipating grief means the internal preparation a person does, often without much conscious awareness, in preparing psychologically for change in one's life. Examples include the death of a loved one after a long, slow illness, the end of school and graduation, or a long-planned geographic move. Practitioners know that the cycle of Empathic Attachment → Active Involvement → Felt Separation with clients, students, and patients is contained within very specific limits and internally prepare for the change.

Honoring the loss means building in a time and energy commitment for the separation. This is not idle practitioner work. They do it so that they can attach again. Grief work is not about dying. Grief work is for living; it makes intensity in living possible. That is why it is so important. Do not misunderstand. I am not suggesting that every practitioner, after only a short contact with a client, for example, engage in a long mourning ceremony. Professional grieving of the loss reflects the depth of the attachment and involvement, just as in one's personal life; therefore, more contact with the other leads to more time and energy for honoring the loss. For example, a nursing home nurse may go to the funeral of a resident that she cared for over a long period. An elementary teacher may devote the last days of the school year to honoring the loss of her students and of the class as a living, breathing group that will never reappear in the same way. She may engage in a series of goodbye and transition activities to help the children and herself. A counselor or therapist may spend all of a last session with a client reviewing progress made, talking about goals for the client, and saying goodbye.

Some practitioners develop separation rituals for themselves. These may involve internal thought processes (i.e., thinking about the work with the individual in a certain way) or external events (e.g., a ritualistic walk within one's office area). Using one's own creativity and imagination can be fruitful for doing this. One academic advisor, writing about her ritual, said,

> *It is helpful to think of ways I can say goodbye and separate in ways that leave me feeling renewed and ready for new connections with clients. My own ritual is to picture each client as a great novel, one that I have the pleasure of reading as I become engrossed in the character's life. But always I know that I am merely a page-turner, a facilitator, an active reader who both affects and is affected by the humanness of the words on the page. Upon termination, I envision closing "the book," my access to the client's life, and place it on an important shelf in my mind. (J. Langer, personal communication, July 1998)*

The Cycle in Summary

I have learned one important thing in my life—how to begin again.
—SAM KEEN *(cited by Goodyear, 1981, p. 347)*

Sustaining oneself, being vital, and being active in the caring professions means being fully present for the other. But how does the practitioner maintain such a presence for person after person? How does the practitioner empathically attach with the "underside of the turtle" side, get involved in working with the client, student, or patient, then end the work in a felt and positive way, only to start again with another and then another? Being able to do this well is a central focus of this book. The exact nature of the cycle differs across occupations and the nature of the contact within occupations. Yet, whatever the differences, the principle of proficiency with the endless caring cycle remains a measure of a successful practitioner.

4

The Long, Textured
Path from Novice to
Senior Practitioner

Thomas Skovholt and M. Helge Rønnestad

Ellis Island is an important place in American history. Situated near the Statue of Liberty, here the immigrant entered the new land. The immigrant had to first leave the homeland, often a painful decision. After finding and entering Ellis Island, the new immigrant would explore the land to find a specific location to live. For some, this meant a long road across the American landscape to a place later called home.

Entering a career in helping, teaching, or healing is like the immigrant experience. Who am I? Where do I fit? What do I want? What can I do well? What provides opportunity? These immigrant questions are also the questions for someone considering a caring profession. And like the new immigrant, the person seeking to enter a field cannot envision or understand the whole picture. Walking along a path, in life or in a career, is like a long hike on a challenging trail. It is step by step.

As research colleagues, we have tried to describe the steps along the bigger occupational hike. In a book, a series of articles, and a book chapter, we have tried to describe the long path of professional development traveled by practitioners (Rønnestad & Skovholt, 1991, 1993, 1997, 1999; Skovholt & Rønnestad, 1995; Skovholt, Rønnestad, & Jennings, 1997). In this research and writing, we have focused on the career of the counselor and psychotherapist and have used an extensive six-year research process including 160 practitioner interviews. In the present chapter, however, we use our work in this one career field and apply it broadly to a wide rainbow of helping, teaching, and healing careers.

This chapter is divided into four sections: a section describing themes of professional growth, one describing stages of practitioner development, another describing a model of development versus stagnation, and a section describing elements of supervision that promote practitioner growth.

Themes in Professional Development

Organizing content according to stages, which we describe later, has advantages and disadvantages. One disadvantage is that the stage concept seems to communicate sharp breaks between time periods; however, in real life, change is more gradual, like with seasons. To combat the disadvantages of stages, we have also organized the content according to themes, which comprise this section of the chapter.

Theme 1. Professional Development Is Growth toward Professional Individuation

If we were to hike together on the long, textured career path, we would come across experienced hikers, each with his or her own style of hiking. The stride, pace, body slope, and use of walking stick could vary greatly among hikers. With time and experience, a hiker develops an individual style. So do practitioners. It is, in fact, the process of developing an individual style that is so important to practitioner identity. The embracing of a unique, individual style can, we believe, be an important factor in career vitality. Let us mention the long career of the great painter Georgia O'Keeffe. Her work changed as she changed, and with it, her originality emerged (Lisle, 1987). Although it may seem simple and painless, the winnowing of the professional self can be difficult. It involves the merging of one's values, theoretical beliefs, and skills. It involves shedding values, beliefs, and skills that no longer fit and adding others. Like hiking, this individuation process requires constant effort.

Theme 2. An External, Rigid Orientation in Role, Working Style, and Conceptualizing Issues Increases throughout Training, Then Declines Continuously

There are three parts of this theme that describe changes over time in the practitioner's development:

1. *Pretraining*—the conventional mode. Just as hikers hike without instruction, so do untrained helpers, teachers, and healers who operate according to conventional and nonprofessional ways of helping, teaching, and healing.

Natural rules and personal experience govern role, working style, and methods used.

2. *Training*—the external, rigid mode. Suddenly, the path meets a bridge between the lay world of high touch work and the high touch professions. On the other side of the bridge, there are experts in professional hiking who believe strongly in only using certain methods, skills, attitudes, and approaches. These experts teach people to be qualified for practitioner fields (such as counseling, advising, social work, psychotherapy, human resource development, elementary and secondary teaching, college teaching, nursing, physical therapy, and medicine). All of these fields attempt to help people, although the focus may vary greatly.

Getting off the bus at basic training, Marine recruits are suddenly enveloped by the right way to do things. So too are recruits to the high touch professions after they cross the bridge. The recruit's reaction to criticism of lay methods is to try to do everything correctly according to professional standards. We call this the external, rigid mode. The novice helper, teacher, or healer is often trying desperately to do things the correct way to pass through gates and jump over hurdles on the training part of the path. This is an exhausting process that takes much of the person's energy.

3. *Post-training*—the loosening, internal mode. *Commencement* celebrates the end of school, but the term really means the beginning. Now, the practitioner begins the self-directed professional development process. During this long period after training, which lasts decades, there is a moving away from prescribed ways taught during the externalizing period. There is shedding and adding as part of the sculpting of the professional self.

Theme 3. As the Professional Matures, Continuous Professional Reflection Becomes the Central Developmental Process

Learning from experience, a powerful possibility, is not always a reality. Professional experience does not always increase expertise. Why, you may ask? There seem to be two routes on the path. The practitioner can have years of experience—rich, textured, illuminating, practice-changing professional experience in a helping, teaching, or health occupation. Or a person can have one year of experience repeated over and over. This happens because feedback from the work with clients, students, or patients is not used to transform practice. Too often the second route is chosen.

In our view, bountiful learning from experience, a wonderful part of the practitioner years, only occurs when three conditions are present:

1. *Professional and personal experience.* Researchers of expertise development (Chi, Glaser, & Farr, 1988) studied chess players, taxi drivers, and physicians and concluded that experience is essential to develop expertise in a domain. So one ingredient of increased competence is experience in the domain. Some teachers in a domain (e.g., counseling, teaching, health care) also practice. Others do not and risk teaching in a way that is not effectively honed by practice.

2. *Open, supportive work environment.* A dogmatic work environment, one where certain truth is already known, does not permit the essential searching process. The novice in such an environment quickly learns that certain answers are better than others. Whereas some certainty and structure are helpful in sorting out the complex, ambiguous data of the work, too much leads to a process that we call pseudodevelopment. Administrative and supervisor support for an open work climate is an important feature. In such a setting, the practitioner can bring in the data from the work and dwell with it.

3. *Reflective stance.* "Dwelling with it" is called reflectivity in the literature on professional development (Neufeldt, Karno, & Nelson, 1996). This dwelling means thinking about, pondering, considering, and processing the reality of the profound experience of meeting with a client, student, or patient. The reflective stance is described well by Benner and Wrubel (1982).

> *Experience is necessary for moving from one level of expertise to another, but experience is not the equivalent of longevity, seniority, or the simple passage of time. Experience means living through actual situations in such a way that it informs the practitioner's perception and understanding of all subsequent situations. (p. 28)*

One challenge to the dwelling is the frantic work pace for many practitioners. If one is so busy *doing*, there is no chance to *be*. Yet, it is the *being* that produces the chance to learn. The supervision process, if done right, also provides an environment for reflection.

Theme 4. Beginning Practitioners Rely on External Expertise; Senior Practitioners Rely on Internal Expertise

A full-of-wonder reality gradually emerges for the practitioner as he or she walks down the path over the years. Instruction books on walking are gradually discarded as the practitioner discovers a method that works for him- or herself. Lessons from the instruction books have been combined with the rich knowledge gained from one's own hiking.

You may ask what has happened. We contend that external expertise has been replaced by internal expertise. It is a positive change in a practitioner's professional life. Experience-based generalizations and accumulated wisdom have replaced global theory developed by others. Expertise entails a "rich structure of domain specific knowledge" (Glaser & Chi, 1988, p. xxi).

The practitioner now has this expertise after hundreds and hundreds of hours of practice in a domain and the active use of reflection about that practice. Using Winston Churchill's words from a more extreme situation, it has come from "blood, sweat and toil."

Dreyfus and Dreyfus (1986) describe this progression from external to internal expertise as:

> ...*the progression from the analytic behavior of a detached subject, consciously decomposing his environment into recognizable elements, and following abstract rules, to involved skilled behavior based on an accumulation of concrete experiences and the unconscious recognition of new situations as similar to whole remembered ones. (p. 35)*

The external to internal change is one of the most profound ways that the path is altered during the long, textured hike.

Theme 5. Conceptual System and Role-Working Style Become Increasingly Congruent with One's Personality and Cognitive Schema

This shedding and adding process is described by Sammons and Gravitz (1990) when they say, "Among individuals, theoretical orientations are not very stable over time. The longer the time elapsed since training, the more likely that a change in orientation will occur" (p. 133). When the practitioner has more autonomy after graduation, shedding and adding occurs. In fact, we believe that this shaping process is necessary for ideal practitioner performance.

There is a grieving process in the shedding and adding. It is important to realize that the grief process is to enhance living. For example, a scab over a cut brings on new skin, pruning a tree brings new branches, and the licking of one's wounds brings forth new functioning. So too does the grief process bring on life and personal revitalization. In *Necessary Losses,* Viorst (1998) describes the grief that is part of normal human development. Here, in this theme, we are attempting to describe the shedding and adding as part of a grief process, with grief defined as a necessity for growth.

Theme 6. There Is Movement from Received Knowledge toward Constructed Knowledge

In *Women's Ways of Knowing* (Belenky, Clinchy, Goldberger, & Tarule, 1986), received knowledge is the entry level, and constructed knowledge is the highest of seven levels of knowing. We think that this work effectively explains practitioner development for both genders. Beginning practitioners, as new students, seem to fit the entry level: "While received knowers can be very open to take in what others have to offer, they have very little confidence in their own ability to speak. Believing that truth comes from others, they still their own voices to hear the voices of others" (p. 37). Senior practitioners seem to fit the highest level.

> *All knowledge is constructed, and the knower is an intimate part of the known.... To see that all knowledge is a construction and that truth is a matter of the context in which it is embedded is to greatly expand the possibilities of how to think about anything...theories become not truth but models for approximate experience. (pp. 137–139)*

Just as the quality of the hard drive dramatically affects how the computer performs, this movement through the seven levels of knowing profoundly affects the practitioner's functioning.

Theme 7. Development Is Impacted by Multiple Sources That Are Experienced in Both Common and Unique Ways

In hiking on a long, textured trail, factors can change the experience. Cumulative experience in hiking has a big impact on hiking approach and style. A stranger may appear on the trail and make the experience better or worse. The work of hiking can also get easier or harder depending on conditions, such as rain, that are beyond the hiker's control. The same multiple factors affect practitioners. These include professional elders such as mentors, supervisors, and teachers; clients, students, and patients; theories and research; peers and colleagues; and the larger social-cultural environment in the profession and the larger society. In our research, we found all of these factors present in practitioner growth. Yet, we also found that the timing and dose of one influence versus another vary greatly across practitioners.

Theme 8. Optimal Professional Development Is a Long, Slow, and Erratic Process

Lewis and Clark had quite an adventure in their journey across the American frontier. Ambrose (1996) describes this adventure of making a path through the wilderness. Sometimes things went well for these explorers; other times there was great uncertainty and danger. Hardship was always around the next corner. A route would appear and then disappear, and it took so much time for them to progress. In the end, however, they traversed the American continent. It was a spectacular result.

Each practitioner, as a Lewis or Clark, encounters a similar long, slow, and erratic trek on the professional development path. It takes a long time to make real progress. The development of expertise in the complex ambiguity of difficult human work takes hours and hours. Understanding the reality of the long journey can help pale the coupled novice feelings of frantic insecurity and lusting for quick competence.

The practitioner's pace through his or her own competence wilderness is also erratic. Sometimes, like with Lewis and Clark, the pace is quick. There can be sudden illumination after a critical incident (Skovholt & McCarthy, 1988). There can be recycling loops through issues, such as feeling skilled, then less skilled, then more skilled. Then there can be periods when digestion must come before more eating. Piaget (1972) calls this change in cognitive complexity assimilation followed by accommodation.

Theme 9. Posttraining Years Are Crucial for Optimal Development

This theme follows closely on the previous one. The importance of the postgraduate years was a notable result from our research because so much literature concentrates on student growth. It reminds us of human development models that emphasize the early years without much attention to the events of adult life. For example, Freud's last stage covered all events from adolescence to the senior years. The consequence, as Borders states, is that "little is known about the postgraduate counselor" (1989, p. 21).

This concentration on student growth makes it appear that most of the path is walked during those days; however, the reality is more like Lewis and Clark. In the first weeks of their trek across the American continent, they got started, but that was about it. The cold winter of 1805 was ahead, as was dysentery and a grizzly attack. So was seeing, for the first time in the same week, the grandeur of the great falls of the Missouri River and the beauty of the Rocky Mountains (Ambrose, 1996). If the practitioner trek is more a marathon than a sprint, it is important for those who want to achieve higher levels of competence to approach it this way.

Theme 10. As the Professional Develops, There Is a Decline of Pervasive Anxiety

Like tiny seeds prudently sown and nurtured, professional experience in helping, teaching, and healing can lead to a rich harvest. The harvest brings a competent practitioner who can skillfully perform multiple professional tasks. One result of the harvest is a major decline in performance anxiety from novice to senior practitioner. It is a wonderful part of the harvest. Describing the underpinnings for the decline in anxiety and increase in confidence, Martin, Slemon, Hiebert, Halberg, and Cummings (1989) say that the work "equips seasoned practitioners with efficient sets of schema that they consistently draw on.... These schemata probably have tremendous practical advantages in both economy of time and energy and felt confidence" (p. 399).

Theme 11. Interpersonal Encounters Are More Influential Than Impersonal Data

Perhaps in the high touch human fields, where intense people contact and caring about the other are central, it is not surprising that the drama of human contact is a great teacher. In fact, we were told from our sample group, in 160 interviews, that interpersonal encounters were more instructive than the theory and research of the profession.

Theme 12. Personal Life Is a Central Component of Professional Functioning

In the high touch human fields, the practitioner's own personal life swirls around the self. Like beautiful butterflies and pesky insects, the swirling presence has positive and negative parts. Motivation for entering the work, for example, often has a personal part. On the butterfly side, there is the novice who was acutely inspired by someone close, such as a relative, or given assistance by a caring and competent practitioner in therapy, education, or physical health at a critical point. Examples here are the college student, at a point of emotional anguish, greatly helped by a skilled therapist, the junior high student awash in an unstable home empowered by a towering teacher, and the child elevated from illness by a dedicated nurse. On the insect side, motivation comes from unended pain, like a child who witnessed the devastation of parental alcoholism or watched poor schooling shrink up opportunity for an older sibling or saw acute physical illness steal life away from a loved one.

These examples concern just one element—motivation for the high touch work. Throughout one's high touch career, the personal life keeps swirling around the practitioner. Bountiful lessons come from the practitioner's normative life events, such as the personal march through aging. Each decade provides so many lessons about emotional, intellectual, or physical development. Equally instructive is the unusual reality, such as acute loss (e.g., job loss) or glorious success (e.g., an award for competence). For optimal professional development, the practitioner illuminates, reflects on, and uses these ongoing personal realities in a highly instructive, nonbiased way to improve his or her work.

Theme 13. Clients [Students, Patients] Are a Continuous Major Source of Influence and Serve as Primary Teachers

Our sample group emphatically told us that their clients served as primary teachers. By extension, students and patients serve the same primary role.

High touch practitioners usually do not talk about learning so directly from the other in the high touch professional interaction. Of course, the learning has to be in an ethical context. The reaction of the client, student, or patient, however, continually gives data for reflection. Openness, especially when the data is part of the "series of humiliations" experienced by all practitioners, is critical. Otherwise, the other is a mute teacher, and nothing is heard.

A common major crisis, often in the beginning years, involves the use of a major, highly valued approach in the field. The novice works hard to learn the approach and then energetically applies it. The result is disappointment, not success. The poor result is sensed by the practitioner because the client, student, or patient does not change. As part of growing, the practitioner must struggle with this stressful information. This is an example, often painful but valuable, of how the client, student, or patient serves as a primary teacher.

Theme 14. Newer Members of the Field View Professional Elders and Graduate Training with Strong Affective Reactions

Professional elders are of extreme importance to new members in any helping/ teaching/healing career field. Beginners are often quite dependent on seniors for career advancement and feel vulnerable to their judgment. This leads to seniors being either idealized or devalued. With more experience and less dependency, the senior can be seen through a more objective lens. This process is parallel to the mature child's transformed view of the parent.

Training programs also receive intense scrutiny by new members of the high touch fields. The student's roller coaster of feelings often starts with a peak of excitement and idealization, leading to a valley of strong disappointment later in training. This disappointment often occurs when the beginner feels unprepared for the rigors of performing after some training. Then much later, long after graduation, the roller coaster hills and valleys diminish and are replaced with a more objective—some good parts, some not so good—evaluation of training.

Theme 15. External Support Is More Important at the Beginning of One's Career and at Transition Points

Hiking a long, textured path for the first time can be difficult, especially at the beginning. Another hard part is when the path changes. Suddenly there may be water on the path or seemingly different options to follow. At these times, the practitioner looks for a professional elder as guide. When the uncertainty or confusion dies down, there just is not the same need for support.

Theme 16. Professional Isolation Becomes an Important Issue with Increased Experience and Age

The novice starts in the back of a big practitioner group hiking on the path. There are so many more experienced and older practitioners in front. Gradually, through the years, those in the front fade away. Professional elders disappear, and the practitioner often has less contact with peers. Unless the individual nurtures professional relationships with younger colleagues, isolation can emerge as a significant professional stressor.

Theme 17. Modeling/Imitation Is a Powerful and Preferred Early—but Not Later—Learning Method

There is often a big surprise for the new student in a high touch training program, and the person is usually innocent about it. The surprise is that the new practitioner comes to school to get educated and enlightened. Instead, when professional theories and methods are introduced, practitioner work becomes more complex and confusing. Suddenly, there are so many ways to look at professional issues, so many options to know about, so many skills to learn. The awareness of complexity leads to a quiet panic and a strong desire for a quick way to learn.

In response, the new practitioner searches for a useful, sure, and quick learning method. It is a teachable moment, and motivation and willingness to learn are high. The new practitioner is ready for the early-in-training great advantages of modeling and imitation. By watching more experienced practitioners hike, the beginner rapidly attains skills for moving down the path. The new practitioner is often eager to watch experienced practitioners and can feel frustrated when there are no opportunities for observation. Effective practitioner training programs usually build in early opportunities for students to do observation learning.

To learn basic skills fast, modeling and imitation have a long history (Rønnestad, 1977) and have been popular in training programs (Newman & Fuqua, 1988). Why, you may ask? It is because watching and copying is a swift and efficient method to attain skills of behavior and action. Later, at more advanced stages, modeling is not desired or used to the same extent by the practitioner.

Theme 18. There Is a Movement toward Increased Boundary Clarity and Responsibility Differentiation

What really is the job? For what am I responsible and not responsible? It takes a long time for the practitioner to hone the subtle distinctions among taking not enough, the proper amount, and too much responsibility. Responsibility for what is also a question in search of an answer. By nature, the high touch career fields are full of complex ambiguity. For example, the question, "What are key positive factors for change?" is very difficult to answer with certainty in all of the high touch fields. With so much unclear about the core of the work, the fuzziness about the work expands out. This reality makes understanding all the boundary and responsibility aspects of the job quite difficult.

In time, for the practitioner, subtle elements regarding boundaries and responsibilities become more clear and easier to implement while on the path. A new walker can easily overestimate capacity and start off too fast. In time, there is more protection of the self from depletion. There is more of an ability to time one's intensity of involvement.

Theme 19. For the Practitioner, There Is a Realignment from a Narcissistic Position to a Therapeutic Position

Practitioners in the high touch caring professions enter the fields of helping, education, and health to positively impact the other. It is a central motivation for being drawn to these occupations. Entering the work world, the new student is unsure of the amount of emotional, intellectual, or physical improvement for the client, student, or patient. Drawn to the field, some new students make an error in believing that the work can bring change more quickly and more completely than is realistic. It takes a long time for the practitioner to sort out the realistic from ideal. This error is often coupled with a narcissistic or grandiose self-perception, meaning a belief by the practitioner that he or she can be an instrument for wondrous change. In time, there is a more textured understanding of the change process, with the practitioner being only one part of success.

Theme 20. Extensive Experience with Suffering Produces Heightened Tolerance and Acceptance of Human Variability

With the passing of professional and personal time and all the experiences life has brought, the practitioner usually becomes less judgmental of others. The practitioner has been a witness to so many lived moments with the client, student, or patient. There have been many attempts and many resolutions to make improvements in the domain (emotional, intellectual, or physical) needing change. One's own life has also been a school in which the lessons have produced a more understanding stance toward self and others.

Stages of Practitioner Development

One way to understand human development is to think in stages, such as the classic stages described by Freud, Piaget, and Erikson. Usually, the stage perspective describes changes that occur suddenly and sequentially. Many stage models are not suited to capturing changes that occur gradually, continually, or chaotically; however, for many human realities, there are no sudden shifts as suggested by stage models. Stage models have strengths and limitations. Yet, we hope that the following descriptions of the stages in our model will be of use for you in understanding your own development as a practitioner.

Conventional Stage

One of the realities of the helping, teaching, and health-care professions is that people, in general, perform these functions for their families, friends, and others. Looking at this picture through a historic and cross-cultural lens, we see patterns of counseling, therapy, teaching, and healing where kin, rather than professionals, fill these roles. For generation after generation, people have cared for each other emotionally and given advice, usually through relationships of blood, marriage, or friendship. In these worlds, parents, older siblings, and other relatives are the primary teachers of children. Health care, as in first aid, is also given by those close to a person.

In recent years, especially within the developed countries, as kin relationships have loosened, professional helping, teaching, and healing occupations have grown. Also, volunteer and paraprofessional relationships of giving through helping, teaching, and healing have increased. These are not primarily blood related. In the United States, for example, most adults volunteer in the community in one capacity or another. Across cultures and across time, there have been different patterns of caring that are not driven by the professional socialization of career fields such as social worker, secondary teacher, or registered nurse. Here, we attempt to describe this pattern of helping, teaching, and healing in the Conventional Stage.

The central task in the Conventional Stage is to use one's abilities and skills to be helpful to the other. For example, an older sister will pass on the skill of doing a family chore to a younger sister. The older sister will usually not be self-conscious or reflective about the teaching process. Rather, there will be a naturalness in the whole process. The older sister will pass on what she knows in a way of teaching that she may not even consider to be teaching; yet, learning by the younger sister, as student, occurs. Although this stage is populated by individuals without training in the high touch professions, the goal is still quite close to that of the caring professions—giving to the other emotional, educational, or health help. Usually there is sympathy toward the other and an interest in assisting the other. Perhaps this is because of kinship obligations, close relationship connections, or a sense of wanting to be a successful volunteer.

The competence to assist another comes from one's life experience. Knowledge, perspective, and approach come from what life, in one way or another, has taught a person. For example, a young woman who is having trouble with her boyfriend turns to a female friend for help. Most often, the friend will give advice based on her own life experience. It is a kind of "based on my life, here is what to do" approach. As much as the friend's life offers useful help, then the Conventional Stage approach is useful. It also has limits, however, because the friend's helping method and solution, based on her own life, may not be a "glove that fits." This same principle of the glove that fits also governs other high touch assisting efforts, such as teaching a child to read, helping an adult to be happy, or treating a snake bite.

At the Conventional Stage, there is usually less self-awareness of the concerns that students in professional training programs have, like "Am I doing this right?" or "Am I any good at this work?" Here, there is a more relaxed, common sense approach to both the work method and evaluation of success.

Transition-to-Professional Training Stage

The high touch career fields are marked by an unusual paradox. The core work of these careers is reserved for only a few yet open to all. For example, the psychotherapist consoles a person enveloped in intense grief. So does the sister, father, or friend. An essential reason for the large overlap between exclusive and inclusive is the core work of caring for the other. The career essential of caring for the other is the occupational glue for the high touch human fields. Of course, caring for the other is also the glue that marks the human bond in families, friendships, and volunteer activities, therefore, the overlap.

The Transition-to-Professional Training Stage is the bridge from a land of the known Conventional Stage to the land of the complex professional world of intense training and exacting standards. The Transition Stage means going across the bridge and entering, via a door, through the walls of the professional field. A person is volunteering to give up old ways of thinking, acting, and feeling for the professionally correct methods, whatever they are. The Transition Stage describes the movement from open to all to reserved for just some, from inclusive to exclusive. Inclusive is teaching a child to count; exclusive is teaching linguistic theory to university students. This stage is marked most of all by the transition from the known to the unknown. The known is the conventional way that the person functions as a helper, teacher, or healer, and the unknown is the prescribed ways of a profession such as mental health counseling, secondary teaching, or nursing.

While walking the bridge, the professional novice-to-be is often filled with excitement and enthusiasm. The person has chosen this field for advanced training, perhaps in part because of positive volunteer experiences, and looks forward to learning new skills. There is also worry about an unpredictable and unknown future.

The approach to this stage and the movement through it and other stages are influenced by factors such as age and life experience. An older person with experience in a high touch field will move through the training stages faster than a younger person with less life experience. A 40-year-old explained how she was different than a 23-year-old when beginning a graduate training program:

> *Perhaps part of this is a function of being older and already having two careers which have been rewarding and engrossing for me: teacher and mother. From these I have brought the knowledge that I could work effectively with people.... I also have the notion that in any field there are many theories and that I can comfortably pick and choose and combine elements.* (Skovholt & Rønnestad, 1995, p. 25)[1]

When school begins, the new student is filled up with theories, ideas, perspectives, facts, approaches, and visions. This formal schooling brings new information cascading onto the student. Two elements, self-assessment of skill level and approach to theory, absorb the novice's time and attention. What is welcomed quickly becomes overwhelming because there is so much to learn and know. One student said, "There was too much data, too many conflicting ideas, and the techniques learned in class seemed kind of wooden and sometimes made things worse" (p. 27).

Two influential groups in school are one's teachers and one's peers. Both of these groups begin to exert a strong influence on the novice. In addition, both the new ideas and the new people serve as catalysts for the novice's life review. The past begins to be examined through a new lens. This is especially true for some occupations such as family therapy, where one's family of origin is examined in new ways, and teaching, where one's own teachers are examined for their strengths and weaknesses as teachers.

In trying on the professional role, a person is often eager but unsure. One student said, "I was very motivated to be in the right saddle but didn't know what that saddle felt like" (p. 26). Another said, "If I don't have success I get disillusioned with myself" (p. 29). In time, the transition to professional im-

---

[1]All the quotations in the rest of the chapter are from this source unless otherwise cited.

mersion is complete. Then, the experience of immersion and the fear of drowning bring on the next stage.

Imitation of Experts Stage

The counselor, therapist, teacher, or health professional is now deeply into professional schooling, which has provided so much new information—research, theory, technique, skill, and approach—that the student is swimming in it, swimming in a swirling pool that is rising and growing in strength. The possibility of drowning in the professional newness is a suddenly felt threat. In reaction, the high touch professional-in-training searches for a life vest to use in the swirling water, turmoil, and confusion. Two popular life vests are (1) modeling oneself after an expert and (2) searching for a theoretical model that explains the intellectual confusion yet is readily mastered.

The central task at this stage is to grab onto a life vest and use it to keep from drowning, while realizing that authentic practitioner development means that eventually one must swim without a life vest. Translating the metaphor, this means that the challenge for the student is to remain open at the meta level while closing off at the micro level. Closing off provides a temporary vaccination from the overwhelming anxiety that can threaten to stop the student. The anxiety is about not knowing. There has been an increase in understanding the complexity of the professional world, like the difference between looking at a leaf from a distance and under a microscope. If the anxiety of not knowing is too strong, the student will retreat. Leaving the field or rigidly clinging to one way of understanding reality (one theoretical approach) are two retreat styles that reduce anxiety but, unfortunately, also reduce the capacity for cognitive complexity, a long-term key to senior expertise.

If a life vest is used, the anxiety of bewilderment gives way to temporary relief and calm; therefore, searching for a life vest has the built-in motivation of a teachable moment. The student is ready and often frustrated when the life vest is not available. One counseling student stated this simply: "I wanted to absorb from the counselors I observed" (p. 31).

Life vest #1 is a senior practitioner to use as a model. Students of teaching watch their teachers teach, students of medicine watch their teachers interact with patients, and teachers of counseling are intensely observed while demonstrating a client interview. The style, mannerisms, thinking method, and approach of positive models—national or local experts and even admired peers—are readily adopted. It is a quick way to feeling more competent. Video or live demonstrations are popular. As a profession, marriage and family therapy has led the way in the use of modeling to learn the profession.

Negative models are also used to cut down the complexity of choice. If something can be eliminated, then confusion can be lessened. Negative models, usually more advanced practitioners judged harshly by the student, provide a movie of "things I do not want to do." A classic example is the teacher of teaching methods judged to be a poor teacher by the student of teaching. A more general negative model in the caring professions is the senior practitioner who no longer seems to care about the client, student, or patient. Such a practitioner, perceived to be burned out, is sternly judged and avoided. There is a strong factor in the negative view; the student fears, "I may end up like that."

For *life vest* #2, the search is on for a theoretical approach to lessen the confusion. It is another teachable moment. First, a reminder that the larger task is to be open to the confusion and to create gradually one's own professional identity. It is a painfully slow process. Here is one student's description of this process:

> *I'm putting together a jigsaw puzzle. First I pick up a piece to see how it fits with another. I turn it around and try to get it to fit. I try lots of different combinations. If a piece fits, I keep it and it becomes a natural part of the puzzle. If it doesn't fit, I keep trying to find a place for it. Eventually with no place, it gets dropped. (p. 33)*

The life vest is an easily learned method that suggests "pay attention to this" and "do this." How, for example, should the nursing student provide care to an elderly patient during a routine health visit? The theoretical model, read in a text or heard about in class, suggests a few key variables. In the mental health professions, students quickly grab a simple theoretical model such as versions of the Rogerian helping skills or cognitive therapy. A simple cognitive approach, for example, suggests that, in the great complexity of the human being, one can be an effective helper by just paying attention to faulty thinking patterns with a goal of correcting "stinking thinking."

If neither of the two life vests are made available to students, they usually begin criticizing their training. The initial excitement of being in school turns to disappointment and frustration, feelings most often voiced to one's peers. Without a life vest, rather than being more prepared for the work, the student feels more vulnerable. One person expressed it this way: "The intensity of the anger comes from the next set of challenges. The person must perform at a consistent level and often feels unprepared" (p. 35).

The central task here—being open to professional complexity while finding safety in temporary solutions—continues as the student enters the next stage.

Conditional Autonomy Stage

The high touch professions (e.g., university counseling, elementary teaching, physical therapy) differ in many important ways. As an occupational core, however, all focus is on caring for the other, which occurs within the practitioner role. The most intense practitioner training usually occurs in this stage. Here, the practitioner-in-training needs a supportive guide for the long, challenging, difficult career path. The supervisor as guide does not do the work of the novice or carry the novice along the path; however, the supervisor does watch as the novice struggles while hiking and points out hazards and pitfalls on the path, suggesting alternative methods of hiking during arduous parts. When a person hikes with a guide for the first time, it goes by different names, such as field placement, internship, externship, practicum, student teaching, clerkship, and residency.

The central task here is to look, act, think, feel, and perform like a high touch professional. Passing for a "grown-up" takes enormous amounts of student energy, time, and effort. In this attempt to "pass as one of them," the student practitioner usually has a seriousness and rigidity in role and function. Later, down the path, the task is to shed aspects of this professional rigidity. Now, however, the task is to show professional gatekeepers that one has what it takes to pass through the gate.

Professional gatekeepers are also the supervisors who guide the student practitioner. This dual role of guide and evaluator leads to deep levels of student ambivalence toward gatekeepers at the Conditional Autonomy Stage. Most loved are the wise and expert gatekeepers who adroitly teach the trade with large doses of emotional support and small doses of evaluation fear. Most despised are the opposite—incompetent practitioners who unfairly evaluate the student as inadequate. The student dream is for the former. Most supervisor-gatekeepers fall in between these extremes.

The reaction of the client, student, or patient lies at the center of the drama at this point. Practitioners-in-training ask, Can I do it? Am I any good at this? Can I help, teach, or heal anyone? Will the person think that I am good at this? The variable confidence at this stage is expressed by these individuals. One said, "There weren't many times I felt highly competent. I questioned, am I in the right place, is this what I should do?" Said another, "I've gone from being petrified to being comfortable." Another stated, "I'm less afraid of losing patients than in the past" (p. 43).

At this stage, the practitioner-in-training is most interested in pragmatic information, which is what will immediately help the person with the current client, student, or patient. The psychology student with the teenage client suffering from a psychotic break wonders, "What can I read to help me interview her?" The secondary teacher-in-training eagerly seeks out a method to keep order in a class of thirty-five highly distractable students. Before stitching a wound for the first time, the medical student, like a dry sponge, eagerly soaks up lessons given by the supervisor. Practical, useful information is valued; confusing, impractical theory is read only when there is the external, anxiety-based motivation of a looming exam.

Practicing like a professional makes the person eager to move beyond the student role to the world of professional practice. It is, in fact, the act of leaving the halls of the academy that ushers in the next stage on the long practitioner road.

Exploration Stage

At commencement, the ritual of graduation celebrates the end of school, and students are happy because they are escaping from the demands of formal training. The dictionary, however, does not define commencement as an ending. It defines commencement as the beginning. The Exploration Stage is about this beginning. It is the dawn of a new time, a time for discovery of a new part of the novice to senior practitioner path. It is a time of freedom. The central task of this stage is searching onward beyond what the individual has already successfully explored.

The new practitioner is excited to finally leave the student role and be a professional in the world of helping, teaching, and healing. The person is eager to use all of the new skills that were gleaned through hard work during the stress and grind of student life. We call this the Confirmation Substage because the new professional is eager to confirm the usefulness of formal training and the status of the school or university.

In the preceding stage, the practitioner had a supervisor as guide. The supervisor and the built-in structure of the practicum, internship, or clerkship are there to help ensure a positive learning experience. Good developmental supervision is part of this equation. The ideal does not always happen; sometimes the guide and the structure of the training experience are not ideal. Now, with the freedom of the exploration stage comes the path, often confusing and dangerous, without the guide. The long dreamed about freedom may also produce a surprise reaction of anxiety, loss, and confusion. Individuals at this stage commented: "Having less guidance from professors and supervisors was scary," "People weren't protecting you from taking on too much anymore," and

> *I didn't anticipate all of this. I was concerned all the time that things wouldn't work if I didn't finish [my degree]. I used to think that my doubts about me and my despair would go away with the degree.... It is a disorienting process because I don't know anymore now except that there are more expectations.... I didn't expect the formal training would lead to feeling adequate until I felt inadequate and then realized how much I expected to know by now. My professional training was over and I lacked so much. (pp. 51–52)*

The realization that one's schooling was not enough usually comes to the practitioner while performing work tasks. The person starts getting hit with challenges that he or she is not prepared to meet. This most often happens when the feedback from those served—clients, students, and patients—clearly tells the practitioner that his or her work is not successful. This may come through what we call "a series of humiliations" that are painfully experienced by the practitioner. The painfully experienced element comes because there is a demand to succeed at helping, teaching, and healing and because the vast majority of high touch professionals are highly motivated to provide service to the other. Failure is distressing.

The realization that one's training was insufficient brings on the Disillusionment Substage. This realization of inadequacy often correlates with anger at not being better prepared. One of our sample group wrote to her clinical psychology training program to tell them all the things that she should have been taught. Others point the finger inward and go through painful self-examination of the inadequacy.

The developmental challenge is to continue down the path with self as the primary guide. The key is to be open and searching, to use the reflection process to learn, and to continue to rely on peers for support and professional elders for guidance. Practitioner development is a long process. The Exploration Stage practitioner who embraces this reality continues the step-by-step process of growth.

Integration Stage

In some developmental theories (e.g., Levinson, Darrow, Klein, Levinson, & McKee, 1978), the decade from age 30 to 40 is considered a time to reconcile and integrate. Childhood and adolescent themes from birth to age 20 merge with the individually directed travel of the age 20 to 30 decade. We realize that such a map is culture bound, yet in our view, it still has some value. In fact, it can be useful to understand the central task of the career journey during the Integration Stage.

The central task, on this part of the path, is the development of a more authentic, genuine, true professional self. The practitioner, now a number of years beyond the external structure of formal schooling, is no longer guided on the path by professional gatekeepers. The Integration Stage requires the practitioner to continue to develop the professional self. A shedding and adding process is key to forming and shaping an authentic professional self. Consolidation is a major part of the shedding and adding. Examining the professional life of Georgia O'Keeffe shows strong evidence of this shedding and adding process as part of developing the authentic professional self (Lisle, 1987).

One practitioner at this stage called it "throwing out the clutter" (p. 62). A second practitioner said, "There was a time I had an investment in one approach in part due to training but exposure to clients, other approaches, and my own therapy led me to change" (p. 64). Another said

I learned all the rules [practice guidelines] and so I came to a point—after lots of effort—where I knew the rules very well. Gradually I modified the rules. Then I began to use the rules to let me go where I wanted to go. Lately I haven't been talking so much in terms of rules. (pp. 66–67)

This personalization of the professional self lets the practitioner express the helping, teaching, and healing self at a higher level of creativity. One person expressed it this way: "If I know my pieces really well I can then play them individually with ease. Played well together there is a unifying and coherent quality that is difficult to achieve but is beautiful when it occurs" (p. 68).

Data to shape the professional self has been coming to the practitioner from a variety of sources for a number of years. The disillusionment of the previous stage has been replaced by active building of the self through these sources and the adding and shedding process described earlier: trying out a wide variety of methods, approaches, and techniques; insights from direct and indirect feedback from clients, students, and patients; learning from a variety of supervisors and other professional elders; and learning from admired peers.

A more general category of influence is the practitioner's own personal maturation and life experience. This is an impactful arena because the high touch occupations are, by their nature, focused on human themes of emotional, intellectual, and physical development and health. In addition, the practitioner at the Integration Stage has now lived more years and has more personal history data on which to draw. For example, becoming a parent—a powerful personal experience—can potentially affect any helper, teacher, or healer in how they do their work. Another example is the death of a close relative or friend and the resulting profound mourning. These are examples from the two ends of the profound attachment–loss process of human life.

Satisfaction is a common practitioner emotion at this stage. It seems to result from all the effort over the years that has now produced a practitioner who feels competent at many complex professional tasks and is paid, at a modest level or above, for the work. Also, practitioner joy seems to come now because of more realistic expectations. Those who have entered the career field to "change the world" either have left the work out of frustration or have modified their expectations. Wanting to have a big impact may be a good way to begin a heroic occupation, that is, one that aims to reduce human suffering. Yet, in time, veteran practitioners see these strivings as dangerous, foolish versions of perfectionism and grandiosity. Thus, in a paradoxical way, the reduction of expectations makes satisfaction and sprinkles of joy more possible.

Individuation Stage

At this stage, the practitioner is highly experienced. Formal schooling occurred years ago, and a lot of shoe leather has been worn out on the career path. The practitioner must continue moving forward toward more professional maturity while dodging hazardous elements on the path (dangerous branches, rocks, and roots), translated as becoming stale, exhausted, and apathetic. The great challenge at this stage is to both settle down into a consistent style of walking along the path and to push oneself to explore more and develop further. Together, these two forces combine to form the central task of deeper authenticity and individuation.

Authenticity means more use of one's own professional experience as the epistemological base for the work. The truth about how to do effective helping, teaching, and healing now comes predominantly from one's own experience-based generalizations and accumulated wisdom. Practitioners at this point voiced this.

> *I think that the more you [work]…you find out more ways of what works. So I think with experience, what you end up doing…you do, with all your experience, what you know works, what has worked in the past.… It leaves you with a model that you developed, that fits your personality, and also from your experience, you know that it works. You start out with a theory and you eventually modify it. (p. 75)*

> *With a new client I think about cases I've had. I think about how they have gone. Themes come in a case and this stimulates a memory in me. The memory is usually in the form of a collection of vignettes, stories and scripts. It isn't fully conscious but new cases do kick off the memory. The memory of how things went before provides a foundation to begin the current case. (p. 77)*

To get to this often deeply satisfying professional level, the practitioner must have moved far down the path. First, there is the absorption from professional elders and theory and research in the field; then there is the agony of early practice when the novice is lost and confused; then comes the shedding and adding and, most of all, listening to the lessons from experience. With the lessons from practice and the active use of reflection, deeper professional personalization occurs, as described in the previous quotations.

As a source of influence for the practitioner, professional elders have receded from the illuminated part of the stage and are now in the background. Life is different, and the individuation stage practitioner is now in the front of the professional parade. This does not mean, however, that one's own professional elders are absent. No, they have just been internalized and live on in that manner. Concerning the influence of John, a supervisor 20 years ago, one practitioner said, "I have running around in my mind words, phrases, quotes that I periodically pull back to…and sometimes I say to myself, how would John handle this situation?" (p. 79).

This professional development process is analogous to a similar process in personal human development. Here is one description:

[I was] talking with an elderly man who was explaining to me that his wife, whom he cared for deeply, wasn't really dead because the pleasure of their time together lived on inside him. While he spoke these words,...I began to feel that all the people I'd ever known who had died or left me had not in fact gone away, but continued to live on inside me just as the man's wife lived on inside him. (Golden, 1997, p. 427)

The personal human development of a practitioner of human development—emotional, intellectual, or physical—is quite naturally a source of influence. It is true, however, that some practitioners are not very self-aware or reflective about the impact of personal life on work. Georgia O'Keeffe seemed to be in this camp regarding her flower paintings. She denied that the lush flower paintings had a sexual component although they were painted during the most intensely romantic part of her life (Lisle, 1987). Others are quite aware of the power of personal life. One practitioner stated,

Certainly my experience has been an important factor.... My experience in the Peace Corps for a few years has taught me...a sense of relativity of this culture. Raising children I think is so important. I got a chance to go back through development with my own children, and to be able to see what it felt like to be them. (p. 79)

The learning process at the Individuation Stage is highly self-directed. The pace, the direction, the focus, and the content are all self-directed. Continuing education requirements must be met, but they usually are structured in a very conventional method of "seat time" with a formal, one-way distribution of information. In fact, now real, continuing education is broader in method and focus. Serious learning may come through watching movies, an intense cross-cultural experience, having personal therapy, teaching a class, or making pottery. The key part for development versus stagnation is an ongoing, self-directed effort.

Integrity Stage

To describe the work of the last stage, we are using the terms of the famous psychologist Eric Erikson. Erikson (1968) said that the psychological focus at this point is either integrity or despair. From our research, we have concluded that the central career task at this stage means *integrity* defined as maintaining the fullness of one's individuality. The task here, within the metaphor of the long, textured path, is to keep on trekking using the skilled style that the senior practitioner has developed during decades of practice.

While practicing within the ethical standards of the profession, this stage represents a profound acceptance and full expression of the self. As one senior practitioner said, "I think I am more myself than I have ever been" (p. 87). This full expression by the practitioner requires a chiseling of the professional self over the years of the postgraduate stages: exploration, integration, individuation, and now integrity. With self as director, there has been shedding of unwanted exterior influences while other influences have been added.

Acceptance, the predominant practitioner emotion, comes from the "fruit of one's labor." Related emotions are serenity, security, humility, and confidence. One practitioner described it this way: "The longer I've been at it the more I've become accepting of my limitations. That is just the way it is. Some things I do well, other things not so well" (p. 88). A secondary emotion is regret, which is related to time gone and the missed opportunities.

Performance anxiety is greatly reduced from the early years. The practitioner does not have the dreaded feeling of not knowing what to do or the strong dependence on professional elders as guides. Contributing to the reduced anxiety is the internal expertise, the experience-based generalizations and accumulated wisdom, that is now the autopilot guiding the work. An Integrity Stage practitioner expressed this feeling when saying, "Almost never do I feel anxious about my work. I've done everything before and it has turned out all right" (p. 88).

The cascade of influences for the novice practitioner—theory and research, the client, student, and patient, professional elders, and peers and colleagues—is different now. These sources of influence are not absorbed during this stage with the same straw-gulping urgency of a thirsty adolescent drinking a malt. Why is this? Things are different because so many of these influences have been internalized. They now reside internally and are forceful in role and working style in that way. The senior practitioner tends not to get excited about new ideas in the field. As one practitioner at this point said,

> By the time a person reaches the end of one's work life, he/she has seen the wheel reinvented so many times.... Old ideas emerge under new names and it can be frustrating...to see people make a big fuss about something he/she has known for years. This contributes to cynicism for the person. (p. 95)

One source of influence has expanded, which is from the classes of the "school of hard knocks." With more life, there have been more lessons from life. Perhaps of most significance is the depth and wisdom gained from the loss of human attachments. These losses can be instructive for a practitioner in a human field. The practitioner must, however, do his or her own grief work and get to a point of resolution (Rønnestad & Skovholt, 2000). Then he or she can speak from this depth and wisdom, as described by the leading character in a recent bestseller who said, "I don't think any of us can speak frankly about pain until we are no longer enduring it" (Golden, 1997, p. 419). So this source of influence, using the depth and wisdom gained from enduring profound human loss, can be of great value to the senior practitioner in helping, teaching, and healing.

Many forces converge to make the work satisfying for numerous senior practitioners. Performance anxiety is greatly diminished; there is often a strong feeling of competence in the work and control in the work setting. New energy is not needed for miles of hiking on the path, yet the work brings success with clients, students, and patients. One Integrity-Stage practitioner stated it this way:

> *With diminished anxiety, I became less and less afraid of my clients and with that came an ease for me in using my own wide repertoire of skills and procedures. They became more available to me when I needed them. And during those moments it became remarkable to me that someone would have the willingness to share their private world with me and that my work with them would bring very positive results for them. This brought a sense of immense pleasure to me. (p. 96)*

Here we see, in this quotation, the joy of practice described in Chapter 2 of this book. Now, at the Integrity Stage, the most dangerous hiking elements— tree branches, steep incline, dangerous overlooks, and sharp-edged rocks— have been managed. The end is near, and the professional hiker can enjoy the final miles of the long, textured path.

Practitioner Development versus Stagnation

Moving down the path by day, week, month, year, and decade, what factors propel the practitioner forward? What factors retard the ongoing hiking? These are questions we have asked for over a decade through our joint research. An early version of the process model of development and stagnation can be found in Rønnestad and Skovholt (1991). Many of the ideas presented here came from Rønnestad's supervision seminars for Norwegian practitioners. This fertile ground for reflection led to numerous concepts.

Education and Experience

When people think of the ingredients for increased practitioner competence, they usually list education and experience as the essentials. We agree that these are necessary. We do not, however, believe that they are sufficient for optimal practitioner development. Many other factors increase one's chances of choosing the development path versus the stagnation path. These include the motivation pattern of the practitioner, whether the work organization supports an open searching process versus a rigid set of beliefs regarding the complexity, and the ratio of support versus challenge for the practitioner.

Processing

For us, there is an often overlooked, key ingredient for practitioner growth. It is the processing of professional experience by the practitioner through awareness of complexity and a reflective attitude. This factor is omitted when education and experience are considered the only factors. You may ask, why is processing omitted? Perhaps because it is hard to measure. An example is the use of grades to measure student learning. Each of us knows that grades are not always an accurate indicator of what we have learned; however, grades continue to be used because they provide measurable information.

Awareness of Complexity

First, let's start with the idea of complexity. By this, we mean that human beings are the most complicated of all species, and so much about human life is unclear and ill defined. For centuries, poets, physicians, theologians, and everyday people have been trying to figure us out. The results to date are incomplete because the subject, people, is so complicated. Awareness of complexity means seeking a more comprehensive, nuanced, and deeper understanding of this complexity and an ability to transform this understanding into better practice. Reductionistic and simplistic conceptions of reality, attractive to practitioners because they offer clarity, must be resisted. Rather, an attitude of adventure into the complexity must take hold. One must have an openness to all of the information and feedback that comes to the practitioner. To develop rather than stagnate, the practitioner must tolerate not knowing and ambiguity. Sound easy? It is not. The achievement and mastery culture of the professional world treasures knowing and clarity. Not knowing and ambiguity are considered undesirable. Consequently, it is hard for practitioners to seek the undesirable. Yet, such seeking, on the road less traveled, leads to practitioner growth.

Premature Closure

Often, the practitioner and the supervisor engage in premature closure. This is a simplifying, defensive process that is especially attractive when there is strong performance anxiety and when difficulties occur. It is easy in such a situation to retreat from the complexity. This premature closure can be done in many ways. For example, one does this by using only one theoretical approach to view all professional interactions in helping, teaching, or health care. A person can shut off feedback and not attend to it, or a person can attend to the feedback in a way that maximizes a possible bias in interpretation. These are schema avoidance strategies.

In our view, these reactions to complexity reduce the anxiety of not knowing but do so in a premature closure style. This way leads a practitioner down the path toward stagnation because of reduction of reality or distortion. In fact, any change in professional behavior that is based on premature closure can be seen as pseudodevelopment. It is stressful for practitioners to not know, yet the reality is that the work—intensive involvement with a complicated species—often means not knowing. The not knowing can be felt in many ways, as in what to do, how to proceed, what something means. Of course, this not knowing is not global. The seasoned practitioner knows a lot. Yet, if a practitioner is engaged in the searching process, there are always questions to be addressed and feedback to process. Being open to all the data, as it comes in its complex form, is a key to finding the developmental path.

Reflective Attitude

Reflection is a focused, persistent search for a greater understanding of the practitioner's world, especially of the challenges and difficulties encountered in the work. There are an infinite number of phenomena and processes in the practitioner's universe that are ripe for reflection. In reflective searching, there is intentional depth. Growth occurs when the individual churns information through the reflection process. Then cognitive and emotional learning is possible.

Summary

We have presented a model that attempts to explain the critical factors in practitioner development versus stagnation (Figure 4.1). These factors include the practitioner's own characteristics and the searching or nonsearching approach within the work environment. Active processing is central to development. This is done through awareness of complexity and a reflective attitude. As a consequence, the premature closure, stagnation, and pseudodevelopment route is avoided.

Stagnation versus Development Model

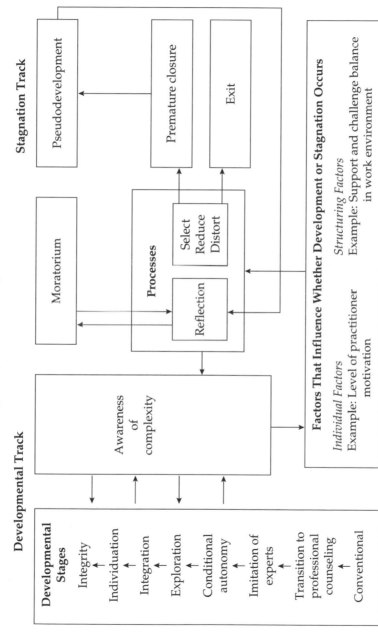

FIGURE 4.1   Stagnation versus Development Model

Source: Modified from Skovholt, T. M., & Rønnestad, M. H. (1995). *The evolving professional self: Stages and themes in therapist and counselor development.* New York: John Wiley & Sons.

Supervision for Development[2]

Here we address important elements of the relationship between a practitioner and a supervisor. We suggest that these elements can serve as catalysts to help the practitioner move energetically along the development rather than the stagnation path. The quality of the supervision relationship is a central element for development. The practitioner often has a fragile *practitionerself*, to use a term described in Chapter 5. In addition, there is often an evaluation component to the supervisor–practitioner relationship. As Doehrman (1976) said, "Supervisors are not only admired teachers, but feared judges who have real power" (p. 11). These two components, the fragile practitionerself and the evaluation component, easily lead the practitioner to a protective, defensive stance. For example, in one study, 97 percent of practitioners withheld information from their supervisors (Ladany, Hill, Corbett, & Nutt, 1996). With a strong defensive stance, development stops, and the stagnation route beckons.

A key to development is the "holding environment" created by the supervisor. A strong holding environment comforts the practitionerself against negative forces within and outside the self. As discussed in Chapter 5, the holding environment acts to promote originality and creativity, aspects of development. As stated by Torrence (1996), a leading scholar of creativity, the "mentor [or supervisor] protects the mentee [practitioner] from the reactions of their peers long enough for the mentee to try out some of their ideas and modify them. The mentor can keep the structure open enough so that originality can occur" (p. ii). When describing ideal supervision, Worthen and McNeill (1996) said, "All trainees described the supervisor as conveying an attitude of manifested empathy, a nonjudgmental stance toward them, a sense of validation or affirmation, and encouragement to explore and experiment" (p. 29).

The Uncertainty/Certainty Principle of Practitioner Development

In addition to a positive supervision relationship, it is important for the supervisor to use a version of what we call The Uncertainty/Certainty Principle of Practitioner Development. The supervisor must encourage the practitioner to explore within the uncertainty of the great unknown, while also helping the practitioner by giving tips within the certainty of the known. For example, the supervising teacher encourages and supports the new teacher to reflect on the work of the day—what happened, what seemed to work, what didn't seem to work, and feelings about the ups and downs. In response to

[2]Earlier and longer versions of this material, in progressively more complete form, have been published in English, German, and Norwegian (Rønnestad & Skovholt, 1993, 1997, 1999).

difficulties, the supervising teacher encourages the new practitioner to keep searching into the ambiguous complexity and to then reflect about it. The use of reflection in this way has been strongly linked to increases in practitioner competence (Baltes & Smith, 1990; Neufeldt et al., 1996; Perry, 1981; Schön, 1983). The supervisor may also give tips about ways to manage certain difficult situations. Examples include a way to teach a group of students who vary greatly in ability or a behavior management approach for disruptive students. Here, then, is an example of the supervisor's approach to searching through both uncertainty and certainty.

Supervision within Experience Levels

For the beginner there are three prominent issues we wish to discuss here. First, managing the pervasive anxiety of the beginner (Skovholt & Rønnestad, 1995) is an important supervision issue at this stage. In this regard, a positive supervision relationship is very important. Supervisor caring and support act like a sponge in soaking up excessive novice anxiety, which can easily seep out and spill. The converse, a negative and distant supervisor relationship, tends to spike up the anxiety. Orphan distress, a condition discussed in Chapter 5, also increases novice anxiety.

Second, the certainty part of The Uncertainty/Certainty Principle needs emphasis. This is done by the supervisor through direct teaching and modeling of ready-to-use methods and techniques. These tips are a great help to the novice working hard to navigate through heavy seas. Direct teaching and modeling by the supervisor of ready-to-use methods is, according to research, a preferred novice learning style (Fisher, 1989; Heppner & Roehlke, 1984).

Supervisor experience level is also an issue in novice development. Often the novice supervisor can provide a likeness in experience and age for the novice practitioner, and this can be a plus. However, the anxiety of the new supervisor, present because of inexperience, can have a contagious effect on the novice practitioner.

Conversely, a strength for the senior supervisor is a low level of performance anxiety. The challenge for the senior supervisor is to translate expertise, gained through years of work, into the language of the beginner. Sometimes the highly experienced supervisor is not able to make a good translation. Benner (1982) describes it this way: "The expert operates from a deep understanding of the situation, much like the chess master who, when asked why he made a particularly masterful move, will just say, 'Because it felt right. It looked good'" (p. 405). In this kind of situation, the consequence for the beginner can easily be lost in terms of the pragmatics of "what to do."

For the advanced trainee, confidence, which ebbs and flows in strong up and down waves, appears to be a common characteristic of the advanced trainee (Skovholt & Rønnestad, 1995). Providing the right amount of supervision structure—a lot of support and instruction or less of both—can be a demanding dance for the supervisor. Yet, high-quality supervision, at this level of trainee development, demands such dancing.

At the advanced level, the practitioner wants more complex supervision. This usually translates into going beyond instruction on the basics and providing emotional support. For example, more complex theory regarding client, student, and patient motivation and readiness for change can be a valuable supervision topic at this point. Other useful topics at the advanced trainee level include regulating roles and boundaries, judging success and managing failure, and trying out more elaborate methods. A supervision constant is the use of the reflective process to translate professional experience into internal theory. This is an always important step on the path to senior level expertise.

Summary

Good supervision can be defined as providing a holding environment by the supervisor as the beginner enters the practitioner world. This relationship can be a great help to the beginner in growing and moving down the path. Some practitioner fields have extensive developmental versus purely evaluative supervision built into the career field. In other fields, there is much more orphan distress as the beginner enters the bigger world. Generally, most students and practitioners assess supervision to play an important role in optimal practitioner development.

5

The Elevated Stressors
of the Novice
Practitioner

The formation of a professional self can be and often is quite frightening.
—M. J. ADOLSON (1995, p. 35)

There is no gathering the rose, without being pricked by the thorns.
—PILPAY (1872, p. 67)

Praemonitus, praemunitas—forewarned, forearmed.

—LATIN PROVERB

Articles connected to students' [and novices'] experiences serve an important function. If only for a moment, they provide validation, clarity, and hope in the midst of great anxiety, discomfort and uncertainty.
—M. PICA (1998, p. 362)

Introduction: An Innocent Entrance into the Complex Ambiguity of Human Interaction

Over and over, Pica (1998) expresses surprise at his lack of preparation for all the ambiguity of practice: "Struggling with ambiguity is one of those unspoken aspects of clinical training that students do not comprehend until they begin their graduate programs" (p. 361). Yes, we are all surprised and unprepared while on our own Lewis and Clark exploration through life's wilderness. Perhaps Emily Dickinson said it best: "To live is so startling, it leaves but little room" (Johnson & Ward, 1958, p. 380). The new practitioner certainly deserves one chapter in the life journey of surprises.

Students are usually accepted into graduate training in the helping professions because they are so good at using compulsive strategies to gain control. This is expressed by getting high grades in classes. Then they decide to be trained in a high touch human field, in part because people are interesting. If only they knew how interesting the most evolved of all species really is, if only they know how hard it is to control ambiguity? For each of us, when taking our turn as a novice, this is when innocence hits reality.

Our work involves close contact with this highly evolved species. The good and bad news, mostly bad for the novice, is that *Homo sapiens* are very complicated. After many centuries of effort, the world's playwrights, head doctors, and spiritual leaders are still trying to figure them out. The kind of problems we attempt to solve are full of complexity and ambiguity (i.e., What is human competence, and how do we get there? What is effective counseling? What is the genesis or cure for either depression or anxiety?). To understand this complexity and ambiguity, as practitioners we often use thinking patterns that are not logical, linear, or sequential. Expertise within these webs takes years to develop because complex ambiguity is difficult to master. The innocence of the novice helps produce an assortment of elevated stressors. Here is one description of these stressors.

Trekking with a Crude Map

I didn't teach long enough to know what I was doing.   —J. SMILEY (1991, p. 384)

Experience is a good teacher, but she sends in terrific bills.
                              —ANTRIM (quoted in Anonymous, 1982, p. 317)

The requirements for the novice to access, integrate, synthesize and adapt information are exhausting.
                              —M. MULLENBACH (personal
                              communication, March 1999)

The novice enters practice as a new canoeist enters white water—with anxiety, some instruction, a crude map, and some previous life experience. All of a sudden, for example, there is the client in front of the counselor, telling a very personal, real story. The story often comes in a complex ambiguity form. The experience is like the sudden rush of water, rocks, and rapids demanding instant understanding and reaction. The novice often has the urge both to call 911 and appear calm, collected, and professional—whatever that is. In a study of novices in the related practitioner field of medicine, the most stressful situation was the white water experience—having to make clinical decisions while very confused (Zeigler, Kanas, Strull, & Bennet, 1984).

The map is, most of all, a cognitive plan in one's head. It is based on a combination of databases used by the novice (Skovholt & Rønnestad, 1995), including theories learned in class or procedures and techniques acquired in a practice lab. There is also the intense psychologizing and introspection of the new helping professional, such as medical or nursing students wondering about any relationships between diseases they study and their own bodies. There is modeling, too, of advanced practitioners, which is an age-old method, like how the apprentice bricklayer learns by watching the senior craftsman. One's personal life enters the cognitive map regarding how to react to human situations. With more age, one may also have had a parallel career or two that provide part of the map. Most of the map is outside of the novice's professional experience. For the novice in the white water, this is not good enough. The status of novice equals an inadequate cognitive map.

Lack of professional experience makes everything more difficult. Inexperience creates a host of problems, and "I didn't know what I was doing" summarizes them. But what does not knowing really mean? It means many things. The novice teacher, for example, does not have a professional, internal cognitive map to navigate the task at hand, such as managing a classroom of bored students. Like much of the work in counseling, therapy, teaching, and health care, confronting this complex ambiguity requires multiple well-timed reactions in the right dose. It is a difficult dance that all beginners struggle to perform.

The theory and research map used by the inexperienced practitioner comes from others, be they writers of theories, supervisors, teachers, or mentors. This is the classic gap between theory and practice that hits all novices in fields such as counseling, therapy, teaching, and health. All of this happens after the practitioner in training has worked hard while attending numerous classes, reading countless books and articles, writing many papers, and taking scores of tests. All of a sudden, what one has learned seems irrelevant in practice. Why?

This happens because the cognitive map was developed by someone else as a *broad* guide to cover a *variety* of situations, not the particular situation the novice has now encountered. Also, the roadmap gleaned from one's personal life is often not adequate for the specific challenge. It is like comparing virtual reality to actual reality or learning a foreign language and then going where they speak that language. All of a sudden, the book learning hits the practical world; language is used differently than in the text in terms of usage, style, and syntax. Another problem is that one must continually try to access the expert's cognitive map, the theory of another, and *spontaneously* use it. So the combination of the theory of experts as a broad guide, the fact that it is the theory of others or personal self-theory and not professional self-theory, and that it must be applied spontaneously in novel situations means that the novice will have, at most, only limited success. It is a cumbersome process. For example, the new therapist sits with a new client who is highly self-critical. The therapist decides that this data fits with a cognitive therapy approach and then tries to apply the theory to the problem; however, the unique elements of the client's presentation puzzle the novice who struggles to find a useful approach.

After realizing that the practice world of unique situations is different from the academic models that often seemed adequate while a student, the novice searches for an explanation for this distressing reality. This searching often coincides with a sense of frustration or disillusionment with one's training. In fact, there is often an intense disappointment with one's educational program, whether an undergraduate or graduate program. We suggest that, in the posttraining exploration stage of professional development, a phase of disillusionment follows a phase of confirmation and confidence regarding the adequacy and worth of one's training (Skovholt & Rønnestad, 1995). Most often, the novice, whether in training or soon after, while searching for an explanation for this often overwhelming sense of inadequacy, focuses on the inadequacy of the training program in the helping professions. There is almost universal criticism by individuals at this point, with either specific or general criticism directed to the courses, the professors, or the entire program. It is as if the novice is saying, "If I were better trained, I wouldn't feel so lost and so incompetent just when I need to perform well!"

The novice often points a finger of blame also toward the self. When directed toward the self, the novice is saying, "It is me. I am no good at this and just an imposter in this field. Nothing I try seems to work!" Pointing the finger at these two fault lines—the inadequacy of one's education and the inadequacy of the self—is captured in a description from life as a novice:

> *Even after having graduated from an accredited master's program, I didn't learn nearly enough to actually be a school counselor. I sometimes wonder if I really paid enough attention in class or if I read my text books too casually. Maybe I just forgot the important concepts that I need to be a helper of children. Yet if I'm asked, I can glibly explain the core conditions necessary for change. I can give a mini-lecture on irrational beliefs and how they impair daily functioning. I can even describe outcome research studies that begin to pinpoint the actual reasons clients do change. Perhaps I studied the theories with the assumption I would be helping insightful clients who know what changes they want. Does the source of this problem lie in my personal shortcomings or in my training? (Bandhauer, 1997, p. 7)*

With extensive experience, one shifts from external expertise to internal expertise, from the theories of others to one's own complex, experience-based rules, procedures, and guidelines for situations. Benner (1982), studying nurses, describes the expert nurse who examines a patient and knows that he is in danger, not because theory says so but because extensive experience says so. Through hundreds of hours of experience, internalized theory has developed. The nurse uses these experience-based generalizations to quickly assess the needed approach.

The problem is that there is just too much to know, and one does not really know what will be needed at what point. An analogy is that of a traveler to a foreign country. One packs the suitcases before traveling, hoping to bring the right clothes and articles. Inevitably, necessary items are omitted. The traveler gets anxious and has to compensate in some way. The novice often feels the same. Rodolfa, Kraft, and Reilley (1988) found that, in comparison with professionals, practicum students and interns in psychology experienced significant stress related to a variety of very specific client behaviors that confused them, such as the client's lack of motivation or crying in session. How does one learn how to handle these very specific situations? Bandhauer (1997) responds to this question when describing his development as a counselor:

> *I remember someone once telling me that good judgment comes from those experiences brought on by bad judgment. I'm seeking to become a part of the fraternity of wise people who consistently make confident, appropriate decisions. Since wisdom comes from experience, perhaps the confidence I seek must slowly develop over time. To find my way, I must promise to examine my feelings and reactions to my experiences. When I feel overwhelmed, I must attempt to figure out why. I must try to figure out who owns the problem I'm being asked to solve. I must delve into my experiences to identify what or whom I'm reminded of from the past. Maybe in 10 years wisdom will have arrived. (p. 9)*

The professional journey for all means studying long and hard *and also* attending the "school of hard knocks." This school is necessary but difficult. Heitzmann (1988) gives an example:[1]

> A few years ago, at a large midwestern university, I had my initial opportunity to counsel clients in a practicum setting. My recollections about one of the first clients bring back an assortment of panicked thoughts at the time: Check the recorder beforehand. Keep nodding so she knows you're with her, and don't say something that might provoke your advisor. You're being taped. You're being taped.... And so it was. Despite a choppy beginning, after a few sessions I was doing, in a fumbling, naive sort of way, what was supposed to be done. I did not sound too atypical from the dialogues I had read or heard. My style was forming. I was becoming a therapist.
>   My dealings with Sandra, age 29, seemed to be proceeding nicely. (At least she didn't terminate like other counselors' clients had.) We got along, talked about innumerable issues, and enjoyed a mutually valued

[1]Reprinted from *Journal of Counseling and Development, 67,* page 76. Copyright © ACA. Reprinted with permission. No further reproduction authorized without written permission of the American Counseling Association.

relationship. Indeed, we figured out quite a few things for her during our times together. We coasted.

In the meantime, I had developed a respect and admiration for her remarkable ability to see through to things, all the while maintaining a sense of calm and coolness that encouraged a facile exchange of ideas. She was making it easy for me. Oh, yes, I was taking no small credit for the general smoothness with which we were progressing. I felt reassured and satisfied, and glad to have chosen a career that suited me.

I don't know what it was that got her off on a tangent that day, but Sandra was speaking of a childhood incident. She had a lisp back then, not uncommon for a 4-year-old, but she found it particularly troublesome. It would always irritate her when she couldn't express herself properly, or worse, when *they* weren't able to translate. I was in the middle of relating this to some of my ideas regarding self-concept when I was interrupted. I almost didn't hear her at first, because it was an unusual way for her to act. The implicit rule was that when I spoke, Sandra listened. But this time she persisted.

Sandra went on to speak of the time she was playing on her tricycle in the backyard and saw the milkman coming to her house on his weekly stop. She kind of liked him, she said, because he was always smiling and seemed so important in his uniform, and her mother told her once that milkmen are always nice to people. She had been a bit afraid of him because he was, after all, an important person, and she would shy away whenever he came near. But this time she was determined to say "Hi" to him. So she mustered up her courage, confronted him as he walked up the stairs, and uttered: "Hi! I'm Thandra." (Her lisp was more evident when she was uneasy.) He reacted with the expected smile, but the words that accompanied it were unexpected: "Well, isn't that a strange name, 'Thandra.'"

I detected a twinge of bitterness in Sandra's voice as she mimicked the milkman. She was bristling at the recollection of the event. She continued: "I said, Thandra!" And he countered: "Yes, I know, 'Thandra!'" "No! Thandra!" she insisted, being unable to distinguish for herself between what she said and what she meant. "Yes, I understand, Thandra," he repeated. And then he just laughed.

Sandra sat across from me, visibly shaken by her story, different from what I had come to expect from her. Her eyes were puffed and she gritted her teeth. She was looking directly at me in a most disconcerting manner. "I'm Thandra! I'm Thandra! Sandra! Sandra! Sandra!" And the milkman smiled and smiled and didn't know what to do, which made her even angrier. She was no longer the 4-year-old—she was here with me, and there was deep sadness in those eyes. As she leaned toward me: "I'm Sandra…and you…. Do you know me? Sandra?… No…. I know you don't…. I am still, so…so alone."

The words were piercing. I could only open my mouth—I couldn't speak. I knew now that Sandra was providing a message in words and a story so simple and direct that I could not avoid the impact of their eloquence. Indeed, I was the delivery man so important in his uniform, smiling and nice in his perfunctory manner. As I sat helplessly watching her cry out for the first time, my thoughts raced wildly in trying to comprehend what had happened, how I had failed Sandra. I suppose I wouldn't let her be what she truly felt herself to be—a hurt, misunderstood, and isolated person.

Perhaps it doesn't matter that Sandra never returned. I'm not sure that I would have been much good for her after that. It is peculiarly difficult at times to show the one who taught you that you have learned after all. She will never know, but Sandra had made tangible an entire realm of psychotherapy for me. I had been painfully instructed that the therapeutic encounter is not the place to show polish, not for self-aggrandizement, not for artful defense, not for "looking good." Rather, it is where the person across from you can expect to be heard and understood in a manner that is rarely possible in other relationships.

Since my initial awakening, I have had other jolts to my professional and personal perspective. I am now confident, however, that they can be processed and incorporated into the core that I had help in forming sometime ago by a most articulate teacher. (p. 76)

Here, in this one painful example, one of the "series of humiliations" by which the novice can learn, Heitzmann is gradually building his experience base. It is a long, slow, erratic process (Skovholt & Rønnestad, 1995) that the novice often wants to speed up to reach the safety of competence. Is it the same wish we ask for in our personal lives? Wouldn't it be wonderful to know the lessons of the last decade without going through the 10 years? I am reminded of the Norwegian saying, "Too soon old, too late smart," which describes this very human dilemma. Another example is that of the youngest child in the family who wants desperately to be as old and mature as his or her siblings but can do nothing to speed up the process.

Experience, lots of it, perhaps 15 years (Skovholt, et al., 1997), is necessary to make the shift to an internal base. The experience must also be of a certain quality, as described by Benner and Wrubel (1982):

Experience is necessary for moving from one level of expertise to another, but experience is not the equivalent of longevity, seniority, or the simple passage of time. Experience means living through actual situations in such a way that it informs the practitioner's perception and understanding of all subsequent situations. (p. 28)

Until experience gives one the internal cognitive map, the novice experiences the elevated stress of inexperience. Not knowing what they are doing is a painful rite of passage for all practitioners who attempt to counsel, teach, or heal. The complexity and ambiguity of so many practitioner interactions makes the life of the novice, like the teen years in one's personal life, a folder for memories in later years. Some accept their own rookie mistakes. Others, like the now experienced college teacher from Tennessee, suffer from guilt and regret:

> *I vividly remember thinking of the song title, "If it wasn't for my bad luck, I'd have no luck at all," when I was told that I'd be teaching 47 under-graduates.... The hundreds of unsuspecting college freshmen who endured my initial teaching...should receive a coupon redeemable for three hours of instruction. (Eison, 1985, p. 3)*

Acute Need for Positive Mentoring

Mentors and apprentices are partners in an ancient human dance.... It is the dance of the spiraling generations, in which the old empower the young with their experience and the young empower the old with new life, reweaving the fabric of the human community as they touch and turn.
—*P. J. PALMER (1998, p. 25)*

Thrown into the tumultuous sea of professional practice, the novice very eagerly seeks safety from the unpredictable, powerful, and frightening forces that seem to quickly envelop the self. Seeking safety while on the high rolling seas, the novice hopes desperately for a mentor who will quell the danger and let the novice practice steering and captaining the ship. Captain-ing here translates to conducting a 50-minute counseling session, teaching a class of lively children, or doing an important health procedure—and then doing it again and again. Ward and House (1998) describe the rough seas for the novice as "increased levels of emotional and cognitive dissonance" (p. 23), which can be translated as the novice not knowing what he or she is doing—the inexperience factor. Help is sought from a wise elder—a super-visor, teacher, or mentor—who "knows the ropes" through experience and has developed expertise.

At this point, the novice badly needs and wants a supportive relation-ship with a seasoned practitioner, who we can call a mentor, just as in life, one at times really needs a parent. Yet, we do not choose our parents, and we do not have the power to have them be what we want when we want it. The saying, "the teacher will appear when the student is ready," is a truism that, unfortunately, is only sometimes true. The novice wants and needs the mentor to be a certain way—supportive, positive, helpful in specific ways of managing the voyage, and available (Rønnestad & Skovholt, 1993). The ab-sence of a mentor leaves the novice with orphan distress, searching for his or her way on the high seas without experience. Equally distressing is the novice's disillusionment with a mentor who has failed to provide what is desperately needed. Examples include the absent mentor, the critical mentor, the confusing and convoluted (while giving instructions) mentor. The terms *orphan stress* and *novice neglect* summarize the fear.

The most effective mentors seem to operate by a structure similar to what we have called The Uncertainty/Certainty Principle of Practitioner Development (Rønnestad & Skovholt, 1997). Here, the mentor, perhaps as teacher or supervisor, introduces the novice to the process of searching through the uncertainty. Searching through uncertainty via reflection has been described as the best method of novice professional growth (Neufeldt, 1999). The novice is taught to proceed on the voyage within a framework of there being more than one right way to counsel, teach, or heal the other. Yet, within uncertainty, the mentor also introduces certainty, as in specific techniques, methods, and procedures that can be very helpful to the confused novice. This mentor approach is sometimes hard to find. This increases the difficulty that the novice has in finding the best growth-producing mentoring at the exact right time of great need.

A key to development is the "holding environment" created by the mentor. A strong holding environment comforts the novice against negative forces within and outside the self and acts to promote originality and creativity. Torrence (1996), a leading scholar of creativity, said, the "mentor protects the mentee from the reactions of their peers long enough for the mentee to try out some of their ideas and modify them. The mentor can keep the structure open enough so that originality can occur" (p. ii).

The importance of the mentor, at this point of high vulnerability, can be assessed by asking veteran practitioners of counseling and therapy, teaching, and health services to describe the quality of the mentoring that they received during the critical period of their lives as novices. Through the emotional intensity, either positive or negative, and the acute memory recall of events decades earlier one can ascertain the importance of mentoring for the novice. Specific situations are described, and strong emotions of affection, appreciation, and adoration or anger, criticism, and disappointment are expressed. Here are three retrospective stories. First, Brinson (1997) writes:

> When I catapulted out of the womb of graduate school...it seemed as if I spent much of my time babbling, drooling, crawling and falling on my rear end.
>
> Still wet behind the ears and suffering the after-effects of that traumatic birth experience, I longed for the support and nurturing of a trusted confidant to help me adjust to this new and exciting profession. This guidance became increasingly necessary for me the more I realized that my graduate experience had not prepared me for the "political" dimensions of the profession....

Obviously, anyone who is just starting out in a profession would value the support of individuals who lend their knowledge and expertise toward helping him or her achieve success. While this was certainly true in my situation, I did, however, approach this relationship with a degree of skepticism. Although there was nothing about the behavior or attitude of the individual that gave me reason for pause, the fact that he was a member of a different ethnic group presented a dilemma for me. Since the historical relationship between our ethnic groups has been strained, I was inclined to ask myself, "Why is this person interested in seeing me succeed?" Yet, through spending time and getting to know him as a person, I eventually rid myself of the stereotypes that otherwise would have made it impossible to foster a productive mentoring relationship.

Having a mentor made a world of difference in my growth.... Not only did I find someone who could provide me with the wisdom, knowledge and experience of many years in the profession, but I found someone who was willing to serve as an advocate on my behalf when I faced certain crossroads in my career.

I also found someone to confide in about my fears and concerns of being a novice in the profession, without feeling as if I would be judged as incompetent.... I am grateful for several other ways in which my mentor helped me, especially during times of professional and personal crises when I felt discouraged and dispirited. It made all the difference to have someone in my corner....

Years later, I now share my experiences with you in hopes of reaching other beginning professionals who are trying to find their way and don't know where to turn. (pp. 165–166)

In this next retrospective account, Lange (1988) describes the emotional intensity of a positive mentoring experience years earlier, in the context of her being a novice in professional writing and the impact of Bruce, her professor and mentor:

Bruce remarked that he thought a paper I had written recently for one of his classes was of publishable quality. He suggested that I make several revisions and submit it for publication. After those few casual comments directed to me, the conversation took a different direction.

I still remember the physical sensations that I experienced as Bruce was speaking. I stopped breathing, and it seemed as if everything in the environment stopped, too. After a few seconds of being frozen in time, I remember feeling energized. The colors and sounds around me took on new intensity.... My critical incident reflected my taking on an identity as a professional and leaving behind the role of graduate student. That shift in perceiving myself as who I wanted to be represented a significant change in my personal and professional life.

Bruce's public affirmation of my writing potential gave me the encouragement I needed to revise and submit the article, which was accepted for publication. In addition, I overcame my academic inertia, invested new energy in my dissertation, and graduated 9 months later.... No one else felt the impact of the moment as I did. For many reasons I was the person who needed and wanted to hear something special. (p. 109)

Conversely, Walsh (1988) describes a negative experience vividly recalled a decade later. The example again is with the skill area of professional writing, but it could be from any of many new skill areas confronted by practitioners in the caring professions.

After reading my fourth revision, the professor returned the paper, with minor changes, suggesting that it was about time to submit the manuscript for publication. In the same breath he also suggested that his name should be listed first on the manuscript. Nothing more was said, and I left his office in "shock." I had developed the project, I had executed the project, I had written numerous versions (with blood and tears), and I had only had editorial suggestions from him. I was so angry that I never touched the manuscript again.... I'm sad that it has taken more than 10 years to write about my first project. Old hurts die hard. (p. 88)

The acute need for positive mentoring is an elevated stressor for the novice practitioner because it often does not happen in the measured-out degree and intensity desired by the novice exactly when needed. The difficulty is often related to the narrow match needed by the novice and the lack of structural or financial considerations built into this novice need. The orphaned novice or the novice with an indifferent, incompetent, or hostile mentor suffers an elevated level of stress. Other novices are more fortunate.

Glamorized Expectations

A vast deal may be done by those who dare to act.
                                    —*JANE AUSTEN (cited by Maggio, 1997, p. 176)*

One of the classic distinctions in vocational decision making is the separation between being interested in "people" and in "things," with things related to jobs like engineering and people related to jobs like counseling. Being drawn to working with people often involves the daydream of making a difference in the lives of others. I remember reading as a child about the work of doctors in developing countries—Albert Schweitzer in Africa and Tom Dooley in Southeast Asia—and also hearing stories of my Uncle Erling, a doctor in rural India. All of these stories, in my mind, were about heroic efforts to dramatically reduce the suffering of impoverished people. They were inspiring! I wanted to someday have work of equal worth.

The models we tend to use for inspiration to enter a career field seem to excel at miracles. They may be a teacher who cared so much for us and taught us so much, a nurse who seemed so exceptional, an addictions counselor who helped us to quit, a physical therapist who brought the limbs of a loved one back to full use, or a professor who was so good at the work. Idealized models who seem so competent also feed the idea of glamorized expectations as realistic.

For people drawn to helping people, who does not want to enter an occupation where one's efforts produce wondrous results? Isn't this human nature? It propels the individual to study the content of the counseling, therapy, teaching, or health field in an endurance contest of tests, papers, and reports, and to read hundreds of pages of textbooks while filling many notebooks with lecture notes. In the caring professions, novices are highly motivated to find a way to help others.

Without full awareness, the novice often is more hopeful about the impact of one's efforts to counsel, teach, or heal than is warranted. This overoptimism coexists with fear about one's skill level. They connect in the goal of magnificent change. If this occurs, the work is impactful, and the novice is a successful practitioner. The novice may reason: If I am able enough, skilled enough, warm enough, intelligent enough, powerful enough, knowledgeable enough, caring enough, present enough, then the other will improve. If the other does not improve, then I am not these things, and my successful entrance into this career field is precarious.

The unclear expectations for the work occur in part because the change process is occurring with the most complex of all species and the beginner hinges practitioner competence to client improvement. Success is mostly measured by direct change of the client, student, or patient in the equation: other change equals practitioner competence. The novice is often not fully aware of this self-focus strand in the unrealistic expectations and the translation to something like, "If the client really gets better, expresses appreciation, or likes me, I'm really good at helping."

The following first-person account illustrates the tie between practitioner self-evaluation and client reaction within the vulnerable world of the novice:

Pam was my first client as a professional counselor. I looked forward to meeting her with such unbridled anticipation that I didn't even notice that the air conditioner was broken and the temperature had climbed into the 90s. I fantasized about sitting quietly and listening to Pam with great understanding and much compassion. I just couldn't wait to hear her story.

Pam was already in my office when I arrived. As I stepped through the door she frowned at me, shaking her head. "Excuse me," she said, "nothing against you, but I'm not talking to anyone but Florence." Florence was her previous counselor who had left our clinic for another job.

I was stunned by Pam's rejection of me. Although I attempted to squelch my feelings, it did not work. I was lost.... We sat quietly as I looked at her, waiting for her to make sense of her feelings. I, too, had to come to terms with my own feelings. I was ill-prepared to deal with the assault of my emotions. Despite the pain, I almost wanted to thank Pam for creating this experience for me. If I was going to grow in this field, to find my own way, I had to learn to recognize my interfering feelings and deal with them.

The silence felt more oppressive than the weather. I began to feel anxious, almost faint.... My relationship with Pam began to grow. She was speaking to me, even though she was singing the praises of another counselor, and I no longer felt devaluated or rejected.

I continued to see Pam for a while, though somewhat sporadically. Many of our sessions focused on Pam's mother. She told me how her mother gave her to foster care when she was very little because her new stepfather was so abusive. I could see the anguish in Pam's face as she talked about her foster home. Often I wanted to take her in my arms to comfort her. "No one should have had to go through your kind of torment," I said.

"You know," she said, "I like you better than Florence."

"Why is that?" I asked.

"Because you seem to understand me better than she did."

I wanted to hug her.

—S. PINCUS (1997, pp. 59–60)

The crash occurs and the stress level goes up for the novice when the expectations, often unarticulated, are battered and broken. This occurs when the client, student, or patient does not show much improvement. Now the human change process in the novice's hand often seems bland and unspectacular. The result of "other no growth equals practitioner incompetence" feels too real.

In time, the novice becomes more experienced, in part through a "series of humiliations" while doing the work, and develops much clearer, more realistic and precise, and less glamorous expectations, which tend to lower stress. No longer is one able to cure the other quickly and easily. Rather, human change is seen as a complex, often slow process in which practitioners play only a part. This helps to reduce practitioner stress. But it takes time to get to a place where "realistic" replaces "idealistic."

Only later will the novice really comprehend how so many factors, such as readiness by the other, play such a role in client, student, or patient success. Lange (1988) describes her emerging understanding of readiness:

[Growth] in my professional development has increased my sensitivity in several areas. First is my appreciation of client readiness to change. No matter how brilliant my insights and strategies, the ability to change rests with clients, who will hear what they need to hear and know what they need to know. What may seem insignificant to me may be the critical incident for a particular client. I am a facilitator and an encourager, but the client decides how and when to create a new identity. (p. 109)

In addition to being attracted to a field in which one dreams of magnificent work, with a connection by the novice between client success and practitioner competence, there are other factors that tend to help inflate and glamorize expectations. One factor is the complex, ambiguous nature of people work. What is success? For example, is a doctor successful if the patient lives? Then how about those doctors who work with high-risk patients with deadly diseases? Right away, with just a few sentences about one occupation, we can see that measuring success within each of the caring professions can be difficult. When it is hard to measure something, expectations can get glamorized without the novice realizing it.

Another factor is the confusion in the literature regarding professional experience and practitioner success. For example, Dawes (1994) argues, with strong evidence, that experience does not ensure expertise. In fact, high expectations fueled by enthusiasm can produce impressive results by novices. Every year, thousands of counselors, therapists, teachers, and health professionals in training, individuals still in school, help many people. In an analogous study of helping, college professors did as well as trained counselors (Strupp & Hadley, 1978). These results fuel an element of enhanced hope, a trace of glamour attached to the work, and a sense that, if one is really good at the work, big, magical client, student, or patient improvement will occur. For the veteran practitioner, the paradoxical reality is that significant change is possible when one is not so grandiose and unrealistic.

For the novice, the problem with glamorized expectations, of course, is that they add to the mountain of elevated stressors. It is just not possible to have an impact each of the thousands of times that one meets with the other during a career. When the novice thinks, "I want to have an impact in every session, every class, every health consultation," then there is pressure and stress.

Intense Evaluation and Illuminated Scrutiny by Professional Gatekeepers

You supervisors dance
on the rim of
this machine
certain of your

power, your values
clear and calm in your purpose
I
trainee
am tumbled and
tossed
caught in the spin
jerked about by the hierarchy's
agitation
my vision
clouded by products
that whiten and soften the dark edge
of reality

And you and I know
that
the spinning always stops when
you open the lid to
check.
    —L. MORELAND (Family Therapy Networker, 1993, p. 13)

For trainees, acceptable levels of practitioner skill seem like a "moving target with
an elusive criteria."
    —W. N. ROBINER, M. FUHRMAN, & S. RISTVEDT
    (1993, p. 5)

Every field in counseling, therapy, education, and health care—occupations with interactions with people when they are at vulnerable levels—is ethically obligated to regulate its own practitioners. Even after passing through numerous gates, a small percentage of incompetent and unethical practitioners damage clients, students, or patients. The profession responds to these events by increasing the gates and narrowing them to keep out undesirables. In measurement language, the goal is to reduce the false negatives and increase the false positives snared by the gates. However, because intensive professional work with human beings is, at the core, complex and ambiguous in nature, the process of finding and removing undesirables is quite complicated, confusing, and convoluted.

Enter the novice who must pass through numerous gates. Evaluation is a large factor in the elevated stressors of the novice practitioner. For example, teaching researchers Morton, Vesco, Williams, and Awender (1997) state, "It is clear that evaluation anxiety is paramount for student teachers" (p. 85). As evidence, lack of control is often cited as a major component in occupational stress and burnout (Maslach & Leiter, 1997). Evaluation by others is certainly a "lack of control" factor.

Part of the level of evaluation stress in the helping fields is the lack of task clarity. For example, there is no clear formula for the exact performance of expert practitioners in counseling and psychotherapy. Theoretical differences wash out, and common factors seem to emerge in outcome research (Bergin & Garfield, 1994; Wampold, et al., 1997). Yet, there is more murkiness than clarity in defining expertise (Skovholt, et al., 1997). A classic quote from Raimy (1950) illustrates this: "Psychotherapy is an undefined technique applied to unspecified problems with unpredictable outcome. For this we recommend rigorous training" (p. 150). Similarly, I have heard thoughtful teachers lament the lack of clarity in defining good teaching.

How then can the field evaluate novices when the road to expertise is unknown? Evaluation happens anyway and must because the public and the profession demand it. So the novice, with as much choice of his or her supervisor as his or her parent, and with ambiguous standards to meet, lives under illuminated scrutiny. The difficulty is magnified by the following reality: "Supervisors are not only admired teachers but feared judges who have real power" (Doehrman, 1976, p. 11). Now, that's stress!

The evaluation is often provided by a senior member of the field who may be a seasoned professional but is poorly prepared in supervision competence. For example, the senior member as supervisor may find it difficult to remove him or herself from the normal work, such as the academic advisor helping a student move toward increased clarity about a major, the teacher aiming for increased student fluency in a second language, or the physician helping a patient move toward reduced blood-pressure readings. In contrast to these process goals, supervision involves other skills such as evaluation. Borders (1992) offers remedies to move beyond the natural role, such as counseling, to the supervision role. Supervision has more of a pass-fail mindset, one that practitioners often do not use in their regular work. One conflict is between the helping self and the gatekeeper self. The supervisor is often ambivalent about the grading demands in the supervisor's role (Bernard & Goodyear, 1998). In addition, evaluation by a supervisor is often an added responsibility given, without choice, to the senior practitioner. All of these factors contribute to possible difficulties in the evaluation process and may heighten the evaluation stress experienced by the novice.

Porous Emotional Boundaries

The pain stayed with me residually when returning home.
                                            —*A NOVICE COUNSELOR*

When I first taught, I thought constantly about my classes.
                              —*AN EXPERIENCED HIGH SCHOOL TEACHER*

What passes in the world for tragedies…I hear about them, I see them. I can't be knocked against the wall by each one. I have to construct a coping technique that allows me to survive.   —*C. KLEINMAIER (cited in Garfield, 1995, p. 6)*

The word *boundaries* has entered the lexicon of the contemporary helping professions and is used mostly to describe the not-to-be-crossed line between proper and improper human contact between the practitioner and the client or student or patient. In the shifting sands of culture and the historic times, it is a valuable term in defining the difference between "appropriate" and "inappropriate."

Although the novice is often helped in training and supervision to develop clarity on appropriate physical boundaries (i.e., to touch or not to touch), less attention is paid to emotional boundaries. The term *emotional boundaries* refers to the internal feelings and accompanying thinking of the helper. The ability to strategically detach and reattach is a difficult, advanced skill. Novice teachers often think constantly about their classes while not at work; novice nurses wonder if they did the right thing when working with a patient; novice counselors and therapists can be very preoccupied with the emotional pain of the client. This "off-duty" penetration of the emotional boundaries is one more elevated stress factor for the beginner.

This emotional and cognitive preoccupation can be educational. It serves, in fact, to provide the material for reflection, a central method of professional development (Neufeldt, et al., 1996; Schön, 1987; Skovholt & Rønnestad, 1995). The task here, however, is to learn how to establish and regulate useful emotional boundaries. The novice, flooded with impressions, images, feelings, ideas, worries, and hopes, often has no established dike to withhold all of this.

In studies of practitioner stress, less experienced practitioners report more stress (Ackerley, Burnell, Holder, & Kurdek, 1988; Farber & Heifetz, 1981; Rodolfa, et al., 1988). (One caution about these results is a possible cohort effect. It may be that the most stressed practitioners leave the field so that, at the senior level, the stress profile is lowered, in part, for this reason.) Ackerley and colleagues, for example, reported more stress for less experienced practitioners in their psychologist sample. Results were measured by the emotional exhaustion and depersonalization subscales of the Maslach Burnout Inventory (Maslach & Jackson, 1981). Overinvolvement was a variable that accounted for some of the variance on both emotional exhaustion and depersonalization. Overinvolvement produces porous emotional boundaries that result in elevated stress.

Difficulty with porous emotional boundaries is experienced by novice practitioners working with acute human problems such as trauma. Pearlman and MacIan (1995) found that sexual assault counselors with less than two years of trauma experience had higher overall general distress and more disrupted cognitive schemas on issues such as interpersonal trust and safety. Perhaps most intense of all is the flood of emotions that hits the novice trauma therapist who has a personal history of trauma, such as the female therapist at a sexual assault center who was a victim of such assault herself (Pearlman & MacIan, 1995). This is an extreme example of porous emotional boundaries, one of the factors contributing to the elevated stress of the novice practitioner.

Developing a variety of boundaries takes time. This skill involves learning to constantly monitor the self, like the car owner monitors the fluid levels of the car—oil, power steering, transmission, brakes. One looks for a positive interplay between empathic attachment to the other and one's own very important self-care needs. It takes time and experience, something the novice does not have.

Ethical and Legal Confusion

The novice practitioner is focused on being competent in a professional role. Depending on the career field, this activity focuses on an emotional, intellectual, or physical domain. The goal is to be helpful to the other, to be therapeutic in the broadest sense of that term, that is, to help the client, student, or patient. At the same time as the therapeutic route is being pursued by the novice, there is another route that is important but often out of the novice practitioner's awareness. It is the ethical and legal route.

The therapeutic and the ethical and legal routes are, in fact, quite different and must be thought about differently. The ethical and legal route has a strong dose of self-protection, yet this is not the illuminated part of the stage for the novice. The high touch professions—counseling, therapy, teaching, and health careers—all socialize beginners, while in training, to care for the other. The caring is expressed by focusing on increasing the competence of the client, student, or patient. The ethical and legal route asks the novice to be self-protective. Along this route, the concern must also be for others, such as potential victims of a client's anger. This too is not part of the therapeutic route.

The two-route dilemma is stressful because it makes difficult work even more difficult. Here is an example. In my supervision of a novice counselor, I was listening to her self-report about a session. She was describing the interaction between herself and a teenage client, telling elements of the client's story, which consisted of struggles with self, friends, and family. The counselor told how she worked so hard to understand fully the client and of trying so hard to help by using the right method at the right time in the right dose. She was motivated to help, especially when sensing the client's anguish.

Midstream in a sentence, she told how the client wanted to kill her stepfather. Without pause, she told how she processed this angry feeling with the client. The goal was to help the client feel less anger and to find a more constructive approach to the problem. The counselor was fully engaged in driving down the therapeutic route. When I heard "wants to kill her stepfather," I jumped the median and immediately started driving on another road, the ethical and legal route. The client's anguish and the counselor's intense efforts were no longer dancing in my head; Tarasoff was (*Tarasoff v. Regents of the University of California*, 1974).[2] Suddenly, the task was "duty to warn."

---

[2]Tarasoff is a case in which the client threatened to kill someone and the practitioner did not warn that person. After the person was murdered, the court said that the practitioner was wrong not to warn.

The route mindsets are dramatically different. The legal, ethical focus is on rules and procedures, not therapy. The practitioner changes from being an engaged therapeutic presence to a person of action. No longer is the client, student, patient everything; now the welfare of others, including the practitioner, takes center stage. Knowing and using the two routes add complexity to the work of the novice. This is an unwelcome addition because things are already complex. Analogies are being bicultural or being a switch hitter in baseball. One of the two is hard enough; doing both well and switching back and forth quickly and with grace are more difficult. Yet, competent practice demands both. This adds another stress factor for the novice.

In addition, legal and ethical road signs are often fuzzy because there is so much confusion within the practitioner professions about many important ethical and legal issues. For example, the new communication technologies are quickly being used before we have clear ethical principles about their use (e.g., e-mail, voice mail, fax). One wants to act in an ethical and legal manner but often does not know what that means in certain situations. That is when the practitioner goes to conferences on ethics or consults with colleagues; however, often this input increases one's anxiety rather than decreases it.

Together, the need to integrate the two routes into one profession and the fuzzy and changing nature of many ethical and legal issues make for novice confusion. As if the novice is not already confused enough!

Acute Performance Anxiety and Fear

As a young teacher, I yearned for the day when I would know my craft so well, be so competent, so experienced, and so powerful, that I would walk into any classroom without feeling afraid.

—*P. J. PALMER (1998, p. 57)*

Fear stops all forward movement.

—*AXIOM*

Anxiety about the unknown and fear about the known are like a one-two punch. The novice can feel so inadequate when stepping into the professional role. The result is acute anxiety cascading upon the person. These moments can be unforgettable. As if it were yesterday, I remember entering my first college classroom with the students, and as they sat down, I went forward, turned around, and saw 46 eyes in close proximity staring at me. Thus, with no professional training, my college teaching career began.

Usually, the acute anxiety occurs when the novice is trekking on a mountain path that is too narrow and the situation is novel (i.e., doing a specific professional task for the first time). Perhaps there is a strong evaluation climate. The situation often becomes arduous because the anxiety of self-consciousness and focusing on oneself makes it more difficult to attend to the complex work tasks. A moderate level of anxiety can improve performance, but high levels of anxiety reduce performance by directing the individual's attention to both reducing the external, visible effects (e.g., trembling and wet hands, unsteady voice) and lowering the internal anxiety level so that one can think effectively.

Opposed to pervasive performance anxiety, hovering like a menacing rain cloud, are fears about specific things. The list can be endless, although there are some specific favorites, for example, being speechless with no idea what to say to one's client, losing control of a classroom of active students, using a health procedure that causes unpredicted pain. Together, anxiety and fear can seriously heighten the stress level for the novice.

The Fragile and Incomplete Practitionerself

At the beginning of any new human role—walking a bridge along the mountain path from the known and secure competence of the past to the unknown and insecurity of the future—we usually feel unsure. Examples abound: the first time with a new date, landing at the airport of a city on a foreign continent, the first day at a new job, or the early days of parenting. The novice is trying on new clothes and new ways of being in the world to create a *practitionerself*. I am using this term, related to one used by Ellwein, Grace, and Comfort (1990), to describe the vigorous interior construction work of the novice in creating a professional practitioner identity. Trying on clothes takes many forms over many days, weeks, and months. With the awkwardness of a new adolescent play-acting in the adult world, the novice is trying to act like an advanced practitioner. All of us as novices, like all of us as adolescents, go through it. A classic method used here is what we call "imitation of experts" (Skovholt & Rønnestad, 1995).

Like an adolescent, the fragile and incomplete practitionerself shifts through a series of moods: elation, fear, relief, frustration, delight, despair, pride, shame. This raw mixture of emotions is a predictable outcome when the novice practitionerself steps into the practitioner world. Although this world produces valuable food for the slow development of practitioner expertise, it is also the context for the series of humiliations experienced by the rookie in the practice world. The novice self is fragile and, therefore, highly reactive to negative feedback. There is not much muscle, and the immunology system is stressed. Age and experience in allied jobs tend to mute the various novice effects. For example, the 40-year-old counseling student who has worked as a hospital aide tends to have a less intense reaction to this elevated stressor than does the inexperienced 23-year-old counseling student.

The following accounts from new student teachers, taken from student diaries by Galluzzo and Kacer (1991), show the emotional reactivity I am discussing here:

The students began asking me questions over my head. Questions that I found no material on. I handled it wrongly.... I was embarrassed and getting worked up. The students laughed at me and that really hurt. (p. 15)

It was the dullest, driest lesson that was ever recited...the students were bored out of their minds...I felt like crying. The lesson was over in about a half hour. I thought that it would last two days. Worst of all the students were saying I was boring. That was the worst insult of all. They didn't like me. (p. 16)

I felt very disgusted and almost indignant toward the kids because they could not grasp the things I was trying to explain. (p. 21)

This preoccupation with self by the novice and the sense that the practitionerself is on stage are analogous of the adolescent sense of being exposed and illuminated while on stage. There is then, of necessity, a self-focus for the novice because of a need to protect and nourish the fragileness. The difficulty is that this occurs at the same time that one is preparing for an occupation where the needs of the other, the client, student, or patient, are the central focus of the work. A supportive senior practitioner as mentor can mute the self-protective, defensive focus and help keep the novice open to learning and growing while focusing on the needs of the other. This clash between a self-focus and an other-focus while creating a practitionerself produces another elevated stressor for the novice.

Summary

Two phrases in high touch work, "talking about the elephant in the corner" and "finding a voice," describe the value of articulating the unarticulated. This powerful curative result within groups has been called the "universality of experience effect" (Yalom, 1985). The aim of this chapter is to produce this universality of experience effect by describing a landscape peopled by each of us when a novice. More specifically, the intention is to provide a positive trinity of validity, clarity, and hope for current novices, their teachers, and their supervisors. The goal is a recognition reflex to terrain descriptions, like of the valleys and hills, the rocks and soil, and the watering holes. Hopefully, the map of terrain descriptors will help in navigating the journey that all of us, as novices, must take.

6

Hazards of Practice

I am interviewing my new outpatient, Lisa, a fidgety young woman with darting eyes that avoid contact with my own. She perches on the edge of her seat, seemingly ready to bolt, her left leg jiggling fervently as she describes to me the circumstances leading up to her most recent psychiatric hospitalization.

"I sat on my bed in the dark with a loaded gun to my head, completely numb, just getting the courage to pull the trigger. And then, out of nowhere, my cat jumped on my lap! I dropped the gun and just started crying. And then I called my boyfriend. I couldn't even talk, but he just knew it was me. He came right over and drove me to the hospital."

When I suggest that her cat could have just as easily startled her into pulling the trigger, Lisa's leg motions cease and, for the first time, she meets my gaze head-on.

"That would have been OK, too."

My adrenalin gives a mild surge, but my eyes meet hers unflinchingly. We have our work cut out for us, I think. "So what do you imagine would have to change in your life for you to feel differently about that?" I say out loud, alert to every nuance, verbal and nonverbal. She meets this question with a long, thoughtful pause.

As Lisa ponders her response, I marvel at the social and historical forces that have propelled the two of us together: she the help-seeker, semiattached to her life as if it were a half-severed limb, and I, the salaried healer, paid to be committed to her life, at least within the allotted time, until the next patient takes her place and I focus on that person's anguish. A clock silently logs the minutes on my desk, its glowing red numbers managing the procession of patients in and out of my office in this busy HMO health center, where a multitude of lives in turmoil intersect with my own. My time is a semiprecious commodity to the insurance company that pays for it. My patient's time? She clearly puts no value to it at all.

—G. GARFUNKEL (1995, pp. 148–149)

The Difficult Nature of the Work with Clients, Students, and Patients

High touch work means making a highly skilled professional attachment, involvement, and separation over and over again. What makes this work difficult? It often has to do with expectations—with our hope to make a difference, with our ability to tolerate so much ambiguity, with the distress we vicariously feel from those we attempt to assist. What are the hazards that make work difficult with clients, students, and patients?

Hazard 1. They Have an Unsolvable Problem That Must Be Solved

A person may be stuck, as in "can't live with him, can't live without him." Neither approach nor avoidance works. These are the ingredients of hopelessness and demoralization that Frank and Frank (1991) suggest are central when individuals seek help. When we are stuck in life and unable to find a solution, the result is often a feeling of low self-efficacy and high despair. It is almost always difficult for helpers to have an impact on this condition, especially in a quick way.

Examples here include the counselor's work with the parent of a very rebellious teenager. The parent will not abandon the teenager but is unable to reach the team to stop the angry, rebellious activity. A counselor can be effective here but not in the sense of finding an immediate, positive solution. A teacher of learning-disabled children struggles to help them get up to grade level, a difficult task given the children's abilities. The physical therapist works to increase the mobility of a patient with osteoporosis who needs to get past a hip fracture. The possibility for improvement is limited. All of these practitioners are operating within the common arena of an unsolvable problem that must be solved.

Hazard 2. They Are Not "Honors Students"

Honors students can get better, improve, and learn anywhere. Harvard professors may do little for the students who come in brimming with resources and skills. If the professors do not harm them, the students will be successful, and the professors can later bask in their success. Schoefield's (1974) term *YAVIS* (the acronym for young, attractive, verbal, intelligent, and socially skilled) was a way to describe desirable psychotherapy clients, that is, those who could improve rapidly. As a practitioner, if one does not get in the way, one can take credit for the successes. There is a natural tendency for practitioners in the helping fields to want clients, students, or patients who have resources (e.g., motivation, ability, limited problems) that will fuel the success of the helping effort. This way, there is improvement, and the practitioner, feeling competent, can bask in the positive change. For example, one of the ironies of the modern university is that there is more status attached to teaching honors courses or advanced doctoral seminars, in which the students have so many skills, than in teaching basic, developmental courses in which the students are less able and the instructor's work can be more difficult.

Hazard 3. They Have Motivational Conflicts

Motivational conflicts in the helping professions have historically been discussed under the concept of "secondary gains." In some government programs, when one gets better, he or she may lose benefits. For example, a Veterans Affairs patient gets money while disabled but loses funding when able to work again. Imagine being a helper there and trying to make an impact.

In the past, I had a counseling client who received monthly disability payments because of a mental health diagnosis. Losing the diagnosis meant losing the payments and becoming vulnerable to the legal demands for funds from a former business partner. As a younger practitioner, I would not have understood the profound impact this situation had on my ability to help the client change. I would have charged ahead thinking I could do it. Now I am more realistic.

I remember the grieving of a disadvantaged minority woman getting her B.A. degree. It confused me because success meant triumph over long odds in an oppressive environment. Success, however, also meant losing her welfare mothers' peer group, a rich source of friendship.

In one research study, we interviewed advanced undergraduates who were unable to decide on a college major. We found that they were often frozen in the decision-making process, not by simple issues such as lack of information or decision-making skills, but by a highly complex set of conflicts that were difficult to resolve (Hagstrom, Skovholt, & Rivers, 1997).

Motivational conflicts also refer to being sent by others, such as parents or the court system (e.g., for remedial classes, domestic violence counseling, nutritional information). The motivation is outside oneself: outplacement—*sent by others;* driving while intoxicated and chemical abuse classes—*sent by others;* academic probation and mandated work with an academic advisor—*sent by others;* dragged to marriage counseling by one's spouse—*sent by others.* One of the classic red flags predicting limited success in human services is external, not internal, motivation for seeking help.

Hazard 4. There Is Often a Readiness Gap between Them and Us

Helping, wellness, outplacement, advising, physical therapy, teaching, therapy—these are all developmental processes. This means that the goal of the counselor, therapist, teacher, or health professional is to facilitate improvement in the person's functioning, a movement on a continuum. How would you have done as a new, first-year college student at age 15? Would 25 be a much better age to begin college because of academic readiness? Ten years can make a big difference. Some 30-year-old new parents would have been inadequate at 16, and some 16-year-old parents would be great at 30.

Readiness can also be a matter of first experiencing the "school of hard knocks." As examples: A friend's daughter was more receptive to his ideas after she had been out on her own and *knew more* than when she was home and *knew less*. Helping others as a career counselor may work better—the client may be more receptive—when the client's own career search process has first failed.

In the caring professions, we often worry about our undercommitment, disinterest, and burnout, but overcommitment is also an issue. Readiness is also, therefore, about matching our commitment and readiness to work at change with the client's, student's, or patient's commitment and readiness. This "readiness dance," which in its best form closely matches the helper's efforts to that of the helpee, is especially difficult for the novice who is trying to judge "dose" and "timing" without much practice.

A classic problem in counseling, therapy, teaching, and healing is the offering of programs to people who are not ready. Prochaska, DiClemente, and Norcross (1992) developed a five-stage model of change: precontemplation (no plans to change), contemplation (awareness of the problem but no decision to change), preparation (awareness of the problem and some attempts to be different), action (actively engaged in change processes), and maintenance (work to maintain changes made). They described a Health Maintenance Organization (HMO) in which 70 percent of the eligible smokers said that they wanted help with smoking cessation. A program was developed and offered, but only 4 percent of the smokers signed up. Like firefighters ready to fight a fire, high touch practitioners often misread smoke for fire.

Our own research suggests that this happens with beginners in the helping professions (Skovholt & Rønnestad, 1995), a sentiment shared by Prochaska and colleagues (1992): "Probably the most obvious and direct implication of our research is the need to assess the stage of a client's readiness for change and to tailor interventions accordingly" (p. 1110). Charting the gap between client, student, or patient readiness and counselor, therapist, teacher, or healer readiness could look like Table 6.1 on page 80, which I call The Readiness Gap.

Like those health professionals who prepared materials for smoking cessation but were disappointed when few people showed up for help, the helping impulse is thwarted for us, too. Training programs select counselors, therapists, teachers, and healers who yearn to help and share a deep desire to care for others. We can easily be more ready than the client, student, or patient. This is a natural occupational hazard.

TABLE 6.1   The Readiness Gap

Stages of Change	Client, Student, and Patient	Counselor, Therapist, Teacher or Healer
Precontemplation		
Contemplation		
Preparation	The Readiness Gap	
Action		
Maintenance		

Sources: Prochaska, J. O., DiClemente, C. C., & Norcross, J. C. (1992). In search of how people change: Applications to addictive behavior. *American Psychologist, 47*(9), 1102–1114; Prochaska, J. O. (1999). How do people change, and how can we change to help more people? In M. A. Hubble, B. A. Duncan, & S. M. Miller (Eds.), *The heart and soul of change: What works in therapy* (pp. 227–255). Washington, DC: American Psychological Association.

Finding the right blend of professional attachment with the helpee is difficult. One can be uninvolved in the attachment, and this, of course, is not good. One can be overinvolved, and this too is not optimal. The self-centered impulse among counselors, therapists, teachers, and health professionals is more destructive to clients than excesses of the helping impulse. Examples here include charismatic encounter group leaders (Lieberman, Yalom, & Miles, 1973) and sexually exploitive therapists (Pope & Vasquez, 1991).

I remember being an academic advisor for high-risk college freshmen. At the time, I was teaching career development theory and practice to graduate students and a career planning class to freshmen. I was an experienced academic advisor and career counselor and had written articles on career counseling in professional journals. In fact, I was very overprepared for the academic advisor task compared to other faculty member advisors who had preparation in areas such as English, physics, and mathematics.

I was really ready to help these high-risk college freshmen advisees, but the task "went South," as Minnesota Twins' manager Tom Kelly says when things go bad. I would give these advisees my time, talent, and energy in looking at the big picture of their educational and career futures. After all, we value the work of helpers who assist disadvantaged individuals to find their way through the American reward maze. But in time, I changed my behavior when my efforts were consistently met by advisees with only, "Would you sign the paper for the classes?" They did not come for a deluxe version of educational and vocational guidance. They came because bureaucratic regulations forced them to get my signature. The readiness gap! My own excessive helping impulse produced the gap.

Earlier in my career at the University of Florida, I joined other new faculty members from many parts of the country to start a Department of Behavioral Studies. We were to offer innovative, cross-disciplinary courses to honors undergraduates. We had spent years in graduate school preparing for the task. At fall orientation, we sat at tables to meet the new students— some of the best and brightest graduates of Florida's high schools. With great animation, we described the content of new cross-disciplinary courses such as Power and Violence. The new students responded by asking, "What courses do you have before lunch?" Again, the readiness gap!

Readiness is also a matter of cognitive complexity—when the client, student, or patient can understand in a broader, deeper, less egocentric way. Readiness is critical, and sometimes we have little power to affect it. After all, "you can lead the horse to water, but you can't make it drink," and "the teacher will appear when the student is ready." Until then, you, the helper, are *invisible, unrecognizable,* and *inaudible:* "I can't hear a word you are saying, only the echo of my mind."

We can't all be lucky enough to have the attention and commitment of the airplane passenger listening to instructions on the use of oxygen in the midst of intense turbulence and cabin depressurization. This is exactly why the work can be difficult. Counselors, therapists, teachers, and health professionals want to believe that they make a difference in human life, but sometimes they do not. At times, we feel ineffective; that is why the work is difficult. The key is that, in time, the counselor, therapist, teacher, or healer, like the veteran athlete, learns when to expend energy and when to preserve energy, when effort matters and when it does not.

Hazard 5. Sometimes They Project Negative Feelings onto Us

Veteran teachers call this *excess baggage,* a term meaning that the student brings extra, painful feelings from interactions with adults in the past. In school, did teachers treat you as if you were your older brother or sister? Did they give you his or her name, his or her characteristics?

Communication can get worse with new lovers as they get more serious because projections from their past can enter in. These are examples of the dynamic of projection and transference. So our clients, students, and patients can bring intense transference reactions to us with their past pain, hurt, anger, and fear related to helpers and authority figures. We get their unrecognized stubbornness, resentment, anger, and lack of cooperation. Teachers often experience angry, disappointed, distressed parents and personalize the parental reaction. It can be difficult to understand the transference element and not be personally hurt. The mark of an expert at attachment and connection may be the ability to do this well even when the client, student, or patient brings excess baggage (e.g., Mallinckrodt, 1992).

I was unaware of my innocence when first teaching disadvantaged, historically unsuccessful students. I thought that they would welcome me as Tom, the good guy ready to help them. I did not know that I represented all the teachers from the past who had flunked, humiliated, and shamed them in school, the mandatory prison they attended for years. To them, I was often just another oppressive adult.

Hazard 6. Sometimes We Cannot Help because We Are Not Good Enough

Their needs and our competence as practitioners may not fit. The demographic variables may be wrong. As I get older, I get more right for some clients, more wrong for others. I am the wrong gender for some women clients who are seeking a female therapist and the right gender for some women clients who seek a male therapist. We may not have the right experiential background or the specific competence needed. Maslow's famous quote, "If the only tool you have is a hammer, [you tend] to treat everything as if it were a nail" (cited by Goldfried, 1980, p. 994), symbolizes the effect of limited competence. In time, practitioners experience a "series of humiliations" when their wrong demographics, life experience, or competence level does not meet the needs of the client, student, or patient. This is difficult for the practitioner because of a basic occupational need to feel that one is making a positive difference in human life.

Hazard 7. They Have Needs Greater than the Social Service, Educational, or Health System Can Meet

All practitioners have examples of how success would be enhanced with more resources. Years ago, I remember a high school boy pleading for tutoring help at a school where there were no tutors. In physical and mental health, practitioners are constantly trying to squeeze out resources for patients and clients within the arid world of managed care, HMOs, and limited funds. Difficult clients can be those who fail because the system does not provide enough resources for success.

In contrast, easy clients, students, and patients are those who quickly succeed at the task. They have the motivation, skills, and resources to get better, and we as practitioners can bask in their success and be nourished by successfully helping another human being. Even now, let us imagine a world of clients, students, and patients who are easy to assist. Let us dream; bring them on. But of course, the world is not that way.

Managing Major Professional Stressors

Hazard 8. Our Inability to Say No—The Treadmill Effect

She [the special education teacher]...felt her enthusiasm ebb in the face of over-whelming problems presented by dozens of students.
—M. J. SMETANKA (1992, p. 1B)

Counselors in the sample overwhelmingly thought that job demands and expecta-tions were too great. For many, this meant serving for too many students in one or more schools. For others, it meant required involvement in a variety of duties that, they thought, had little or nothing to do with the professional school counselor's role and may, in fact, seriously detract from it. For still others, the sheer amount of work, even if professionally appropriate, was overwhelming and eventually exhaustive.
—R. KENDRICK, J. CHANDLER,
& W. HATCHER (1994, p. 369)

The practitioner tries to keep up with constant demands by running faster and faster. Soon the pace is dizzying, and the surroundings blur. The practitioner gets numb and can't think or process experience or feedback. On the treadmill, the pace just seems to increase.

This major professional stressor concerns our desire to help, our diffi-culty in saying no, and the resulting overload. In "The Heroic Syndrome," Stone (1988)[1] described his "good intentions and heroic strivings" as ulti-mately an Achilles' heel that needed to be changed for long-term profes-sional vitality. His prescription: "The word 'no' belongs in the helping vocabulary." Here is his description:

My incident deals with a situation I encountered during the first weeks in my new position as director of a university counseling service. My incident provides a useful example of the heroic syndrome, a common neurotic tendency prevalent among counselors.

I received a call from a resident assistant (RA) at about 1:00 a.m. on a Saturday night after a football game. He stated that "a young man was in his room, dripping blood from cuts in his arms and acting very strange." He pleaded, "Couldn't you come down?" I was still some-where in the twilight zone as I heard this description, yet responded, "Sure." I went to get my John Wayne uniform and wake up the trusty steed. As I was motoring to the rescue, I became aware of how little I knew of the situation. Such things as name of RA, specific residence hall, security issues, medical needs, and so on drew a blank. I finally woke up and lowered my Superman cape, and went to the security office to gather some information.

---

[1]Reprinted from *Journal of Counseling and Development, 67,* page 108. Copyright © ACA. Re-printed with permission. No further reproduction authorized without written permission of the American Counseling Association.

Although the situation was resolved in a positive manner, the potential for harm was also present, regardless of my heroic although misguided intentions. The incident crystallized for me the importance of becoming informed before blindly attempting to save the world. My good intentions and heroic strivings are no substitute for informed and competent practice. There are limits!

My personal incident also sensitized me to the potential for the heroic phenomenon within the counseling profession and higher education. I have witnessed the heroic drive among counseling center leaders and practitioners as I listen to them describe their responses to their unique campus situations—24-hour on-call duty, treating long-term clients with limited resources, serving as the hero on campus by becoming all things to various campus constituencies. For example, a counseling center may find it difficult to say "no" to a part of the campus community needing long-term treatment, although the center does not have the necessary resources—24-hour on-call service, sufficient staff, and easy access to inpatient facilities. Given the limited resources, long wait lists, and a brief therapy orientation to student developmental tasks, many counseling centers may not be an appropriate treatment facility; that is, use of such a center may be countertherapeutic for long-term clients. Of course, the long-term treatment question for counseling centers is more complex (e.g., a question of availability of appropriate referral sources), but to the degree that heroic intentions of counseling centers are not matched by adequate resources and competent practice, they become prone to the heroic syndrome.

On our campuses, the heroic trend also seems to be present. It seems that the social progress expectations of the "Great Society" of the 1960s have been transferred to the "Great University" of the 1980s. We hear about the expanded mission of the university as it is frequently called on to address the social ills of economic hardships, racism, and war. For instance, the role of the university in fostering economic development has become a hot topic.

The heroic symptoms seem to be everywhere—personally, professionally, and institutionally. I wonder if Karen Horney might be right; namely, the feeling of being outside the camp, feeling inferior, and isolated instigates the need to "search for glory." Horney's insight seems on the mark for a counseling profession perpetually seeking an identity, counseling centers trying to justify their existence, higher education struggling with criticism and new mandates, and even the larger society that has lost some of its moral and economic leadership in the world; there seems to be a focus on heroic actions. Each of these entities seems preoccupied at the moment with its perceived inferior status and related heroic aspirations.

I am not troubled by heroism, but I have relearned that the heroic drive needs to be tempered by realizing the necessity of limits. The word "no" belongs in the helping vocabulary.

My discussion has to end here because I just received an emergency call. I've got to roll. The struggle continues. (p. 108)

Stone's dilemma is the dilemma of all of us in human services, education and health care. It concerns the tension between two elements: good intentions/heroic strivings and the "no" of turning one's back on human need. These two pulls on the heart and mind of the practitioner are extremely difficult to reconcile, especially for the novice counselor, therapist, teacher, or health professional who is often confused about how hard to try in the helping role. Practicum, clerkship, practice teaching, and internship sites often receive excessive services from students in training whose strong intentions and heroic striving naturally lead to overextension. This process occurs year after year, like the swallows returning to San Juan Capistrano, with each new wave of students in training. It happened with me and my classmates; did it with you and your classmates? Learning boundaries and saying no seem to come later.

There was the public-health nurse in Chicago (L. Smith, personal communication, 1982) who had a 550 person caseload, and the school counselor in New York (R. Severson, personal communication, 1987) who tried to be fully available for 400 students and to please all the relevant groups—the school administrators, his counseling colleagues, the students, and the parents. Often the ability to set limits and say no only occurs with exhaustion and the realization that the individual cannot physically or emotionally maintain the pace over the long haul of 30 to 40 years or even a shorter haul of months or weeks. For Hill (1988), it came only after she had become totally overwhelmed as *the* college counselor for hundreds of students. She wrote:

Nine years ago I accepted the position of college counselor at a private liberal arts college of 800 students. I entered with 4 years of community counseling experience but was new to the needs and expectations of a college system. Seventy percent of the position was designated for directing and providing personal counseling and programs, and 30% was designated for teaching one psychology course each semester and serving on departmental committees. In addition to the college counselor, there was one career counselor.

My first year was chaos. Ongoing, and at times simultaneous, situations occurred that required immediate attention be given to students, staff, and faculty. For example, class lecture preparations and test design and evaluations were left to the late evenings because of the high demand of 35 to 40 hours of psychotherapy per week. (There were times when 3 or 4 students were simultaneously needing immediate counseling.) I was called out for approximately two middle-of-the-night emergency calls per weekend because a poorly trained housing staff was unable to identify, respond to, and refer students with problems in their early stages of development.

Needless to say, I felt exhausted, angry, hurt, and numb. I wanted the college system to reward me for my hard work and to rescue me from the overload. Neither occurred. I went to an extreme, working lunches, evenings, and weekends before I was willing to say to myself; [sic] "I have done all I can do and it's not enough." At the end of the first year I faced a cathartic moment, which became a turning point in my life. I realized that I had the choice of quitting or rescuing myself and the position. I chose the latter. (p. 105)

How does one learn to say no yet avoid indifference and apathy? For many, as Hill said, the proper point of tension only occurs after becoming overextended and exhausted. This process inspired the first work on burnout by Freudenberger (1974) and the subsequent work by many others, including a book with a poignant title, *Burnout: The Cost of Caring*, by Maslach (1982).

Hazard 9. Living in an Ocean of Stress Emotions

The capacity for compassion and empathy seems to be at the core of our ability to be wounded by the work.
—B. H. STAMM (1995, p. ix)

The incidence of stress-related problems for teachers has been dramatic in studies that have investigated this phenomenon. Surveys have demonstrated that up to 90% of all teachers may suffer from job-related stress and 50% of all teachers indicate that stress is a serious problem for them.
—M. T. SCHELSKE & J. L. ROMANO (1994, p. 21)

Practitioners often work with those who are experiencing some kind of difficulty. It may be a physical, academic, or emotional problem. Often a component of the need is emotional distress. Confusion, frustration, discouragement, anxiety, and anger are common. Unable to solve their own problems, helpees often experience a strong dose of the distress we could call *demoralized hopelessness*. Frank (1974) states that it is the job of the professional helper to work with demoralization. Hopelessness is a strong predictive sign of suicidal ideation. I use the term *demoralized hopelessness* to communicate the level of human distress that we are often asked to address.

One reason it is important to describe the intensity of client, student, and patient distress is that "forewarned is forearmed" helps us prepare to practice self-care over the long haul. When we understand that the task is stressful, we can prepare for it. The job of the counselor, therapist, teacher, and health professional often involves attaching and being wired emotionally to the other. That is the essence of empathy, being wired as if one's battery is connected to the other's battery to jumpstart it. The wiring often involves the negative emotions, meaning the stress emotions, resulting in the practitioner living in an "ocean of stress emotions." In time, practitioners learn how to be both wired to these distress emotions and separate from them. Learning this skill is complex and takes time.

Being wired to these stress emotions can be professionally toxic and a threat to the helper's emotional immunological system. Support for this idea comes from research on the immunological systems of individuals experiencing chronic stress, such as caregivers of Alzheimer's patients (Kiecolt-Glaser & Glaser, 1989). While working as a practitioner, which of these client, student, or patient stress emotions is most toxic for you: fear, confusion, rage, helplessness, cynicism, sorrow, isolation, loneliness, estrangement, anomie, lack of motivation, hopelessness, anger, desperation, or bitterness? To understand the poisonous qualities of these negative emotions on you as a practitioner, imagine each of these as a toxic agent attempting to enter your body. Which are most powerful and compelling? What is difficult or debilitating about these emotions for you?

Because working in this ocean of stress emotions is taxing, practitioners sometimes wish to remove themselves. For example, I once thought of opening a joy clinic, a place of only happy emotions where people would come when everything was going well, but I realized that business might be kind of slow. Later I thought of a flower shop, an ice cream store, a candy shop, or a plaque and awards store. At these kinds of places, everybody seems happy. There are many positive emotions.

The intensity and scope of human distress that comes to practitioners should not be underemphasized. Human beings are an extremely intelligent, able, and creative species and have the capacity to solve many complex problems (D'Zurilla & Nezu, 1982). All of us are very skilled at problem solving. Often, people seek out helpers *only* when they can't solve their problems by themselves, that is, when they have *unsolvable* problems that must be *solved*. It is the combination of *unsolvable* and must be *solved* that leads people to experience demoralized hopelessness.

In the work relationship—in the intensity and vividness of the counseling session, the educational classroom, or the hospital room—what is too much involvement and what is too little involvement in the negative emotions of the other person? We know that lack of empathic involvement in the emotions of the other is often considered poor practice in the helping professions. An uninvolved, callous, disengaged, "burned out" helper is what every counselor, therapist, teacher, and health professional hopes to avoid becoming. Yet, the other extreme, overinvolvement in these stress emotions, may be more precarious and dangerous for the helping process and our own well-being. How then does one regulate emotional involvement in the flow of human data, the life stories, of our clients, students, and patients? What is too much involvement; what is too little in this ocean of negative emotions? Cousins (1979) has made a compelling case for the impact of positive emotions and laughter on the health of the individual. In contrast, does the intensity of negative emotions change the helper's emotional immunological system? Are there analogies here to the effect of passive smoke on the non-smoker or asbestos fibers on the person in the room?

Hazard 10. Ambiguous Professional Loss— Ending before the Ending

In studies with families of missing-in-action (MIA) soldiers or Alzheimer patients, Boss says that ambiguous loss produces extreme stress (Boss, 1999; Boss, Caron, Horbal, & Mortimer, 1990). The family member is missing but not gone, present but not present. This can be extremely stressful. I have modified the term *ambiguous loss* to *ambiguous professional loss* to describe the constant lack of concrete results and closure for those in the counseling, therapy, teaching, and health professions. Lately, I have been hearing stories of this ambiguous professional loss, the times when there is an ending before the ending.

- A counselor at a residential treatment center worked very hard with a teenage female runaway, and he and his wife became very committed to this young, troubled teen. They got attached. Then one day, the teenager suddenly left the center, and they never heard from her again.
- A counselor in training told her supervisor that she wanted to have a different supervisor, but the counselor would not say why. The supervisor had to deal with this rejection—this attachment and then separation—without knowing why.
- A teacher spent the year with an at-risk fourth grade boy, trying amidst a room full of 31 children to give him enough attention to improve his poor academic performance. She was very invested in his progress. Just as he started to finally make major strides in April of the school year, after months of effort by the teacher, he was suddenly removed from his home and put in a foster home in another town. She never saw him again.
- A nurse was working intensely with a seriously ill patient. Upon returning after two days off, the nurse discovered that the patient was discharged because of insurance problems.

• A few years ago, a counselor saw one of her clients at a social event. The client seemed uncomfortable and later did not come back for counseling. Why? Did the social situation make a difference? The counselor never knew.

An elementary teacher told this story of ambiguous professional loss:

Recently I was reminded of…a third grader in my room a few years back. She came to me as a new student the day before Christmas vacation, with no school supplies, late, wearing dirty clothes, and smelling strongly of urine. In a day I learned she had been sexually abused as a preschooler, had severe psychological problems that had never been treated, soiled herself constantly, and had lacking social and motor skills. I attempted to involve school personnel and the parents immediately and continually, with little success. I spent much time working one-on-one with [her], documented daily her behaviors, etc. She was difficult to work with and I was exhausted at the end of each day. After one month, she was put into the psychiatric ward in our local hospital. I was concerned for her but hoped she would receive the care she needed.

She was there for one month, and when she returned to school, she was changed; she appeared to be happy, healthy, and clean. She did better in academic and social areas. I was excited and happy for her! She was with me for one week. One day her parents called on the way to [the West Coast] to say she wouldn't be returning to school.

I remember feeling very uncomfortable, sad, and angry. I had "lost" Cristina when we were just making progress. While she had been a challenging student to work with, her sudden disappearance truly bothered me. I had no opportunity to say good-bye or to wish her well. I felt like I wasn't "finished with her"; we still had more things to do.… I still occasionally think about her and wonder how she is doing. I believe I am also realistic in knowing that there will be similar incidents regarding lack of closure during my teaching career. (Smith, 1996)

Reflecting on ambiguous professional loss, S. Hage (personal communication, February 1994), a counselor in campus ministry, said: "Perhaps here lies one of the most difficult personal challenges of being a counselor. We most likely will never know the fruits of our work. We are very often the sowers or the waterers of a harvest we will never see."

A few years ago, I saw a TV documentary about an old, illiterate man who, earlier in his life, had a job making bricks one by one in a little machine. Now, decades later, he was walking around his city with great pride, showing his grandson all the bricks that he had made. They were in buildings all over town and obvious for all to see. I felt pity for helpers when watching him because he had this solid evidence of his work, the bricks, that helpers lack. Where are your bricks? Where are the obvious, concrete signs of your labor?

The constant demand for helping professionals to attach, be involved, and then separate over and over means that this process must be done in a way that is energizing to the individual practitioner. Ambiguous professional loss produces the opposite result; it drains the practitioner. This is analogous to descriptions of how ambiguous loss in the family and the confusion and lack of closure about "who is psychologically in and who is psychologically out of the family system can block family reorganization and accommodation to chronic stress" (Boss, et al., 1990, p. 246).

> *Caregivers have difficulty accepting the loss of their loved ones (because the loss is only partial) and they cannot grieve and move on to restructure the family as they could if the person were no longer physically present.... Caregivers' boundary ambiguity and sense of mastery are important correlates in understanding the development of caregiver depression. (Boss, et al., 1990, pp. 247, 253)*

The lack of closure can be quite stressful for practitioners. Being sensitive enough to be affected by such experiences is, I contend, part of the "soft side of the turtle" issue. An exceptional capacity to attach demands emotional sensitivity. A medical doctor described the dilemma this way:

> *I suppose one has to have a fairly conscientious type of personality to be a good doctor. It is a caring and painstaking approach which endears doctors to their patients. The problem is that this same personality can make a person very conscious of failure, which in turn leads to depression. I also found that my sensitive nature, which fitted me so well for my profession, caused me to feel hurt over matters I have seen others shrug off without apparent injury. (By a general practitioner, 1985, p. 63)*

Hazard 11. The Covert Nature of the Work

The previous hazard suggests that ambiguity and lack of closure can make success feel elusive. This hazard introduces another element that interferes with work satisfaction. Practitioners in the counseling, therapy, teaching, and health professions can't talk about their work! For example, the psychotherapist may have achieved an incredible breakthrough with a client that is life changing, yet the practitioner must return home and remain quiet about the day's success. Imagine that! You want to tell friends and family about your day—doesn't everybody want to do that?—but you cannot because of confidentiality provisions that protect the privacy of the client, student, or patient.

Confidentiality is an important and valuable aspect of these professions and is a catalyst for the work to occur, such as with psychotherapy in which the client reveals very personal information. Although this is a very positive aspect of the work overall, it binds practitioners to not talk about the work, therefore, the covert nature of the work. Counselors, therapists and Central Intelligence Agency (CIA) agents share a common bond, a secret life they cannot reveal. The negative side of this is that a practitioner in these fields is unable to share the successes, failures, frustrations, and confusion of the work outside of the professional context; therefore, the value of social support, connection, and understanding as ways to reduce work stress gets greatly compromised in these fields.

Hazard 12. Constant Empathy, Interpersonal Sensitivity, and One-Way Caring

Empathy is a double-edged sword; it is simultaneously your greatest asset and a point of real vulnerability.

—D. G. LARSON (1993, p. 30)

Individuals in the high touch (vs. high tech) occupations are successful only because they can do "high touch"—relate to others by way of expert people skills. Yet, this work takes effort. The practitioner must concentrate, be involved, and work at it until depletion—not total depletion but relative depletion. Interpersonal sensitivity demands that the practitioner understand the complexity of human relationships, including concepts such as projection and transference, which mean the feelings that the other projects, like in a movie, onto the practitioner. For example, if you followed an older sibling in school and the teachers seemed to keep treating you like the sibling rather than yourself, then you have experienced projection or transference.

The psychoanalytic-psychodynamic tradition has been most useful in illuminating transference-countertransference concepts (Corsini & Wedding, 1989). Maintaining a clear awareness of transference-countertransference issues is not always easy for counselors, therapists, teachers, and health professionals trying to establish positive human relationships with individuals that they attempt to assist. Working in the high touch professional relationship amidst the transference-countertransference flotsam is very difficult but critical in achieving excellent human relationships, a marker that sets apart those in the caring professions. But it is "swimming upstream" and hard work. Working free of our own distortions is a difficult goal because it means that we must take off the layperson's perceptual lens.

Mitchell and Anderson (1983) describe the stress of the transference re-action in the professional lives of an allied helping field, the clergy. They write, "At the best of times, people project on their pastor their fears of judg-ment, their anger at God, and many other feelings. In moments of severe stress, the tendency to misperceive the pastor is even stronger" (p. 118). Members of the clergy, wanting like other helpers to be perceived positively, can often be confused and distressed when those that they seek to help react to them with strong negative emotions.

With countertransference, which is our own distorted reactions to the other (Sexton & Whiston, 1994), we must work to understand the wide array of perceptual filters that we bring to the helping relationship—our own per-sonal history; our own major demographic variables such as age, race, religion, sex, and Social Economic Status (SES); our own family of origin genogram and its biases; our own trauma and pain; and our own cultural encapsulation within geographic and national boundaries. Understanding all of these per-ceptual filters and their impact on our reaction to the other is hard, hard work.

Thus, although transference and countertransference provide rich data for the helper of others, making use of this data means swimming against the cur-rent. The temptation is always to turn around and go with the current, with the lay reaction of just being human. This is both a primary stressor and hard work. Excellent high touch practitioners, however, maintain the interpersonal sensitivity within the one-way caring relationship.

Hazard 13. Elusive Measures of Success

In complex, ambiguous caring for others, it is difficult to gauge success. If the professional impulse is to counsel, teach, or heal, then success must relate to the amount of counseling, teaching, or healing. Or does it relate more to the amount of improvement by the client, student, or patient? Or is it some com-bination of these qualities—effort by the practitioner multiplied times im-provement by the recipient? Then is it the quantity of the practitioner's effort or the quality? Is it improvement by the recipient compared to self or to the general population? If the person in need is significantly impaired, do we ex-pect less? If he or she is highly functional, do we expect more? For example, should the doctor of terminally ill cancer patients judge success or failure by whether the patients stay alive? If not this criteria, what?

Professional stress comes in part from the elusiveness of concrete results and the difficulty in measuring success. In the ambiguous and murky world of counseling, therapy, teaching, and healing, who is responsible for im-provement? A graduate student in the helping professions wrote:

Related to feelings of success and failure in the helping professions is the issue of responsibility.... My own natural inclinations have been to rescue the client and to work from my own set of assumptions about what the goals and expectations ought to be. The supervision I had...was very useful in helping me see that tendency in my approach with clients. Not only was the overresponsibility sometimes unproductive, or even counterproductive, with the clients, it was horribly frustrating to me to often feel like a "failure" with my clients. I too frequently imposed my view of success, then beat myself up when they couldn't achieve it. (Thorson, 1994, p. 3)

Maybe we are doing a good job if our supervisor says we are, but then maybe the supervisor is in error. Maybe we are doing a good job if our clients, students, or patients like us, but then maybe liking us is irrelevant to having a significant impact on their lives. Haven't we all, with time, come to appreciate and gain from practitioners, such as a demanding teacher in high school, whom we disliked at the time that they were pushing us hard?

Perhaps success is related not to results but rather to skilled effort. In other words, the counselor of acting out, angry adolescents can measure success by how much an adolescent client becomes more cooperative, social, and achieving, or the counselor can measure success by how much he or she practices professional skills to a maximum level. Do we focus on outcome (the client's changes) or process (our own professional effort), or is it a combination of these two? Should one reduce expectations regarding outcome if the level of need, dysfunction, disease, or dis-ease is greater? When do reduced expectations help to fuel the cycle of failure, rather than interrupt it, so that the practitioner colludes in the failure rather than attempting to stop it?

Even if we decide that realism rather than idealism should be a goal, how do we move in that direction? This question often emerges for practitioners from the older dilemma of realizing that one's professional efforts (one's power-influence-commitment-energy-competence coupled with feelings of inadequacy) are not enough. This realization usually occurs through a "series of professional humiliations," which occur when one's best efforts produce only failure (Skovholt & Rønnestad, 1995).

Even when avoiding unmeetable expectations, the practitioner faces a new dilemma of how to transform expectations. How is the practitioner to distinguish between being realistic and giving up? Giving up is a process in which the counseling, teaching, or healing practitioner colludes in the cycle of failure and becomes, in the end, the official reporter that the system tried but the inadequate client, student, or patient failed. This is when helping becomes toxic, the victim becomes revictimized, and blaming the victim becomes a powerful, destructive enterprise. The liberators have become prison guards who continue on because they like the salary and retirement benefits, the security, and the status, but they no longer care enough to really be powerful helpers of others. They are no longer attached, and without the attachment, the helping relationship, so well documented as an instrument of human change and transformation (Sexton & Whiston, 1994), is unplugged. Powerlessness results. How can this destructive process be distinguished from the very different process of becoming realistic; that is, gaining a more elaborate, textured understanding of the difficulty of human change and moving to less grand expectations of oneself as a practitioner?

Hazard 14. Normative Failure

A common experience of teachers is to feel the pain of opportunities missed, potential unrealized, students untouched.

—W. AYERS (1993, p. 7)

[Sometimes] the classroom is so lifeless or painful or confused—and I am so powerless to do anything about it—that my claim to be a teacher seems a transparent sham. Then the enemy is everywhere: in those students from some alien planet, in that subject I thought I knew, and in the personal pathology that keeps me earning my living this way. What a fool I was to imagine that I had mastered this occult art—harder to divine than tea leaves and impossible for mortals to do even passably well!

—P. J. PALMER (1998, p. 1)

One of the most distressing parts of being a practitioner in counseling, therapy, teaching, and healing is the often desperate search for concrete standards of success versus failure. The personal threat is often severe, and one's career search and occupational identity are at stake. Also, there is often a sense of ambiguous but pervasive anxiety related to this question. One element of this dis-ease is the need to differentiate normative failure from excessive failure. Resolving this question is very important for the novice practitioner, and increased professional experience often brings more clarity to the distinction. This, in turn, tends to greatly reduce pervasive professional anxiety as one moves from novice to advanced practitioner (Skovholt & Rønnestad, 1995). After learning to define normative failure versus excessive failure, the novice must begin to clarify whether he or she is on the normative or excessive side of the competence fence. Being able to place oneself on the normative side also reduces one's free-floating worries about professional skill.

A second element here is the term *normative failure*. It is a startling term. People most often enter counseling, therapy, teaching, and the healing arts with an intense desire to make a significant impact in the lives of others—to heal, educate, reduce hurt, stop pain, increase competence, provide insights. Accompanying this desire, there is often an only partially understood sense of using a powerful method of change, a feeling of one's own potence in helping others make positive changes. Related to this, there can also be an urgent attempt to rescue the other. Thus, the concept of normative failure can be a startling jolt.

Those in the caring professions can be extremely distressed when they feel that they have failed in helping. Linville (1988) describes such an experience:[2]

> I was in my first position as a school counselor and soon found that I was expected to do much more than talk with students who had problems. I learned that I was also the director of the school district's home-bound program. I tried to be conscientious, but my world seemed to be a jumble of interviews with students, parents, and teachers; of trying to deal with classroom and playground emergencies; and of jumping from one thing to another. I was not quite sure who or what I was supposed to be.
>
> One morning I found a note on my desk. A boy in the upper grades who had leukemia now required home-bound instruction. He was only a name and an added responsibility for me, part of my duties. I shook my head. I had begun fitting students into categories, "Problems" and "Duties," and I slipped Tim, the boy with leukemia, neatly into the "Duties" category.
>
> I made my telephone calls. I called the teacher who worked with home-bound students and asked when she and I could visit the boy. I called Tim's mother, and we set up a time for the visit.
>
> The teacher and I visited the home. I didn't know what to expect, but Tim was dressed and he was up and around, a little pale perhaps, wearing a brown sweater to keep warm, but happy to see the teacher.
>
> "I'll be back on Friday," the teacher said. "Maybe you can have all of your assignment done by then."
>
> Tim came up to me. "When will you be back?" he asked.
>
> "I'll come back a month from today," I said cheerfully. "That will be Tuesday, the 28th. I'll see how everything's working out."
>
> "What time will you be here?" Tim's mother asked.
>
> "About one o'clock," I said.
>
> "Come back," Tim said.
>
> He stood just inside the door, holding one of his books.
>
> Arrangements had been properly made. Another of my assignments had been completed. When I was back in the office, I made a note in my appointment book about the visit on the 28th.
>
> I was soon involved with Parents Night, with some boys who were leaving school at recess, and with two teachers on a teaching team who had stopped speaking to one another. The month went fast. The day I was to visit Tim came, but the school superintendent came by to talk to me,

[2]Reprinted from *Journal of Counseling and Development, 67,* page 101. Copyright © ACA. Reprinted with permission. No further reproduction authorized without written permission of the American Counseling Association.

and I forgot to check the appointment book. Then the superintendent asked me to go to lunch, and when I got back to the office it was two o'clock.

"Tim seemed all right," I said to myself. "I'll stop by another day when I'm in the neighborhood."

Another day became another day, and Tim was a forgotten note in an appointment book. The days were blurs of conferences and telephone calls and bits and pieces of advice and admonition, all shaped by duty and expectations. A month passed, and I stopped at a grocery store on my way home from school. It was an evening in early winter, and I was glad to walk down the brightly lit aisles of the store after walking through the evening darkness outside. I stopped by the produce counter and picked up a head of lettuce.

I looked up and there was Tim's mother, pushing a grocery cart. She pushed it slowly, and her lips moved as if she were trying to remember something. There was a large orange box of cereal in her basket with a picture of a baseball player hitting a home run on the side.

I said cheerfully, "Hello. Do you remember me?"

"Yes," she answered.

"How's Tim doing?"

This time she didn't answer. She only looked at me.

"I hope.... " I started talking because everything seemed so quiet.

Suddenly she spoke. "He died," she said in a harsh voice.

I gathered up the usual words of sympathy and smoothed them out. She kept looking at me, and I shifted the head of lettuce in my hands. I stepped back a little. I thought she was looking at me as if she hated me.

"He thought you were coming," she said. "He waited for you. He had his work ready to show you."

I still remember every sharp detail of the scene—her face with the tight lines of grief by her mouth, the stacks of produce, the bright lights of the store. Her hands were gripping the round handle on the grocery cart. She looked at me and said softly, "You hurt him."

She pushed the cart hard and walked away. I stood there. I put down the lettuce and walked out of the store. It was dark outside, no touch of evening left. The lights fell across the parking lot in pale and wavering lines. I waited a while before I opened the door of my car. I felt as if I had turned my back on another human being.

Since then I have kept duplicate appointment books, but, far more than that, I began to think about what I was really doing. I realized that I had a responsibility to others, that I could not keep people waiting through long afternoons, that being busy (often idle busyness) was no excuse. My essential function was to be there and not leave people all alone, waiting for a word from me. I saw that failure in my work could go far beyond not meeting job specifications. I realized that children were not Problems and Duties, that human contact was more than making proper arrangements, that beyond the performance of assignments were human needs reaching toward me—and I had not been there. A little boy in a brown sweater had been waiting, and the afternoon was long. (p. 101)

We may know at one level that the patients of expert doctors sometimes die, but this profound understanding of the reality of professional success and failure doesn't penetrate our own professional self-concept. Somehow, we believe that we will succeed in our own healing of others, and our clients, students, patients will change and get better. With further experience and a clearer reality, practitioners must realize that they are like doctors whose patients die. All our will, all our work, all our competence will sometimes not be enough. This means that, in time, the practitioner must develop the capacity to accept lack of success—normative failure—as a component of the work. Being able to come to this realization, accept it, and incorporate it into one's professional self-concept is important for long-term, high-quality professional functioning. In our research, experienced practitioners often were, in effect, talking about acceptance of normative failure when they described their own shift in expectations as they moved toward being "realistic" (Skovholt & Rønnestad, 1995).

Hazard 15. Regulation Oversight and Control by External, Often Unknown Others

A medical doctor told me of being scolded by an administrative clerk the day after admitting an adolescent to the hospital. The evening before, he had seen the adolescent while he was on emergency room duty. He made a medical decision, based on 20 years of practice, that inpatient care was warranted. The next morning, the administrative clerk, an anonymous person in another state, told him that the admission was unwarranted.

This new layer of administration between the practitioner and the client, student, and patient in human services, education, and health care has a positive goal—to reduce excessive costs and increase quality of care. From the practitioner's point of view, however, the main result is often increased stress. The ingredients for the increased stress are less control but increased responsibility by the practitioner, more detailed paperwork without pay for the additional work, and contradictory messages to increase and decrease services at the same time. There are many difficulties. For example, should the mental health practitioner highlight the client's problem areas when asking for authorization of more treatment? To do so may increase the stigma of emotional illness; to not do so decreases the chance for authorization.

Hazard 16. Cognitive Deprivation and Boredom

The novice, at sea in heavy waters, tries hard to maintain the craft and avoid sinking. It is often an anxiety-filled voyage, composed of quick changes, new challenges, occasional calm, and a veneer depth of professional confidence. Like a powerful, churning sea, the novice is never sure of the professional challenge to be faced in the upcoming minutes, hours, and days. It is often intense, involving, and engrossing and sometimes very exciting in a positive vein. It is *not* boring.

For the senior practitioner in the high touch fields, the challenge can be 180 degrees from that facing the novice. For the veteran with years of experience, the sea is calm, the route predictable, and the work tasks, now mastered, the same as before and before and before. This situation is especially true for a practitioner working in a very prescribed arena in terms of the scope of the work and the job environment. Sure, the payoff is reduced anxiety and increased professional confidence. That counts for a lot. The problem is that the intellectual stimulation is lessened, the routine has become boring, and task repetition grates like an old wound. The stimulation of novelty, with its sugar coat, is gone. The obnoxious, unpleasant, unwanted tasks, which did not seem too bad for the novice who was simply trying to stay afloat, now can be felt aptly in the phrase, "You can take this job and shove it."

This drama for the senior practitioner occurs in the bigger drama of the dance between the practitioner and the client, student, or patient. The client, student, or patient is, of course, fully invested in his or her personal needs, as should be the case, and wants very much to have a practitioner who is fully invested too. The unwritten, unspoken contract desired by the one in need is that the practitioner be strongly engaged in the caring cycle of empathic attachment, active involvement, and felt separation. For example, remember in Chapter 3 the research study of teachers that found that, most of all, people want a caring teacher. They want to feel that they matter to the practitioner.

With boredom, there is a lack of novelty to stimulate the practitioner. One kind of novelty relates to the practitioner as a cultural anthropologist. One vocational choice inventory asks if the person is more interested in people or things. For counselors, therapists, teachers, and health-care workers, it is people. People—their lives, choices, thoughts, feelings, and ways in the world—enchant them. It can be exciting, like a big tip for a taxi driver. Being with people, therefore, is very rewarding because the practitioner keeps learning about these beings called people. When one knows enough about one aspect of human life and the curiosity factor is satiated, then the cultural anthropologist reward disappears. I remember being an advisor and counselor for 18-year-old college freshmen. It was interesting to try to understand all the permutations and combinations of their lives, but after four years of it, I felt that I knew more than enough about being 18. I was getting bored with the same thinking, struggles, worries, and developmental vistas. I wanted out.

Aside from learning about people through involvement with them, practitioners are stimulated in their search for more professional competence. Good practitioners always want to find ways to work effectively with those that they serve. Using one's own human computer and attempting to work effectively with the most complex of all species can be immensely stimulating intellectually. For example, imagine that there is a seventh grade boy in front of you. He is in school but not doing well. You, the teacher, are charged with charging him up. What route will you take? Or imagine that you are a physical therapist with a patient who fails to do critical exercises at home. What will you do? Or you are a school counselor leading a group of children from divorcing families. These children have never been together before to discuss this difficult topic. How will you lead the group so that the children will benefit?

These challenges stimulate the practitioner; however, at some point, especially with a narrow population or problem, the practitioner has seen and done it all before, and *boredom sets in.* The counselor has heard the story many times before; the teacher has taught the subject over and over; the physician has performed the medical procedure again and again. The rub is that the client, student, or patient needs an energized practitioner, but the practitioner is bored. The practitioner can be engaged by new work but may be trapped by "golden handcuffs," the financial benefits given to those who stay in a position for many years. In short, this problem of cognitive deprivation and boredom is a significant hazard in the counseling, therapy, teaching, and health fields.

Hazard 17. Cynical, Critical, Negative Colleagues and Managers

> *It is not unusual to see faculty in midcareer don the armor of cynicism against students, education, and any sign of hope. It is the cynicism that comes when the high hopes one once had for teaching have been dashed by experience—or by the failure to interpret one's experience accurately.*
>
> —P. J. PALMER (1998, p. 48)

The work can be hard, and those that we try to help can stress us. Yet, with a supportive work group and a good boss, the job can be positive and fulfilling. When the colleagues are negative or the boss is incompetent, reality is more burdensome. Cynical colleagues spread a highly infectious disease. This disease, negativity, is easy to catch. It is also a seductive disease because, when one first gets it, he or she feels better. Venting helps. But like other seductive diseases (smoking, for example), the long-term result brings on a grimmer reaper. Cynicism in the air is especially dangerous in the high touch occupations. Members of the people occupations need the stress-buffering effect of positive colleagues, which is a long distance on a continuum from the nonbuffering effect of negative colleagues.

A second factor relates to the needs of those we serve. The "touch" desired by the other, whether client, student, or patient, is most empowering when it contains the active ingredient of hopefulness. In fact, Frank and Frank (1991) argue that helpers are sought out when a person feels demoralized, with the chief curative agent being hopefulness. But how can one offer hope within a critical, cynical work environment?

Bosses get paid more because they help create the important work environment. I am reminded of the work of Carkhuff (1969), whose research suggests that the client cannot function psychologically at a higher level than the helper. In a parallel fashion, it is hard for a worker to function at a higher level than the boss. With a great boss, everyone can sail; with a poor boss, the environment leads to no sailing or poor sailing by all on board. In the caring professions, bosses are incompetent if they are very critical or unfair. They also are poor if they do not support ideal conditions that enable counselors, therapists, teachers, or health workers to use the caring cycle with those that they serve. And remember that only energized people can continually care for the other in need and do it over and over again.

Hazard 18. Legal and Ethical Fears

> We used to be on our toes of concern for the kids, now we are on our heels of worry about ethical and legal threats.
> —25-YEAR VETERAN TEACHER AND COUNSELOR
> PARTICIPANT IN OTHER-CARE AND SELF-CARE
> WORKSHOP (1996)

> The combination of grater public awareness of inadequate practice on the part of professionals, ongoing research into the etiology of mental disorders and the efficacy of different treatments, increased third-party financing, and increased corporate practice provide a ripe environment for litigation.
> —R. K. OTTO & W. S. SCHMIDT (1991, p. 319)

It is important to start by noting that legal and ethical complaints have been nurtured by illegal and unethical behavior of practitioners in the counseling, therapy, teaching, and health fields. Misuse of power to meet one's own needs, general incompetence, and other unethical behaviors are not to be tolerated. But here we are talking about the wider arena of potential legal and ethical complaints and instances where the practitioner is wrongly accused.

Hazard 19. Practitioner Emotional Trauma

Last week on one day I had eight appointments, all with people who had been ter-minated from their jobs. After that day I wanted to crawl in a hole [to escape the painful feelings].

—MATT JOHNSON, counselor of newly "downsized"
employees (August 1996)

I have described the practitioner dilemma of needing to connect with the other by using one's soft side of the turtle rather than the hard shell. Yet, unfortunately, doing this produces a side effect—practitioner emotional trauma—as surely as strong medicines produce side effects. Chersick (cited by Sussman, 1995) calls it *sadness of the soul.* Cerney (1985) describes it as *secondary trauma.* McCann and Pearlman (1990), Pearlman and MacIan (1995), and Saakvitne (1999) use the term *vicarious traumatization.* All of these terms describe how we hear about, visualize, and experience the events that bring people to caring professionals in counseling, therapy, teaching, and healing.

This construct overlaps the earlier described ocean of distress emotions, but it goes beyond that to experiencing the reality of difficult events in the lives of our clients, students, and patients. These include sexual assault, chronic physical pain, unexpected failure in school, betrayal in friendship, student neglect by parents, severe financial loss, a child's death, physical attack, sudden job loss, deceit within marriage, a fatal car accident, onset of a serious illness, and severe existential anguish. Over the years of a practitioner's career, many of these events and others are heard and described. Often for history taking and diagnostic purposes, the counselor, therapist, teacher, or nurse must hear the details of the experience. Later in counseling or therapy, for example, the desensitization elements of the work may entail countless times of recalling the experience to help the client reduce the traumatic elements of it. The therapeutic process for the client can, over time, produce a vicarious traumatization or secondary trauma experience for the counselor or therapist. Therapist Sussman (1995) describes it this way:

Prone to overidentifying with clients, I tend to experience much of their emotional pain and internal struggles as if they were my own. The permeability of my ego boundaries may facilitate empathic contact, but it also leaves me vulnerable to emotional overload. Especially when working with more disturbed individuals, hearing and digesting their stories of past and present abuse can be highly disturbing. (p. 21)

A parallel process can happen for health professionals who repeatedly hear of the vulnerability of the human body to disease and injury. The human body in front of them that has been attacked by disease or injury is not unlike the body that they themselves possess. Educators also experience versions of this vicarious stress when they interact with struggling students unable to learn and with little family support. Vicarious traumatization or secondary trauma means processing this knowledge and the realization that "there but for the grace of God go I."

Another kind of practitioner emotional trauma involves "taking in" the hostility of the client, student, or patient toward the practitioner. For example, there is the angry reaction of a parent to a teacher at a parent-teacher conference, the intense affect lability of a teenage client to a youth counselor, or the hostile behavior of a patient to a nurse. This negative reaction from those that we try to help can be quite stressful because it can hit the "soft side of the turtle" part of us with which we attach and negates our primary occupational need of being helpful.

Hazard 20. Practitioner Physical Trauma

Sometimes things go beyond severe overload, the ocean of negative emotions, ambiguous professional loss, and normative failure so that the underside of the turtle, the soft defenseless part, the area that attaches, gets physically hurt.

The most frightening form of practitioner physical trauma for psychotherapists is direct attack by clients. In the *Boston Globe* on August 21, 1999, a headline stated, "Social Worker Slain Outside Client's Home." The first paragraph reads, "A social worker whom colleagues described as dedicated to his job counseling troubled youths and trained to deal with violent situations was shot dead yesterday, allegedly by a member of a family he had gone to visit" (Milbouer, 1999, p. B1). And so the nightmare came true for a 30-year-old practitioner, married with children, just trying to do his job!

In research on this topic, Guy and his colleagues (Guy, Brown, & Poelstra, 1990, 1992) discovered that 40 percent of their sample group of 750 predominantly full-time practitioners had been physically attacked by clients during their careers, and 49 percent had received serious verbal threats against their health and safety. These kinds of traumatic events led to many different concerns about safety. For example, 28 percent often or sometimes were concerned about the verbal threats toward their physical safety, 17 percent were often or sometimes concerned about physical attacks on their loved ones, and 7 percent were often or sometimes concerned about being murdered. This in turn led to a variety of protective measures against client threats. For example, this sample group frequently refused to treat certain clients (50 percent), discussed safety issues with loved ones (30 percent), installed a home security alarm system (13 percent), or kept a weapon at home to protect themselves against present or former clients (5 percent). This study provides sobering data regarding this issue of counselor or therapist primary trauma.

Both Kinnetz (1988) and Zeh (1988) describe highly traumatic experiences while they served as counselors. Both were physically attacked by their clients and traumatized by these events. For Kinnetz, it occurred while she worked in a maximum security psychiatric unit; for Zeh, it was in a shelter for runaway adolescents. Kinnetz describes her experience:[3]

At the beginning of my counseling career, I was employed as an art therapist in an adult male, forensic, maximum security psychiatric unit. The job was difficult because I had never before worked with an all-male population, let alone one that was explosively violent. Angry patient outbursts were common. For example, in one scuffle a patient cracked the jawbone of a hospital aide, and, on another occasion, a patient knocked his doctor nearly unconscious in an unprovoked attack. Nearly paralyzed with fear during the first few days, I stayed in the protective nursing station away from the patients, leaving only to come and go from work. My fear of being harmed lessened considerably, however, when I realized that the hospital staff was very tightly knit and could be counted on to work as a team, especially in emergencies. So, despite the limitations imposed by the strict safety requirements, I began to feel challenged to stay on the ward and to establish an art therapy program.

My discomfort did not completely disappear, however, as I sensed tension in the patients as well. Although I never actually observed a blatant example of staff abuse, I became aware that some of the staff's behavior was less than professional. It seemed to me that, at times, their methods of patient restraint were too strong and bordered on abuse. Certainly, the patients were both verbally and physically abusive to staff as well [as] to each other, and any staff intervention was aimed at rapidly defusing a potential fight and reestablishing compliance with hospital routine. A client-centered approach would have been ludicrous in this situation, because immediate control had to be externally imposed to protect other patients. It was obvious that very strong measures were needed. But how strong, and what kind?

My dilemma was this: Do I report my suspicions in an effort to stop overly aggressive restraints, and risk being told that the force was really necessary? Or do I continue to observe the strong-arm control and be ensured of the protection of the staff? I could depend on the staff to promptly come to my aid should a fight threaten to break out, and was afraid that if I reported my suspicions, I might upset some of them and lose their protection. My fear won out; I did not report anyone until I left the unit for another position.

[3]Reprinted from *Journal of Counseling and Development, 67,* page 87. Copyright © ACA. Reprinted with permission. No further reproduction authorized without written permission of the American Counseling Association.

One of the factors that helped me to decide to leave was when a patient attempted to rape me. I had been escorting him to another part of the hospital when he suddenly grabbed me around the neck and twisted my arm behind my back. He held a contraband razor to my throat and dragged me into an empty room. Fortunately, I was able to free myself and run back to the unit for help. But I continue to wonder whether help would have come so quickly if the staff knew that I was considering reporting them for excessive force.

Years later, I still have not come to terms with the issue of whether I should have reported the possible abuse earlier. This incident has sparked many internal dialogues on the general issue of how I can best take care of myself without sacrificing my client's care. I have found that it sometimes becomes necessary for me to pull back momentarily from the continually intense and demanding emotional needs of a client. This is essential to preserve my own emotional reserves and to prevent eventual burnout. These client needs are less life threatening than the attempted rape, but my time-out response to them is no less important over the course of therapy. Certainly, if I withdraw every time the client becomes emotionally demanding, it would be a major therapeutic error, and my effectiveness would be severely compromised.

The ability to be fully engaged with the client in his or her struggles is a powerful curative factor. But if I allow myself to become emotionally overwhelmed and burned out, the long-term result is a compromised effectiveness. Not only is one client affected, but all my clients and even family and friends suffer. Although the strong-arm measures on the unit were extreme, perhaps (but perhaps not) they were justified to preserve the unit's functioning and ultimately to benefit the patients. Similarly, without taking care of myself emotionally, I cannot help clients learn to take care of themselves.

The unresolved nature of this question continues to keep me searching for balance. Too much therapist emotional withdrawal is not in the client's best interests, but continual emotional availability to the client is draining and dangerous, particularly in the absence of sufficient external therapist support. It is imperative that I monitor my own internal state as well as attend to my clients' emotional well-being. I judge my immediate internal state as a balance of present emotional and physical reserve, counterbalanced with the amount of support and replenishment that I can count on in the near future to replace the outgoing supply. This self-monitoring can be considered an extension of caring for my client. Although self-monitoring is not sufficient in itself to prevent therapist burnout, it goes a long way in helping me remain effective in both the short-term and long-term. Nonetheless, it is an ongoing, elusive dilemma—where is the balance between my needs and the needs of those I serve? (p. 87)

These are examples of practitioner physical trauma—acute wounds to the "underside of the turtle" part of the self from work as a practitioner. They include experiences that produce the stress emotions of anger, fear, and despair.

Hazards Summary

For veteran practitioners, there often are especially difficult incidents over the years of practice that lead to a loss of innocence. The most traumatic incidents, such as the suicide of a client, are stressful and, at the time, bring on daydreams of other, hopefully more positive, occupational choices. What are the lessons from these incidents? For one, practice can wound the practitioner. Often the vulnerability is unknown. The person may not have known before that a field that can do so much good can also wound its practitioners. Innocence is not knowing how the "soft side of the turtle" can produce practitioner vulnerability.

Reading this chapter of 20 hazards may lead a person to question the wisdom of entering any of the "people" professions. Bodily experiences can include a pit in one's stomach, an increase in anxiety felt, or the beginnings of a headache. This is my intent. I also tried to communicate the opposite feelings that one can get in Chapter 2, Joys, Rewards, and Gifts of Practice. The overall goal of this whole book is to portray first the wonderful qualities of the work, in contrast, the stressful qualities of the work, and consequently, the need for professional self-care on an ongoing basis.

7

Burnout

A Hemorrhaging of the Self

After working in community mental health for five years, I was burned out, or burned up, by a sense of hopelessness after overextending myself to help people and no one seemingly appreciated my efforts.

—M. E. YOUNG (1997, p. 45)

You may wonder where the term *burnout* came from. In the early 1970s, Herbert Freudenberger was a practitioner in New York City at a community agency focusing on drug abuse. At the time, drug abusers were often called "burnouts." Being called a burnout meant that the person no longer cared about anything except drugs. As a consequence of a slow erosion of motivation and competence, the person was not capable of much. Hence, one became a burnout.

In 1974, Freudenberger published an article titled "Staff Burnout" in a psychology journal. Freudenberger attempted to describe a loss of will among the practitioners who worked with these addicted clients. He used the word *burnout* in this way for the first time, and the term was born! This first article on burnout began:

Some years ago, a few of us who had been working intensively in the free clinic movement began to talk of a concept which we referred to as "burnout." Having experienced this feeling state of burn-out myself, I began to ask myself a number of questions about it. First of all, what is burn-out? (p. 159)

In the 1980s, the term *burnout* hit a cord. It quickly became a popular way to consider exhaustion and disquiet at work. It had what measurement people call face validity, meaning that it captured something that practitioners could identify as real. Soon, a number of authors wrote books on burnout in various occupations, such as human services (Cherniss, 1980), teaching (Cedoline, 1982), nursing (McConnell, 1982), and medicine (Wessells, et al., 1989). From 1980 to 1985, there was an outpouring of 300 academic articles on burnout (Roberts, 1986).

Searching the literature, Söderfeldt, Söderfeldt, and Warg (1995) found many descriptions of the term. Although the descriptions were different, key words reveal commonalities. These key words are *fatigue, frustration, disengagement, stress, depletion, helplessness, hopelessness, emotional drain, emotional exhaustion,* and *cynicism.* These words point to a profound weariness and hemorrhaging of the self as key components of burnout. This profound weariness and hemorrhaging of the self makes the idea of burnout understood by counselors, therapists, teachers, and health professionals.

Lack of Clarity

Paradoxically, although the concept of burnout seems understood by all, it does not seem to really be one specific thing. One could ask, what does it really mean, and what is the research summary at this point many years later? The answers are murky. It has been hard to find strong, consistent statistical relationships regarding burnout. Söderfeldt et al. (1995) wrote, "Overall, there are weak indications of any pattern in the associations, except that they generally seemed job related" (p. 642), and concluded that "burnout should be considered a multidimensional syndrome" (p. 644). A wide variety of variables has been found, in at least one study or another, to be associated with burnout. Table 7.1, is an example from the field of social work.

Work of Maslach

Christine Maslach, a psychology professor in California, is considered one of the leading burnout researchers. (This is opposed to being a burned out researcher. I heard her speak recently, and she was quite energetic.) The Maslach Burnout Inventory, a popular research instrument (Maslach & Jackson, 1981), and her recent book, *The Truth About Burnout* (Maslach & Leiter, 1997), have been well received.

Maslach and Leiter (1997) give their definition of burnout: "Burnout is the index of the dislocation between what people are and what they have to

TABLE 7.1   Factors Associated with Burnout in Social Workers

Work related

Low work autonomy
Lack of challenge on the job
Low degrees of support
Role ambiguity
Work in public sector
Low professional self-esteem, low salary
Dissatisfaction with agency goals and minimal use of coping strategies at work
Difficulties in providing services to clients
Negative attitudes toward the profession, high degree of work pressure, bad
    agency functioning

Client related

Negative impressions of the clients
Empathy
Personal involvement in clients' problems
Involvement in the client-worker relationship

Worker related

Chronic minor hassles of daily living
Family income, attitudes toward the profession, years of experience, low
education

Source: Sölderfeldt, M., Sölderfeldt, B., & Warg, L. E. (1995). Burnout in social work. Copyright © National Association of Social Workers, Inc., *Social Work, 40,* 641.

do. It represents an erosion in values, dignity, spirit, and will—an erosion of
the human soul" (p. 17). They go on to describe three key work dimensions
in which a person could be fully engaged or burned out (p. 24):

Fully Engaged	*vs.*	*Burned Out*
energy	vs.	exhaustion
involvement	vs.	cynicism
efficacy	vs.	ineffectiveness

Regarding the causes of burnout, Maslach and Leiter (1997) take a strong
work-climate view. Instead of blaming the individual, they say that "burnout
is not a problem of the people themselves but of the *social environment* in which
people work" (p. 18). They cite six specific work environment sources of burnout: work overload, lack of control, insufficient reward, unfairness, breakdown of community, and value conflict. As an example of their view of
burnout, I am using a long citation from Maslach and Leiter—their description
of the case of Julie, a public school teacher:[1]

[1]Reprinted from *The Truth about Burnout.* Copyright © 1997. Reprinted by permission of Jossey-
Bass, Inc., a subsidiary of John Wiley & Sons, Inc.

Julie taught history and literature to eighth graders in a public school and had a reputation as an outstanding teacher. Students loved her, parents called to get their child enrolled in her class, and the principal rated her as one of the best. Young and successful, Julie was expected to have a long and distinguished teaching career. But this year, Julie decided to quit. Her decision came as a shock to everyone; some of her colleagues cried when they heard the news.

At one time Julie was completely dedicated to the job because it allowed her to do things she valued highly—to make a difference in the world, to have a positive impact on other people's lives. But today she doesn't feel the job is worth it. At one time she brought enormous energy and commitment to her work, putting in long hours and agreeing to do all sorts of "extras" above and beyond the call of duty. Now she is exhausted just going through the motions and doing the bare minimum. At one time she was deeply involved with her students, attentive to their progress and achievement in learning, sensitive to their individual needs. Now she is more negative and cynical about their motivation and skills. At one time she was confident that her efforts would pay off, that the kids would get a better education and a better start on life because of what she and other teachers were able to accomplish. Now she questions whether the students are really getting what they need; she even worries that children are getting damaged by overworked teachers like herself. To Julie, trying to do good came at too high a price.

What is noteworthy about Julie's case, and many others like it, is that the negative slide to burnout started from a position of strength and success rather than from one of weakness. Julie was not an incompetent, lazy individual who didn't know how to teach. She brought to the job an impressive set of credentials and personal qualities and was able to use these to produce high-quality teaching. In terms of skills and motivation, she was at the top of her class—one could hardly ask for more. As one of her colleagues said, "Julie was 'on fire' from the beginning, not like some of those teachers who never even 'light up' in the first place. She had a passion for teaching, and it is so depressing to see that disappear." Indeed, losing the best and the brightest—people like Julie—is the most devastating cost of burnout.

Six Sources of Burnout

What led to the erosion of Julie's engagement with teaching? A close look at her case reveals the presence of the six mismatches between job and person that we described in Chapter One.

Work overload was a major factor from the beginning. Julie spent intense eight-hour days in the classroom and extra hours—after school, in the evening, and on weekends—to prepare for class, grade homework, and attend meetings. Although she had a great deal of control over how she taught her class ("When I close that door, the class is all mine—just me and the kids"), she had a *lack of control* over the district policies that led to increased class sizes and decreased teaching resources. Like other teachers, she received a low salary that was clearly *insufficient reward;* she didn't mind so much when she was young and single and just starting out in the profession, but later it posed a severe financial burden. Furthermore, low salaries are the most visible symbol of the lack of respect for teaching. Julie's wages fueled her sense that there was an inherent *unfairness* in the system ("Why am I working so hard, doing so much, and yet getting so little in return?"). The bickering, political infighting, and competitiveness between the teachers in her school made her feel alienated from them, and thus there was a *breakdown of community.* Finally, there was a growing *value conflict* between what Julie was trying to achieve in the classroom and the "extras" she was being asked to do by the school. As she put it, "The last straw was when they wanted me to spend a lot of time pulling together all this material to prepare an application for a 'good school' award—there was far more concern about getting the award than actually doing the things that would make us a good school!" (pp. 25–26)

Maslach and Leiter's (1997, p. 149) burnout prevention formula addresses each of the six problem areas described in the case of Julie. I have put the alternatives in a table and labelled them burnout creation and burnout prevention.

Burnout Creation	*vs.*	*Burnout Prevention*
work overload	vs.	sustainable workload
lack of control	vs.	feelings of choice and control
insufficient reward	vs.	recognition and reward
breakdown of community	vs.	a sense of community
unfairness	vs.	fairness, respect, and justice
significant value conflicts	vs.	meaningful, valued work

There is strong research support for the Maslach and Leiter (1997) belief that the cause of burnout is often in the organization, not the individual. Their interventions, therefore, are to change organizations. I think that this approach has merit, but it is also myopic and dangerous for practitioners. Actually, Maslach and Leiter support this caution in their description of the contemporary work environment:

The workplace today is a cold, hostile, demanding environment, both economically and psychologically. People are emotionally, physically and spir-

itually exhausted.... The idea *of the workplace as an efficient machine is returning to undermine the* ideal *of the workplace as a safe and healthy setting in which people may fulfill their potential through intrinsically rewarding work for which they are given fair compensation. (pp. 1–2)*

What if one's work environment is not a place that constantly addresses the psychosocial stress of the staff? It reminds me of the play, *Waiting for Godot* (Beckett, 1997), in which two individuals waited and waited for a man named Godot to show up so that they could go on with their lives. He never did, and the play ended. The moral of the play for practitioners: Be careful about waiting for others to care for you.

Consider the two work settings described by Molassiotis and Haberman (1996) in their research on bone-marrow-transplant nurses. This is a caring profession group at high risk for stress and burnout. They have the grief work that accompanies engaging in the caring cycle with dying patients and their families. In one setting, there was a supportive environment that addressed staff psychosocial needs. This was not present in a second setting, and the stress and burnout level was higher there. Hopefully, in the second setting, some of the nurses took charge of their own self-care and did not "wait for Godot."

I am reminded of many settings where I have worked. Some were burnout creators and some burnout preventers. In the bad settings, no one rescued me. It was up to me to create an environment that worked. That is the point that I make in this book in the chapter on sustaining the professional self, in which I discuss "creating a professional greenhouse at work." In the absence of psychosocial support, counselors, therapists, teachers, or health professionals must create it for themselves.

There are some exceptions to this rule. One successful, systemic, organizational intervention is that of Gysbers and Henderson (1994). Instead of waiting for others to create a positive work environment, they have taught school guidance counselors how to do it for themselves.

Meaning and Caring Burnout

The term *burnout* has helped us lift a shade and see more clearly through a window to the realities of the practitioner's world. The symbolism involved with the word *burnout* relates to the extinguished flame, which is the motivational force in the caring professions.

I like to distinguish between two styles of burnout; one is meaning burnout, the other caring burnout. Meaning burnout occurs when the calling of caring for others and giving to others in an area such as emotional development, intellectual growth, or physical wellness no longer gives sufficient meaning and purpose in one's life. Individuals in the caring professions derive much "psychic income" from helping others. In religious terms, such occupations are often labeled a calling, a calling to something of great value. When the meaning of the work disappears, an existential crisis can develop, and meaning burnout can result. My definition is that meaning burnout occurs when the meaning of the work has been lost and the existential purpose for the work is gone.

This may occur for any number of reasons. It may be that the activity—such as counseling adolescents, teaching children to read, or nursing the frail elderly—becomes routine, boring, and seemingly insignificant for the practitioner. It may be that the practitioner entered the occupation in part to satisfy his or her own personal needs. This in itself is not a negative factor in job choice. Yet, when it is a predominant factor and the need is filled, then the meaning of the work can decrease. Here are some examples. There is the "wounded healer" who feels healed after counselor training and work in the field. A teacher may have entered education to prove that he wasn't dumb, after feeling that way in high school. Now, years later, he feels intellectually competent and no longer has to prove himself. How about the wellness nurse who was attracted to the field because of her own body image distress earlier in life. Now, she has better feelings about herself. Each of these individuals has lost some of the original meaning and purpose in their occupational choice. However, new meaning in the work can emerge. If it does not, meaning burnout can grow.

Another kind of meaning burnout occurs when the practitioner no longer feels that the work is helpful to the client, student, or patient. This can be a "crisis in meaning" time because if the work is not useful, and the point is to be useful, then why continue? Examples here are a job in (1) an agency where too many cases and too much paperwork make good work impossible, (2) a school that seems to promote a "revolving door" of failure rather than student success, and (3) a health setting where the finances do not permit the practitioners to operate in a competent manner. One colleague working with substance abuse talks of the relapse problem bringing on meaning burnout for him. He wondered how the work could be meaningful when relapse seemed to be more of a reality than recovery.

The second type, caring burnout, is the most popular way of describing burnout. This type focuses very strongly on the professional attachment-involvement-separation process that all counselors, therapists, teachers, and health professionals engage in over and over again with their clients, students, and patients. As described in an earlier chapter, the quality of the attachment to the person in need is of central importance for client, student, or patient gains. (For example, think of your favorite teacher. Was his or her interest in you *as a person* a central element of what you treasured about this teacher?) This idea corresponds with research in the helping professions described in Chapter 3: "The major agent of effective psychotherapy is the personality of the therapist, particularly the ability to form a warm, supportive relationship" (Luborsky, McLellan, Woody, O'Brien, & Auerbach, 1985, p. 609).

If the inevitable separation with the client, student, or patient does not too severely deplete the practitioner, then he or she can attach again. But if the process drains the person, perhaps each time just a little—just as the plaque in arteries builds up little by little—then the life force, the blood flow for the counselor, therapist, teacher, or health professional, is gradually choked off. This is the caring burnout process. One could also use the analogy of a battery. The battery keeps getting energized or drained. When drained enough, there is no spark, no life.

Professional attachments and separations that deplete the practitioner, such as too many ambiguous professional losses, can lead to a subsequent inability to attach. The three subscales of the Maslach Burnout Inventory (Maslach & Jackson, 1981) seem to capture this process—emotional exhaustion, depersonalization, and lack of personal accomplishment. Corey and Corey (1989) provide a description that fits with this description of burnout:

> *Continuous contact with clients who are unappreciative, upset and depressed often leads helpers to view all recipients in helping relationships in negative terms. Practitioners may care less, begin to make derogatory comments about their clients, ignore them and want to move away from them. Dehumanized responses are a core ingredient of burnout. (p. 167)*

The most important point that I am making here is that the presence of losses and the absence of gains in the caring cycle of empathic attachment → active involvement → felt separation contribute to burnout. My own definition of caring burnout, as opposed to meaning burnout, is focused specifically on the most important work task in the high touch occupations. Caring burnout is the result of a decreased ability to professionally attach with the next client, student, or patient because of the cumulative depletion and negative energy generated over many previous episodes of work between the practitioner and the client, student, or patient. I define caring burnout as disengagement of the self from the caring cycle of empathic attachment → active involvement → felt separation. Hopefully, there are bountiful joys, rewards, and gifts of practice. It is best when the work itself, active engagement with the other, produces energy rather than depletion. When depletion occurs more than a positive effect, energy is drained from the battery. Without a spark, burnout occurs. That is what Figure 7.1 on the next page represents.

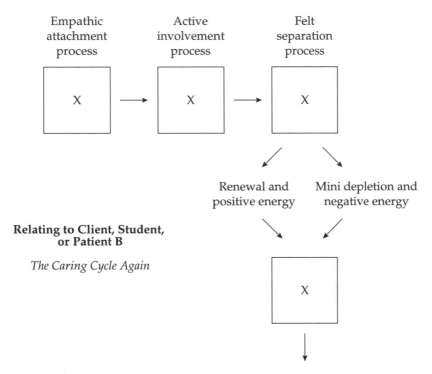

**FIGURE 7.1   Factors in Professional Vitality versus
Caring Burnout**

Both meaning burnout and caring burnout are destructive realities because the end of active engagement by the practitioner means the end of competent practice in counseling, therapy, teaching, or health work. Mediocre work can occur, but expertise in these fields needs the active engagement of the self. You ask, what is one to do about burnout? My attempt to answer that question can be found throughout this book. I hope that you will find some answers or at least some strategies in different places in the book.

8

Codependency
An Idea That Illuminates or Clouds?

High touch practitioners struggle with regulating caring for others and caring for self boundaries. The concept of codependency provides one way to understand this (Beattie, 1986). Although offering some clarity, the term *codependency* is also full of confusion and contradiction. What does it mean? What is the conflict? First, I take a middle position in the controversy (e.g., Collins, 1993) over the concept of codependency.

The term is useful in illuminating self-care concerns for counseling, therapy, teaching, and health professionals. These individuals are distinguished by their high touch capacity, as I have described in the caring cycle: empathic attachment → active involvement → felt separation. Essentially, the codependency concept attempts to describe excessive self-sacrifice. But what is excessive? This is where some of the confusion comes in. Individuals in the caring professions are distinguished by their caring for others, a kind of self-sacrifice. In Chapter 1, I addressed this point while considering the universal human dilemma of caring for others versus self-preservation. A theme in this book is the balancing of other-care and self-care, with the self-sacrifice element as a risk for helpers and others in allied fields.

A historic factor for individuals in the high touch fields is the connection between personal history and career choice. Individuals in the caring professions sometimes have a childhood or youth in which caring for others and sacrificing self was a way to sustain oneself. Not infrequently, this has led to a caring-for-others career. Excessive caring for others, at great cost to oneself, fits with the definition of codependency.

Wells, Glickauf-Hughes, and Bruss (1998) give a description:

Co-dependency has been used to refer to a disturbance in self and relational development.... [It] is marked by enmeshed caretaking patterns that are exercised at the expense of autonomous self development in order to maintain security relationships.... Adult individuals who have developed... [self-sacrificing traits] will be more susceptible to developing flagrant co-dependent characteristics in an intimate relationship as an adult. (pp. 26, 29)

Wells and colleagues conclude their research study by saying:

These results lend support to the author's contention that co-dependency reflects a self-disorder and relational orientation that revolves around burdensome self-sacrifice and caretaking intended to "control" significant others (e.g., by making oneself indispensable, one can avoid being abandoned because one is needed). (p. 34)

I think that there is value in thinking about these ideas and how they may affect the professional resiliency of people in helping and related professions. My objection to the term relates to two issues: unfair criticism of women and cultural encapsulation. Concerning women, the term tends to pathologize women, a concern shared by female scholars such as Collins (1993). Self-sacrifice is often seen as part of women's lives. The term *codependency* views such behavior through a critical lens. Another lens considers self-sacrifice to be one of women's most admired traits. One very powerful word that communicates the value of female self-sacrifice is *mother.* Is anything of more importance than the work and devotion of mothers to the health and evolution of the human species? Is anything more valuable than the mothering that goes on every day in every country by millions of devoted women? In my view, the broad brush of codependency unfairly stains central, positive, traditional female attributes.

Second, through the American cultural lens, codependency does not fare well because of cultural bias. American society puts unusual emphasis on the needs of the individual. Anything that impedes the individual is considered negative. I doubt that the cheerleaders of this term are really aware of the cultural bias. When one is within the cultural bubble and has not been outside of it, the relative seems both absolute and positive.

In America, the needs and rights of the individual are stressed so much more than in other cultures. I have experienced the differences while working in the Middle East and Asia. The focus in those contexts is often on the group, such as the family, rather than on the self. A small example hints at the difference. When Americans eat at a restaurant, they tend to order for themselves and then eat that one order. Many Asians do not order for themselves; they order for all, and all eat from all dishes.

When one is culturally encapsulated, it is hard to see how American society could reflect an unhealthy bias. As a result, in America with the individual on the throne, we have excessive "me-ism" that results in conditions like narcissism and loneliness. Two books that address these issues and are very critical of Americans' self-preoccupation are *The Culture of Narcissism* (Lasch, 1978) and *The Pursuit of Loneliness* (Slater, 1980). A consequence of the emphasis on the individual and criticism of self-sacrifice is a social landscape with problems such as elder neglect, divorce, and teen rebellion.

Overall, I think that the term *codependency* is helpful for counselors, therapists, teachers, and health professionals in pointing out factors in excessive self-sacrifice. It is also a concept that should be used sparingly because much of the self-sacrifice and giving in the caring professions is central to the work, helpful to others, and meaningful to the giver.

Helping professionals at risk for excessive codependency-type behaviors would do well to address the short-term seduction and long-term destruction of an excessive other-care orientation. A core aspect of the term *codependency* is an abandonment of self, and this ultimately has severe implications. Abandonment of self, however, like all strong seductions, can have great appeal. The appeal is often in avoidance of the self and its own growth. There may be unresolved grief, strong ambivalence, or great risks that are avoided through abandonment of the self. It can draw one in like a strong magnet.

Severe codependency, as abandonment of self, is a behavior that should be a warning to high touch practitioners. Years ago, I worked with a client. After her husband was killed, she totally invested herself in her children. After a long period, she stopped running, faced the reality of her grief, and started the healing and moving on process. Yet, for us helpers, running from ourselves and our needs can be a temptation because denial of reality can solve short-term problems. Helldorfer, cited in Robinson (1992), describes the clergy, a helping profession, as composed of many individuals engaged in such "addictive caring."

Women in the helping professions may be most in tune with taking "the role of the other," to use George Herbert Mead's (1934) expression. Women writing about women's lives often describe female socialization as focused on an "ethic of care" and nurturing human life, with concern for others as a strong value. This is a major theme of Gilligan's *In a Different Voice* (1982), Ruddick's *Maternal Thinking* (1989), and Chodorow in *The Reproduction of Mothering* (1978). Montagu (1974) expressed a similar sentiment in *The Natural Superiority of Women*. This ethic of care may be a very positive trait; after all, how can helping professionals not endorse it? But it may also produce extra risk for a high other-care, low self-care focus among those who are oriented this way by the three elements of personality, gender, and membership in a helping profession (e.g., females who are elementary or secondary teachers, social workers, nurses, rehabilitation counselors, psychotherapists, or physical therapists).

The opposite option, too little other-care and too much self-care, also tips the balance. Although understandable, self-absorption carried to an excessive level is also out of balance. To abandon clients, to meet only our needs, to do excessive self-protection, to listen to their struggles and solutions and apply them to us and our problems, or to use the hard side of the turtle to avoid involvement, is excessive self-care. We can listen to client, student, or patient concerns—their struggles and strategies—and use them excessively to bring us back to our own lives. For example, a client loses a job and reacts to it with disbelief and inaction. We say to ourselves that we would handle the situation better if it happens to us. We use the client's behavior to focus on our own well-being. Without knowing it, we are focusing on ourselves.

The ability to naturally turn one's focus onto the other is, we must remember, a wonderful attribute for those we serve. The opposite focus for counselors, therapists, teachers, and health professionals—self-care at the expense of other-care—is potentially unethical and destructive to the well-being of the often vulnerable individuals who we help. Unethical, exploitive helping professionals are often focused on the needs of the self. One example comes from the encounter groups of previous decades where charismatic, self-focused leaders often produced deterioration in group members (Lieberman, et al., 1973). A second example comes from the unethical, exploitive therapists who violate professional boundaries to satisfy personal needs (Pope & Vasquez, 1991).

9

Balancing Caring for Others and Caring for Self

In life, it is important to first take good care of yourself. If you don't, you can't take care of others.

> —MY MOTHER, ELVERA MEYER SKOVHOLT
> *(August 1994)*

If I am not for myself, who will be for me, if I am only for myself, what am I, and if not now, when?

> —HILLEL (*cited in Neusner, 1984, p. 32*)

Overall, we recommend that therapists do for themselves the self-nurturing, self-building things they would have their clients do. Increasing our awareness of our needs and remaining connected with our bodies, our feelings, and other people will strengthen us as individuals and allow us to choose to continue to do this important work.

> —L. A. PEARLMAN (1995, p. 62)

Losing One's Innocence about the Assertive Need for Self-Care

The focus of the first chapters of this book is on some of the difficult elements of the work. Hopefully, with foresight, we can be forewarned! Too often in the helping fields, we focus on the immediate tasks at hand and the intense human needs before us, rather than thinking of how we must take care of ourselves if our self, the healing agent, is to thrive for the decades of our work.

In addition to realizing that the work is difficult, and often very rewarding, one should remember that practitioners are people too, with their own lives that often contain the normal stress and strain of life during these hinge days between the twentieth and twenty-first centuries. That often means time and money pressure, multiple-role demands, and high workplace expectations to perform. The result is often a series of stress-related problems. This can be understood by examining the results of a recent study (Table 9.1) (Mahoney, 1997, p. 15) in which helping practitioners were asked about a variety of personal problems.

The table lists a variety of stress-related conditions, some job related, some personal life based. When one combines the hazards of practice in Chapter 6 with personal life stress, it is clear why there is an assertive need for practitioner self-care.

Ingredients of balancing include:

1. *An attitude of altruistic egotism.* Selye (1974) described the helper of others as needing to also be concerned with the welfare of the self. He called for a stance of altruistic egotism. Given Selye's credibility as a pioneer of the concept of stress and its toxic effects, his ideas warrant attention. Veteran psychology practitioners J. Buchanan (personal communication, 1992, 1995) and E. Nightengale (personal communication, 1995) coined similar concepts—holy selfishness and self-attentiveness. By holy selfishness, Buchanan means that the individual must hold his or her own welfare as a holy or sacred obligation. For Nightengale, self-attentiveness means having a focus on one's needs and concern for others. Here, we are talking about an obligation in attitude that involves a constant allegiance to one's own well-being as necessary for competent other-care.

2. *Continual behavioral monitoring of one's other-care–self-care balance.* Buchanan's holy obligation to oneself is more than attitudinal. It also involves an obligation to monitor oneself and constantly be nurturing of self. When the

TABLE 9.1   Mental Health Professionals' Previous Year Personal Problems Endorsed by 20 Percent or More of the Sample (N = 86)

Problem	Percent
Concerns about the size or severity of their caseload	48.2%
Episodes of irritability or emotional exhaustion	46.5%
Problems in their intimate relationships	41.2%
Doubts about their own therapeutic effectiveness	40.7%
Insufficient or unsatisfactory sleep	39.5%
Chronic fatigue	37.2%
Feelings of loneliness or isolation	33.7%
Episodes of anxiety	31.8%
Feelings of disillusionment about their work	27.1%
Episodes of depression	25.3%
Frequent headaches	20.9%

practitioner works in a highly stressful environment, this means monitoring and nourishing oneself, just as diabetics monitor their own insulin levels. This describes actual behavior engaged in by the practitioner to check for signs—physical, emotional, social, spiritual, and intellectual—that one's self is seriously depleted. Robinson (1992) describes "brownouts," episodes of forgetfulness and inattention, among helping professionals as early warning signs of insufficient self-care. Veteran helping professionals often develop personal signs indicating that they are approaching a point of danger.

The Need for More Self-Care at Times of Personal Crisis or Excessive Stress

Self-care is always important. At times of personal crisis or excessive stress, when ability to function well may be severely compromised, it is even more important. There are, as we all know, bountiful examples of either personal crisis or excessive stress (e.g., the serious injury of one's child, a sudden loss of family income, a major geographic move, the death of one's parent, the emergence of a chronic disease for oneself, the loss of one's intimate partner, destruction of one's property because of the force of nature). Below are two examples of a serious family illness that have had an impact on the practitioner. First, Schorr (1997) discusses how the personal crisis affected his ability to listen to his counseling clients:

> *In my sessions with clients, there would be frequent reminders of our black cloud [my wife's diagnosis of leukemia]. One man complained about a woman he knew—she was weird but that was because she had cancer. Another client had a son who killed himself after he was diagnosed with leukemia. Another came in numb with grief over the recent cancer death of a housemate. When clients would tell stories in which the mention of disease was a minor note, I had to restrain myself from asking questions merely to satisfy my own insecurity. Or to let my mind drift off into worrisome tangents. (p. 57)*

Pollack (1988) describes her own experience as a person in the caring professions who experienced extreme stress:[1]

The timing was right when I entered graduate school. The youngest of my three children had reached age 10, my husband's career was stable, and I was 37 and ready for a new challenge. I was going to explore my long-time goal of working with adults, with an emphasis on older adults. Two years later, during my spring break, I found myself facing

---

[1]Reprinted from *Journal of Counseling and Development, 67,* page 117. Copyright © ACA. Reprinted with permission. No further reproduction authorized without written permission of the American Counseling Association.

the severest challenge of my life. At first we thought it was the altitude of the Colorado ski resort that was making my husband…ill. When the doctor said it was colon cancer we were totally shocked.…

Immediate surgery provided temporary relief. Although we were far away from family and friends, the hospital had become like a cocoon, with its kind and caring staff. I felt a sense of terror when we left. Back at home in Maryland, I felt nearly unbearable anxiety while waiting for the results of further surgery. I will never forget my feeling of devastation when the surgeon told us the cancer had metastasized and the prognosis was poor.

The next 11 months were an emotional roller coaster. Why him? Why me? I felt shock, sadness, and disbelief. I was angry at the doctors who took away our hope, joyful during experimental treatments that shrank the tumor, distressed at the appearance of another malignancy, happy with his recovery from the second surgery, depressed as it became clear that it was only temporary, encouraged by the good days, cheered by the jokes we shared about the situation, and distraught at my impending loss.…

As his condition worsened, I tried to prepare the children, urging them to read books about death and to talk with us.… My grieving started long before his death. Never before did I realize the strength I had. Indeed, I had never before been put to the test.

…As I look back and reexamine my experience in facing his death, I am keenly aware of what helped me to integrate it, of what may similarly help my clients to come through devastating transitions successfully. According to the Transition Model (Schlossberg, 1984), there are three components in how one copes with any transition: the situation, the environment, and oneself. All of these contributed to my understanding of what I was going through and my eventual adaptation. In terms of the situation, I knew what it meant to be an "off-time" or early widow. There were no rules or role models, no one to guide me, and no one who would understand my feelings at a gut level. Consequently, I learned to become more self-reliant, independent, and capable of making decisions.

Not only was the transition off-time, but it was unanticipated and outside my control, so there was a high degree of stress. This was balanced by an environment of tremendous social support from family, friends, and my department at the university. I could not have survived without the constant telephone calls, concern, and continuous offers of help. I was surprised at my initiative in creating a support group of single women to share common concerns.

In terms of myself, I discovered that I used many coping strategies. Giving in to my sad feelings helped me get through them. I jogged every day, which helped me reduce the stress. I talked to myself, reassuring myself that things would get better and that I could handle the situation. I also talked to trusted others and learned it was more helpful to be listened to than rescued. The emotional pain made the world look gray and bleak, but I felt that the pain lifted, and with it, my spirit, when I was able to have a sense of humor. Although not changing anything, it did provide temporary relief. The process took time; there were many setbacks. I discovered that there is no "best" coping strategy that works in all situations, but no matter how difficult the situation, I will eventually find a way to cope with it.

By working through my own loss I feel better able to help others, particularly the elderly population, for whom loss is a common theme. Facing death has enabled me to grieve, to learn, to grow, and to be a better counselor. (p. 117)

For short periods of time, one just tries to "hold on" and get through it. For example, an intern was trying to hold on for three more months before she could leave her internship in a distant city and return home. At the time, though, she was coping with the stress of a major geographical move, the sudden death of her brother in a traffic accident, and an inadequate internship stipend, as well as the demands to perform at a high level to meet the expectations of internship supervisors.

The balancing equation can be especially precarious in times of extreme stress. How do we do adequate self-care during these disequilibrium periods, these times of exhaustion, pain, despair, and disquiet? A short answer to a difficult question is that we must continue self-care but do so at an accelerated pace.

10

Sustaining the
Professional Self

When you open your life to the living [your clients, students, or patients], all things come spilling in on you, and you're flowing like a river, the changer and the changed...it's an endless waterfall, like the rain falling on the ground, all around.
                                   —C. WILLIAMSON (1975, side one, track one)

Sustained by Meaningful Work

Occupation is essential.   —VIRGINIA WOOLF (1990, p. 503)

The only ones among you who will be really happy are those who have sought and found how to serve.   —ALBERT SCHWEITZER (1975, p. 87)

Do all the good you can,
By all the means you can,
In all the ways you can,
In all the places you can,
At all the times you can,
To all the people you can,
As long as ever you can.   —JOHN WESLEY (Oxford Dictionary, 1979, p. 568)

Practitioners often choose their work because they perceive it to be of great value. The work to benefit other members of the species *Homo sapiens* can provide enormous meaning and purpose. You may remember the George Bernard Shaw quotation at the beginning of this book: "This is the true joy in life, the being used for a purpose recognized by yourself as a mighty one;…the being a force of Nature instead of a feverish selfish little clod of ailments and grievances" (cited in Larson, 1993, p. 2).

I know a remarkable public school teacher whose work is infused with meaning. Coming from a home with a shaky foundation, she received needed transfusions from teachers during the difficult hinge days between childhood and adolescence. Now, with great energy, enthusiasm, and competence, she gives content and relationship to young people like her. Her work, of great help to them, is rich in purpose and meaning for her. This inoculates her from burnout. All win.

The sense of purpose and meaning is most at risk when, for example, the case worker senses that her work accomplishes little good and that her clients are caught in destructive, bureaucratic systems. It is when the counseling, therapy, teaching, or healing seems to have little effect that we reach despair because our *raison d'etre* for choosing this work—to make a difference in human life—is threatened. Pines and Aronson (1988) describe this process: "The root cause of burnout lies in our existential need to believe that our lives are meaningful, that the things we do are useful, important and even 'heroic'" (p. 11). I call this meaning burnout.

The problem is not the choice of the work itself, like it is with some other jobs. We could all name occupations that do little to further the development of our species and others that are very destructive to human life. That is not true of our work; at least, it is not true of our intentions. We are trying to make the world a better place, each in our own small way (e.g., to ease the physical pain of a postsurgery patient, to provide safety to mothers and children in a shelter, to reduce the anxiety of a college freshman away from home for the first time, to assist in reducing the shock of sudden joblessness). This means that the search for meaning and purpose in life, such a major life crisis for so many individuals at this time in history, can be less of a crisis for us because our work intrinsically gives us meaning.

For some practitioners, formal religion offers a rich structure of beliefs that provide meaning and purpose and help them confront mortality with answers and assurance. For many others, formal religion seems not to offer assurance or answers for the larger life dilemmas. In either case, I am suggesting that our work can provide meaning because we often sought this work to make a difference. Victor Frankl, in *Man's Search for Meaning* (1963), addresses this concern, as do many powerful existential writers of this century, such as Rollo May, Paul Tillich, Soren Kirkegaard, Irving Yalom, Albert Camus, and Jean-Paul Sartre. Ernest Becker has produced one of the most impactful books of this century in its focus on the meaning and meaninglessness in modern life. In *The Denial of Death*, Becker (1973) suggests that we as a species spend an enormous amount of time and energy in denial of our own mortality.

We all know stories of individuals who, in later life, radically changed their life's work to engage either professionally or as a volunteer in work that nurtures human life. The search here is often for more meaning or purpose and is an attempt to tie oneself more directly to the species and its survival. It is a kind of immortality, an identification with our species' history or future and is analogous to the way that grandparents partake in the future through the lives of their grandchildren.

As practitioners, our crisis of meaning burnout concerns the sense that we are not being very effective. If we can feel effective, we can obtain the kind of meaning that can offer great sustenance to the self. For the sustenance of the self, therefore, we must find a way in our counseling, therapy, teaching, and healing to feel that we are succeeding, even if it is in very small ways.

Maximizing the Experience of Professional Success

One generation plants the tree, another gets the shade.   WARNER (1992, p. 301)

Having an impact…is crucial to [practitioner] career satisfaction. Jobs that allow active, skillful involvement that produce tangible results are inherently sustaining and rewarding.… Constant giving in a one-way relationship, without feedback or perceived success, is hard on anybody.… Unrealistic expectations may be especially manifested in terms of expectations of client growth. The same urge to help and to be seen as helpful that propels many into the therapeutic professions often fosters grandiose notions of completely turning people's lives around.
—*W. N. GROSCH & D. C. OLSEN (1994, pp. 8, 15, 16)*

What is success in the helping professions, education, and the healing arts? How can we judge our success? I discussed this problem earlier. Here, I suggest a perspective that attempts to reduce practitioner stress. There are four different aspects of professional functioning: the changes for the client, student, or patient; external recognition by supervisors, work peers, and others; expert knowledge content; and the professional relationship processes. (See Table 10.1.) We tend to focus on the first one, whether the person we are helping gets better (e.g., learns more, walks better, is less shy). Our validation of professional competence and self-worth seems to come mostly from this dimension. Because our whole reason for professional functioning is to be helpful, the usefulness of our efforts naturally seems most valid. It is the recipient of our help—the client, the student, the patient—to whom we relate most closely and who also can judge our work. Does not the patient of the physical therapist have the most contact and an investment in judging the

TABLE 10.1   How Much Can the Practitioner Control the Outcome in These Dimensions?

Caring Dimension	Control
Client, student, or patient positive change and/or appreciation	Limited
Supervisor or work peers' support and/or appreciation	Limited
Expert knowledge	Yes
Quality of working alliance—the relationship with client, student, or patient	Yes

professional's efforts? Yet, this is the dimension over which we have the *least* control, and so to judge our success by this dimension alone is potentially damaging to long-term sustenance of the professional self. As an example, reviewing results in psychotherapy, Asay and Lambert (1999) concluded that "outcome is determined to a great degree by the client and outside events— not the therapist" (p. 30). In addition, success is so hard to judge. The client, student, or patient may take in the practitioner's help, but like the inside of a dry sponge on water, the absorbed help may go undetected, unexpressed, or unappreciated.

We often choose our supervisors with as much freedom as we choose our parents. Sometimes we are lucky, sometimes not so lucky. Peers too are a mixed bag. They can be friends who give much, but they can also be fierce competition in an arena where jealousy is exchanged more often than support. Excessively tying one's own sense of professional success to either of these external sources can make us feel out of control, which can help produce high levels of job stress.

In contrast, we can control two other dimensions: our professional expertise and the quality of our involvement in the relationship process with the recipients. Professional expertise means knowing about our field and keeping up to date on theories, techniques, methods, research, and strategies. All counseling, therapy, teaching, and health fields continue to explode in knowledge. Although hard work, growing intellectually and in professional knowledge is something we can do.

Of equal importance is the relationship, the working alliance, that we create with those that we serve. It is important for us to be fully present with the other in the counseling, therapy, teaching, and healing process. Do we understand the process of involvement in these kinds of relationships, and are we able to be fully involved? This is an extremely important dimension of professional functioning. It is also, as I described in Chapter 3 (Bachelor & Horvath, 1999; Sexton & Whiston, 1994), a key to practitioner success in professional relationships.

For two of the four dimensions (expertise and process), our efforts dictate our success. We can, therefore, have some control over our work and derive some satisfaction from it. For example, when teaching a college psychology course to prison inmates, I worked on the subject matter, my teaching style, and my relationship skills with the students. It would have been a setup for professional discouragement if I had expected the inmates as students to write excellent papers, do very well on the tests, or praise me as a teacher. I looked for small gains for them and little positive feedback while working to be prepared and teach well. Using this approach, the course went well, and I remain excited and pleased about this teaching experience.

The student may fail; the patient may die; the client may continue with substance abuse. We may be distressed by these results, but we must continually reflect about the other two dimensions, relationship and expert knowledge: "Did I do the relationship work well; was I professionally attached and involved? Was my knowledge base sufficient?"

Sometimes we get external recognition. Savoring it at the moment may be important for long-term professional vitality. What does savor mean, and why is it important? We usually use the term *savor* when discussing food. It means to linger over the food—to enjoy the taste, the smell, the texture—before it is gone. In contrast is the eating method of the adolescent boy who quickly devours large quantities of food in an attempt to fill up. The savoring process gets missed in the mad rush toward a full stomach. So, too, we practitioners sometimes go madly from one occupational responsibility to another, rushing from one thing to the next without savoring the success. I have learned, over time, how transitory are the moments of satisfaction with our work, in part because, at its heart, it often involves the professional attachment-separation process that has, by the nature of the work, few concrete and permanent results (e.g., the twelfth grade English class goes very well but ends and will never be together again; the cardiac rehabilitation patient completes the program and returns home; the displaced worker no longer needs job assistance and emotional support after finding a new job).

Like all other practitioners in the high touch fields, I struggled for a long time while trying to become an adequate practitioner. Just in terms of my teaching role, there were many stress-filled hours. I described this in an article, "Learning to Teach":

I was driving down the freeway from Missouri to Florida, with spouse and baby girl next to me in the Ryder rental truck. Soon I would begin working as an assistant professor at the University of Florida with a split faculty/ psychologist position. One thought kept recurring: "How will I be able to teach? I've received no formal training in the art and science of teaching." ... where was the training to be a professor? I thought of my sister, an elementary teacher in Minnesota, who had received extensive training before beginning to teach. My mind wandered off to other occupations—hairstylist, airplane pilot, bricklayer, surgeon. Did any of these professions let loose their new graduates without any practical training? How was it, then, that I had received no systematic, organized instruction in teaching?

After days of daydreams and driving, I reached Gainesville, and the academic year began. I spent the first year on a do-it-yourself training program.... My self-training was deficient.... There was no systematic, organized sequence of learning experiences and no feedback from experienced master teachers.... In those first years of teaching, traumas and disillusionment coexisted with a few victories. (Skovholt, 1986, p. 8)

There are many factors that impinge on the recipient's reaction to our practitioner attempts. Once I took a time management course. It was difficult to really appreciate the instructor's efforts because I was frustrated by all the time demands in my life. I didn't need time management; I needed more time, less to do, or a culture in which human life was not defined by time-obsessed schedules. None of these was possible. Only time management was an option, and the instructor did his job. But my evaluation expressed my frustration with the bigger picture and, in that sense, was unfair to the instructor. If he judged his success by my reaction, he would be disappointed. As another example, one time in a mediation situation, my colleague was pleased by the work of the mediator but was too exhausted by the conflict and loss that was mediated to be appreciative. If the mediator depended on my colleague's reaction for validation, she would be disappointed and depleted. Do patients in the recovery room, coming out of anesthesia after surgery, ever really express their appreciation for the gentle, expert care that they receive? Probably not. They are confronting their own disorientation and discomfort and are concerned with little else. If the recovery room nurse judges her success by the appreciation of her patients, will she not soon be discouraged by her professional efforts? If she attempts to receive most of her personal self-esteem validation this way, will these relationships sustain her? And what if the high school teacher relies heavily on student reactions for her self-esteem?

Two constructs, control and self-efficacy, have been linked by Schulz, Biegel, Morycz, and Visintainer (1989) in their study of the emotional well-being of caregivers, those who take care of elderly or disabled family members. These two constructs can be thought of as closely related to the ideas here of the dimensions under the control of the practitioner. It is important to add that results do matter in the age of accountability, outcome standards, and managed care. But they have always mattered. Here, we are addressing the intensity of this dimension for practitioner long-term vitality. In the dimension of our efforts related to client, student, or patient outcome, it is important to match our expectations to the possibility of positive change.

Avoid the Grandiosity Impulse, and Relish Small "I Made a Difference" Victories

When considering results, watching one's expectations can be useful. Sometimes if we expect less in terms of client, student, or patient gains, we can be more satisfied. I do not mean here becoming lazy or accepting mediocrity. It can be a paradoxical task. Helping professionals often want so much to help that they get caught up in wanting to make a big difference for many people. Veteran practitioners often learn that satisfaction can consistently come only if the helper reduces expectations and focuses on small changes. This approach is often more empowering for the client, student, or patient and is a form of practitioner self-care.

Think Long-Term

Professional development is a long-term process (see Chapter 4). From the expertise literature of Chi and colleagues (1988), we know that it takes thousands of hours to develop high-level skill in a complex human craft such as counseling and therapy, high school teaching, or nursing. Seeing the long-term map while meeting short-term goals can be useful. Breaking down big educational and career steps into small steps is a well-used personal method and motivational strategy; however, considering the long haul is also important. In the wilderness of northern Minnesota, some canoeists start paddling hard in the first hour of the first day. How about the next five hours and the next day of another six hours of paddling and the day after that and the day after that? Practitioners work 30 to 40 years. Thinking long-term and building professional and personal self-care into this decades-long adventure can change one's perspective and approach. Think of the toddler learning to walk; it is a process, an adventure of attempts, feedback, and more attempts. In time, with experience, the toddler walks and then runs.

Creating and Sustaining an Active, Individually Designed Development Method

To stay alive, one must eat. To stay alive and grow professionally, one must eat voraciously and then digest the new professional food. Not eating or "throwing up" the food—that is, denying it or distorting work-related feedback—can lead to stagnation and pseudodevelopment (Rønnestad & Skovholt, 1991; Skovholt & Rønnestad, 1995). I discuss this topic here and in Chapter 4.

The development method is usually individually designed. In contrast to college and university training in which we are told how to develop through class requirements, as practitioners we are now in charge of our own development. The use of continuing education credits by many fields is an attempt to ensure development, but the requirement of going to classes reflects an earlier, less developed approach. Highly functioning senior practitioners do not vary in the intensity of their efforts over the long run, but they do vary in their development methods (Skovholt & Rønnestad, 1995).

One key element is an openness to new information and to feedback about one's performance. This entails a nondefensive stance, as in Rogers' description of the fully functioning person (Rogers, 1961) and Maslow's (1968) self-actualized personality structure. In both of these descriptions, openness and perceptual accuracy are key. When the individual must distort information or shuts off new information, then development is stifled. This is a reason why experience alone does not seem to increase expertise. We have all met experienced veterans in our field who are seemingly less skilled than newer practitioners. One reason is that the veteran is not growing from the increased experience.

Aside from openness, one must continually feed oneself with data from practice and from the bigger world of ideas and theories. One highly functioning practitioner that I know reads five books at once; another works collaboratively with four other practitioners on different projects to keep developing. Both of these senior practitioners are voraciously feeding themselves professionally with new content, new ideas, and new alternatives that they add, modify, and shed with their ongoing professional working method. Highly respected by their professional peers, each has a finely tuned, individually designed development process.

Lastly, professional reflection as a catalyst for one's development is important. Reflection has recently received much attention as a key developmental process in the professional growth of counselors, therapists, teachers, and health practitioners (Copeland, Birmingham, De La Cruz, & Lewin, 1993; Hoshmand, 1994; Neufeldt, et al., 1996; Schön, 1987; Skovholt & Rønnestad, 1995; van Merriënboer, Jelsma, & Paas, 1992). Neufeldt and colleagues (1996) identify key elements of the process as starting with an initial problem or point where the individual is puzzled and unsure. The individual's personal and cognitive flexibility, plus a supportive work environment, furthers the reflection process, which is guided by a search for understanding. They write:

> *The intent to understand what has occurred, active inquiry, openness to that understanding and vulnerability and risk-taking rather than defensive self-protection, characterize the stance.... To contribute to further development, reflections are profound rather than superficial, and are meaningful. (p. 8)*

The end point, using one's experience and theory, is professional improvement as a practitioner. Benner and Wrubel (1982) describe elements of this process when they say:

> *Experience is necessary for moving from one level of expertise to another, but experience is not the equivalent of longevity, seniority, or the simple*

passage of time. Experience means living through actual situations in such a way that it informs the practitioner's perception and understanding of all subsequent situations. (p. 28)

These viewpoints are similar to our own three-part view of this essential process for professional development—professional and personal experience; an open, supportive work environment; and a reflective stance (Skovholt & Rønnestad, 1995). Receiving uncensored performance feedback and ideas from other sources, being open to it, and taking time for it are essential elements of reflection as a developmental process. The closing off or distorting of feedback, with little time given to it, along with an absence of reflection, provides elements for professional stagnation (Skovholt & Rønnestad, 1995).

One time, thinking about the reflective process, I realized that the spacious campuses of American colleges and universities, the benches and the grass, serve the serious, intellectual reflective function. After class, these environments encourage students to ponder, wonder about, consider, discuss, and contemplate the content of the past class. This is important because the opposite—experience without reflection—does not produce the same amount of professional growth. The requirement that professional psychology doctoral interns spend at least 25 percent time on direct clinical work, rather than 50 or 75 percent, represents this stance; professional development entails more than just direct experience (*Internship and Postdoctoral Programs in Professional Psychology,* 1994).

The reflective process is stunted in work environments in human services, education, and health where productivity is measured by volume and practitioners are kept continually busy and, by necessity, practice in a hectic, repetitive style. The problem is that repetitive practice alone tends to produce the same behaviors, cognitions, and affective reactions, rather than creative professional growth and improved work by the practitioner. There is little evidence that experience alone produces expertise.

Professional Self-Understanding

As important as methods may be, the most practical thing we can achieve in any kind of work is insight into what is happening inside us as we do it. The more familiar we are with our inner terrain, the more sure footed our [work]—and living—becomes.   —P. J. PALMER (1998, p. 5)

Finding healthy ways of maintaining a strong sense of self is a prerequisite for effective functioning as a professional helper.
—W. N. GROSCH & D. C. OLSEN (1994, p. 31)

Self-awareness is a strongly emphasized value in a variety of high touch professions. The psychotherapy professions have especially endorsed one's own counseling and therapy as a method to develop self-awareness and increase personal maturity as a way to make one's professional work more effective. Other helping professions often include training experiences in self-development as part of the education of helping professionals. Along with Guy (1987), Grosch and Olsen (1994) provide a valuable discussion on the personal background of helping professionals. For example, they make a surprising declaration when they say:

> *The great paradox revealed by professional burnout is that, although helping others can and should be a way to transcend ourselves, many of us embark on helping careers not out of a genuine concern for others but rather out of a need to be appreciated by them. (p. 170)*

Using the work of self psychologist Kohut and family theorist Bowen, Grosch and Olsen (1994) suggest that family of origin roles are instrumental in the excessive needs that some helpers bring as adults into their professional work:

> *In dysfunctional families, boundaries may be absent or violated; in fact, parent-child roles are often reversed. Rather than receiving the mirroring [validation] they desperately need for the formation of healthy and cohesive selves, children wind up needing to provide mirroring for their parents. (p. 93)*

Grosch and Olsen point out that many individuals attracted to the helping professions received validation and admiration for their helping attempts early in life. They suggest that these attempts may have occurred in families in which the helper, as a young person, took on the role of an adult, perhaps in a highly stressed family, and received this validation rather than in the normal mirroring and admiration of healthy child and adolescent development, described in self psychology theory (Kohut). If the person then, as an adult, enters one of the helping professions, the style may continue.

The person enters an occupation in which caring for others is a primary role. The individual already knows how to care for others—listening, putting the other's needs first, nurturing the other. These skills are sometimes hard for others who are not socialized this way, but the helper cannot be sustained over the long run just by validation from recipients. If the individual centers his or her life around caring for others and does not develop other, more balanced interpersonal relationships, that is, relationships in which the individual is not the giver but also the receiver, then the benefits from the helping role are the only source of the individual's sustenance. This source of sustenance, however, is limited because the client, student, or patient does not have a primary obligation to care for the helper and meet his or her needs. "The hunger for mirroring and the inability to find it in many work environments are the primary causes of professional burnout" (Grosch & Olsen, 1994, p. 95). Ethical violations, in fact, occur when the helper's needs become primary in the relationship. In addition, the recipient is often not in a place to help the other because he or she is too distressed to focus on the other.

The essential point here is this: When the child does not receive developmentally appropriate validation from significant adults, the self develops in a different way, seeking self-worth through pleasing, supporting, and understanding others. This need for admiration is then sought in adult work by working extra hard to help others. This deep longing for appreciation is so often thwarted, of course, because the client, student, or patient role is not designed to meet the basic self-esteem needs of the professional helper. For those who need admiration, approval, and validation from clients, students, or patients, the situation is quite precarious. Consequently, "when we do not understand and deal with our craving for admiration and need to be seen in given ways, we tend to get angry and resentful" (Grosch & Olsen, 1994, p. 119). These authors suggest that Bowen's concept of differentiation is useful in suggesting how we need to learn to separate our own sense of self and its basic needs from the professional attachments we make with those we serve. Understanding this family of origin dynamic can be important for understanding unrealistic work expectations and preventing emotional depletion.

Berry (1988) uses the terms *messiah* and the *messiah trap* to describe the extreme helping of others as a defensive interpersonal type. Although this messiah idea may be simplistic, Berry does touch on some important ideas, such as family-of-origin roots and expressions of this style in pleasing, rescuing, counseling, and teaching. She described her own awakening as: "I thought I was doing the 'right' thing by helping people. But by helping others, I avoided being intimate with them. We [other helpers and I] were much more comfortable helping than we were asking for help" (p. x). (See Figure 10.1.)

A related area in which professional self-understanding is important concerns attachment. Within developmental psychology, attachment theory is now widely used to understand, explain, and predict interpersonal relationships, such as success at intimacy. One of the premises of this work, which is now being extended to other relationships such as work collaboration, is that past relationship patterns have an impact on present relationships. For example, Bachelor and Horvath (1999) summarize the therapist attachment research to suggest that "therapists tend to re-create earlier interpersonal patterns in the therapy relationship and treat clients accordingly" (p. 158).

This research is very important, in my view, because the important common factor in the high touch fields is the caring cycle of empathic attachment → active involvement → felt separation. If the practitioner has a poor per-

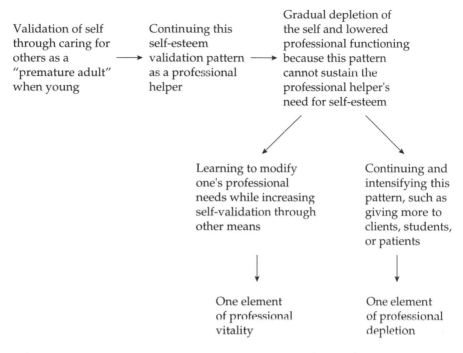

FIGURE 10.1   Possible Outcomes from an Excessive Focus on Helping Others

sonal history of attachments, the chance of doing good work is at risk. This is another reason for professional self-understanding.

Creating a Professional Greenhouse at Work

No man is an island.   —*JOHN DONNE (1975, p. 87)*

The work is hard. We are constantly asked to increase human competence in areas such as social skills, learning, and health. A stressful work environment can make it even harder. As I discussed in Chapter 7, Maslach and Leiter (1997) make a strong case for organizational factors as the key to burnout. I agree; however, I also urge you as a practitioner not to wait for the organization to serve your needs. I urge you to actively create your own greenhouse at work. A greenhouse, as you know, is an environment where many factors—temperature, soil, and water—are ideal for growth. Five elements seem to create a greenhouse effect at work: leadership that promotes a healthy other-care–self-care balance, social support from peers, receiving other-care from mentors, mentoring others, and having fun. These can be hard to find in any work environment. It would be great if all practitioners could describe their work environment like speech pathologist Carole Sellars who works with highly disabled children. She said:

> *It's absolutely the most wonderful place to work. It's spiritually rewarding and mentally rewarding. I bet I laugh more on my job than anyone I know. The children and families with whom I work have literally stolen my heart out of my chest. I'll never have a vacancy in my department. Once you're here, you're here. (Majeski, 1996, p. 5A)*

Leadership That Promotes Balance between Caring for Others and the Self

We pay leaders more because they have the power to create a tone, vision, and direction in an organization. Let's hope that the leader has a symbolic sign that says, "Here, we care for the clients, students, and patients and also the practitioners." Such leadership makes a difference.

Professional Social Support

Many practitioners are social people by nature, and they seek out others. The helping literature is filled with data suggesting that helpers similar to helpees (e.g., Alcoholics Anonymous [AA] group for a newly recovering alcoholic) can be powerful sources of influence. Within the social support research literature, Mallinckrodt and Bennett (1992) found that social support from others who have experienced job loss can be a stress reducer for the newly laid-off worker. The support of one's colleagues can be quite powerful in reducing distress emotions such as depression and anxiety. The same principle holds for high touch practitioners. When we can talk with our colleagues openly and honestly about our work, then the "universality of experience effect," a curative factor in groups (Yalom, 1985), can be a powerful force for our own professional vitality. In this context, the use of peer supervision and consultation groups, popular among professional psychologists (McCarthy, Kulakowski, & Kenfield, 1994), is a natural and important method of renewal.

One source of self-care is the organizational and group atmosphere at work. Johnson (1994), a graduate student in the helping professions, said:

> *At my practicum site, I experienced and observed terrific support among staff members. This helped me feel as though I was a significant contributor and was a strong source of professional and emotional support. Through this experience, I better understand that this support is vital in the helping*

business in order to give the helper a sense that he or she is not alone, a feeling that can occur in this line of work where results are frequently hard to measure. (p. 8)

Another source consists of good work friendships in which one can engage in giving and taking equally with another coworker. These friendships, as we all know, can be rich just in themselves.

Receiving Other-Care from Mentors, Supervisors, or Bosses

The mentoring literature has, of course, developed because of the power of these relationships. Levinson and colleagues (1978) describe the power of mentors in men's lives, just as Kram (1985) describes the importance of mentoring in women's lives.

Being Nurtured from Our Work as Mentors, Supervisors, or Managers

The act of mentoring, supervising, and managing others can be very positive in one's own self-care and professional development. For example, a psychologist in his 70s supervising new interns said, "They get brighter all the time. I feel that I learn as much from the interns as I teach them. They have become my teacher" (Skovholt & Rønnestad, 1995, p. 92).

At Work, Learning How to Be Professional and Playful, Have Fun, Tell Jokes, and Laugh

We need to pump positive emotions into a negative emotions environment. One individual approached this task in the following way:

I continue to try to find ways to make myself laugh and to do small fun things as a way to release tension and to feel more energized. Laughing seems to have a physiological effect. I can feel sad and begin to laugh, and the tension in my chest dissipates. I like to hear humorous stories from people's lives, I like to tease people and sometimes I like to be teased. I also keep toys at work to entertain me. I have a rainbow colored slinky that a friend gave me. I keep it on my desk. The colors are fun and the slow, rhythmic sound it makes when I play with it is relaxing. I also have Play-Doh in my desk drawer. I use it in class as part of a topic on creativity and critical thinking. However, it also is fun to play with in my spare time. I find that kneading Play-Doh when I am tense can help relax me. (S. Renninger, personal communication, February 1995)

Another did it this way:

She kept a tin noisemaker in her pocket, and two or three times a day, when no clients were around, she'd take it out and make a silly little "cricket" sound with it. Finally, curiosity got the best of me, and I asked her about it. "My biggest fault is seriousness," she said, "I need to remember that there's fun in the world, too. So I take out my little cricket and give it a couple of clicks, and it always makes me laugh." (Help for Helpers, 1989, p. 147)

Using Professional Venting to Release Distress Emotions

Venting is cathartic, which is an old word out of the psychodynamic tradition. It describes the usefulness of talking about feelings. Professionals in the high touch fields know that human feelings are powerful. They are not surprised by a study that appeared in the *Journal of the American Medical Association*, in which Smyth and colleagues (1999) found that writing about an emotionally impactful experience could change a person's physical health. In a scientific way, they found what people already know and do. It is called *venting*, a wonderfully descriptive term for the process by which people use words and nonverbal communication to let go of distressing emotions. Venting means, by analogy, to let the air take away one's emotional distress, as through a vent.

Having the skill to do professional venting and then doing it are especially important for practitioners who attempt to help people in the human services, education, or health care. Practitioners hear stories of distress. They need to motivate individuals for change when internal motivation is limited, and they often work in an environment of loss, anxiety, and pain. At work, counselors, therapists, teachers, and health professionals live in an ocean of distress emotions. Their willingness to work in this ocean is a big part of why they get paid.

Let me give you an example. One practitioner told me about her job as an employment counselor for the unemployed. She worked for a government agency with a mandate to help clients move from being unemployed to employed. She described the work as very frustrating because of low client motivation. She said that she was "saved" because she could vent to colleagues about the frustration of being unable to reach her clients.

I am describing venting as a positive professional process that helps the practitioner stay in the work and continue with intense involvement within the caring cycle. I am endorsing professional venting as a method of helping people do better work. This contrasts sharply with chronic complaining and negativity, which often have long-term negative consequences for practitioners, their colleagues, and the organizational climate. Professional venting improves work functioning; chronic complaining and negativity do the opposite. For example, offering hope is an important element of the practitioner's work. Negativity weakens one's ability to be hopeful for clients, students, and patients.

The "Good Enough Practitioner"

Practitioners are often afraid of underperformance and want very much to perform at the 100 percent level, 100 percent of the time. This is impossible, however, and can lead to the dead end experienced by an elementary school principal who told me, "I had to quit after ten years because after I gave and gave and gave, there was nothing left." Now, after five years in moratorium and recovery, she is again trying to do the job, afraid of both underperformance and overperformance.

A few years ago, in a formal mentoring program for new professors at my university, I began to talk with them about B+ teaching. It was shameful and embarrassing to discuss this with them, yet I knew too that there was great value for them in the timing perspective of when to sprint and when to jog, so I pushed myself to vocalize this view. Essentially, these five new assistant professors in music, chemistry, statistics, business, and history—talented, energetic, conscientious individuals—were facing an impossible job. The life of a university professor has no boundaries. There is always much more to do in the domains of the work: teaching, scholarship and research, and service to the university, one's profession, and the community. In addition, the tenure decision clock begins on appointment, and six years later, one either has a job or is fired.

My job as a mentor was to help these new faculty members with their teaching in the context of their larger job that is, by its nature, overwhelming. If they devoted all of their time to their teaching—reading, preparing, presenting, grading, etc.—they could perhaps do almost perfect work. They could almost reach the practitioner's goal of 100 percent effort, 100 percent of the time. Yet, they would be perfect in only one element of the position, avoiding other areas, and would eventually get fired. I have seen young professors take this route, a seemingly good choice that eventually leads to bitterness and an occupational dead end.

Knowing the seduction of the 100 percent effort, 100 percent of the time fantasy, I suggested to these new professors that they entertain the style of the veteran athlete who knows when to sprint and when to jog. For these new professors, this meant *some* B+ teaching. Now, let me suggest that B+ isn't too bad if one thinks of a 12-point continuum (A, A–, B+, B, B–, C+, C,

C–, D+, D, D–, F), yet it is so unattractive as a goal, and I am embarrassed to be associated with it.

The problem is that 100 percent performance, 100 percent of the time, is too exhausting to sustain in the work of the counselor, therapist, teacher, and health professional. For example, the paramedic must give all at critical times but perhaps not always. From the child development literature, there is a related concept, the "good enough mother" (Winnicott, 1965). Professor Alan Sroufe, an expert in child development research, says about Winnicott's expression, "It is actually a very useful idea because it suggests that care does not need to be perfect, it just has to be good enough" (personal communication, January 1996). The idea is that the child *very much* needs the parent to be good enough, but the child does not need the parent to be *everything* for *optimal* development of the child to occur. So perhaps our clients, students, and patients also need us to be "good enough," and anything less is unacceptable. Perhaps, however, they do not need us to try for that which we cannot sustain, a 100 percent effort for 100 percent of the time. It is a wonderful fantasy, but it also leads to the long-term dis-ease of occupational exhaustion and caring burnout, as well as a loss in creativity and growth. This is expressed by Kushner (1996): "If we are afraid to make a mistake because we have to maintain the pretense of perfection…we will never be brave enough to try anything new or anything challenging. We will never learn; we will never grow" (p. 85).

Understanding the Reality of Pervasive Early Professional Anxiety

Fear of failure undermines altruism.   —C. CHERNISS (1995, p. 7)

One of the most important findings in our research study (Skovholt & Rønnestad, 1995) was the high level of pervasive anxiety among beginners and the great reduction in this anxiety among seasoned veterans. Anxiety is the natural emotion when an individual feels threatened and out of control in an important situation. The novice–veteran contrast in pervasive performance anxiety was startling and affected many facets of the work. The high stress level of the beginning practitioner is supported by other research studies. Cherniss (1995) found an elevated stress level for first year human service workers, and others (Ackerley, et al., 1988; Pearlman & MacIan, 1995) have found high stress with new psychotherapists.

Professional experience helps so much in reducing this anxiety because counselors, therapists, teachers, and healers can increasingly rely on their own internalized experience base for professional functioning. The beginner must rely on the expertise of others, such as textbook theories, journal research studies, or the advice of a supervising senior practitioner. These sources can be invaluable. We all are indebted to useful theories and supportive supervisors; thanks, Carl Rogers, for the theory, and Phyllis Eppley and George Meyer, for the supervision years ago! Unfortunately, external expertise often does not quite fit the situation, in the way that foreign language instruction in a college classroom does not quite fit with the language usage of the people of a foreign country. As a visiting professor in Turkey, many Turks would get frustrated when I corrected their English, which they had diligently learned in class, with my comment, "That's really not the way Americans say it." With experience, internal expertise replaces external expertise (Skovholt & Rønnestad, 1995), and pervasive anxiety goes down. A teacher told me that she got through her first year by asking a veteran colleague every day, "What should I do today?" Five years later, she never asked the question.

Relevant, fruitful, and illuminating work has been done in cognitive science. A pivotal book, edited by Chi and colleagues (1988), is *The Nature of Expertise*. Much of this work has contrasted the cognitive processing of novices and experts. Application of novice (with little experience) versus expert (with much experience) distinctions has been done by Benner and Wrubel (1982) in nursing and Etringer, Hillerbrand, and Claiborn (1995) in counseling.

Etringer and colleagues (1995) summarize the cognitive processing distinctions between novices and experts within the categories of memory and knowledge structures, declarative and procedural knowledge, pattern recognition, reasoning processes and goals, and problem structure. In summary, experts can understand more of the complexity of a situation even if it is ambiguous or unique. They know how to use their more accurate judgments more efficiently; their knowledge is both more differentiated and integrated; and they recognize complex patterns more easily through sensing the most critical features of a problem even if it is ill-defined. Examples here include how an expert teacher can more quickly and accurately diagnose student mood level in a classroom and make quick instructional changes or how a nurse can understand the unique expression of a patient's changed pain level and respond with great skill.

This novice-versus-expert work in cognitive science can be highly useful to understanding how pervasive professional anxiety declines with experience in the counseling, therapy, teaching, and health fields because human work often involves complex, ill-defined, and difficult problem situations (e.g., how to introduce court-ordered treatment to a defensive person after a driving-while-intoxicated (DWI) arrest; assessing the maximum level of pain that a physical therapy patient will accept for healing without canceling appointments; finding a midlevel of instruction for a math class widely divergent in ability level). Working with people is so difficult because *Homo sapiens* is the most complex of all living organisms. Practitioners work constantly in ambiguous, confusing contexts. The veteran practitioner's hundreds of hours of experience can radically reduce daily pervasive professional anxiety.

Increasing Intellectual Excitement and Decreasing Boredom by Reinventing Oneself

In Chapter 6, I discussed hazard 16, cognitive deprivation and boredom, which can be very negative forces in the lives of veteran practitioners. Now, I discuss an antidote for the boredom.

High touch practitioners work in the realm of complex ambiguity, or should we call it ambiguous complexity? Swimming in this reality can be very stimulating for the practitioner. For example, a practitioner may wonder how to establish trust with a guarded, defensive teenager. In time, he or she figures it out and creates an internal plan for such situations. The challenge, excitement, and rewarding qualities of the situation lessen. Now, if the practitioner often works in helping, teaching, or healing with such teenagers, the intellectual challenge, over a long period of time, may decrease, and boredom can set in. Such a process often happens with veterans who have a narrow set of clients, teach the same subject term after term, or administer the identical health procedure over and over again.

Some veteran practitioners do not get bored in their work domain. When I asked a 68-year-old veteran practitioner who objected to the boredom idea, she said, "I never get bored because every situation and every person has uniqueness. Like putting a complex puzzle together, the process is always somewhat different. So, this is the uniqueness that prevents the boredom" (H. Roehlke, personal communication, February 23, 2000).

Renewal is a word used to describe a process of freshness. It is like an energy shot that animates the practitioner. Here, I focus specifically on the word *renewal* viewed as reNEWal. Meaningful new work tasks provide stimulation for the practitioner, and the stimulation, in turn, energizes the practitioner and makes high touch work possible. How does the NEW work as an antidote and provide renewal? It seems to me that one of the main issues concerns novelty. The key point is that novelty helps to animate the practitioner.

This is not the novice's problem. For the novice, the novelty provides so much stimulation that boredom is never a reality. In fact, for the novice, there is more than enough stimulation. The novice worries more about being anxious and lost while trying to perform work tasks. For the experienced practitioner who works in a fairly narrow domain, the boredom threat is not too much novelty. It is too little novelty.

One of the satisfactions of the work is cognitive. Helpers, teachers, and health professionals work with the most evolved of all species, human be-

TABLE 10.2 Different Ways Experienced Practitioners Reinvent Themselves

Ways to Create More Novelty, Challenge, and Energy	Examples
Changing the work tasks	Doing supervision instead of direct service
Changing the methods that one uses	Replacing group process with individual process
Changing the population with which one works	Working with adolescents instead of adults
Changing the time allocation	Doing some administration or research rather than 100 percent direct service

ings. These human beings are intricate, complicated, and convoluted. Data from them come in the form of complex ambiguity. This novelty, this complexity, this ambiguity can offer great cognitive stimulation for the practitioner. It is a major reason for the attraction to the field. For example, therapists talk of hearing the person's story and how engaging it can be to try to really understand the world of another.

Let me use the case of motivating the other to show the excitement of the work. In all of the professional fields that I am addressing here—social services, education, and health—motivating the client, student, or patient is a major practitioner challenge. How can a practitioner really motivate the other person to make necessary changes? How can the practitioner motivate the other to become less angry, study harder, or continue with painful but important medical procedures? It is often a very challenging and intellectually stimulating dilemma. Without stimulation, practitioner energy and interest recedes.

This is the process whereby the NEW brings reNEWal. Experienced practitioners must keep reinventing themselves. This can occur through different ways (Table 10.2). The goal of all of this effort, of course, is to have the NEW provide reNEWal.

Minimizing Ambiguous Professional Loss

The lack of closure and concrete evidence of success is a major ongoing stressor for those in the practitioner arts. One way to reduce this stressor is to acknowledge the dimension of ambiguous professional loss. I use this term, *ambiguous professional loss,* to describe the constant series of connections that the practitioner makes with the client, student, or patient that end without an ending. Awareness of this stressor can help us to acknowledge it to ourselves and gain support from colleagues. In addition, we can also try to have as many concrete endings as possible. Termination of the attachment relationship in a formal sense, no matter how brief, is often quite valuable for the professional's vitality.

At the University of Florida Counseling Center, the doctoral interns and the staff are captured in a yearly photo. The photos, year after year, are on the wall of the center in recognition of the training done by the senior practitioners. Year after year, they attach to a new group of enthusiastic and anxious interns. The interns leave at the end of the year and are replaced by a new group of enthusiastic and anxious interns. Is there any evidence of this 15-year effort by the staff? The product, the trained interns, are scattered throughout the United States. Where is the concrete evidence? It is there in the rows of photos of excited and proud interns and staff. What a great idea! What a great way to blunt ambiguous professional loss!

We all need lots of small ways of making the ambiguous concrete. This is the value of concrete achievements, such as a promotion or new certification. Concrete activities such as professional writing can be helpful too. The key words are *tangible* and *permanent.*

Learning to Set Boundaries, Create Limits, and Say No to Unreasonable Helping Requests

As described earlier, learning to set limits *only* after first exhausting themselves early in their professional careers is a normative experience for counselors, therapists, teachers, and health professionals. Stone (1988) described this process in "The Heroic Syndrome." Veteran practitioners, like veteran athletes, learn to pace themselves, always being ready at critical moments but pulling back some at noncritical moments. For some practitioners, finding the appropriate level of letting go is difficult. Samples (1991) describes the letting go process within the context of a twelve-step approach for caregiver self-care.

Summary

In this chapter, I have presented a number of ideas for you to consider in sustaining your professional self. Table 10.3 lists factors that practitioners have told me are important in sustaining or depleting the professional self.

TABLE 10.3   Factors That Sustain and Deplete the Professional Self

Factors That Sustain the Professional Self	Factors That Deplete the Professional Self
Joy in participating in others' growth	Feeling unsuccessful in helping the other
Feeling successful in helping others	
Closely observing human life (creativity, courage, ingenuity, tolerance of pain) and meaningful human contact	Professional boundaries that allow for excessive other-care and too little self-care
Finely tuned professional boundaries	Low peer support
Peer support	Low supervisor support
Supervisor support	High organizational conflict
Low level of organizational conflict	Excessive seriousness in purposes and style
Sense of humor and playfulness	Little attention to long-term professional development
Constant focus on professional development and avoidance of stagnation and pseudodevelopment	Inability to accept any ambiguous professional loss or normative failure
Tolerance of some ambiguous professional loss and normative failure	Neglecting the importance for self and others of a positive closure experience at the time of professional separation
Attempting to have a closure experience at the time of professional separation that is positive for both parties	Insufficient salary and benefits or educational credits if the practitioner is in training
Sufficient salary and benefits or educational credits if the practitioner is in training	Realism and idealism as one
Distinguishing between idealism and realism	

11

Sustaining the Personal Self

A major premise of this book is that helping work requires giving of the self. This capacity to be deeply involved in the caring cycle of empathic attachment → active involvement → felt separation is the core skill for effective work in the high touch human fields such as counseling, therapy, teaching, and health care. The opposite reaction—an inability for deep involvement in giving of the self and the caring cycle—is, in my view, the strongest indicator of caring burnout. Without deep involvement of the self in the cycle, effective high touch work cannot occur.

This chapter flows directly from this central premise. Sustaining the personal self is a serious obligation because the work, giving of the self, cannot successfully proceed without it. Many practitioners in the high touch fields struggle with feelings of selfishness when they think of trying to meet their own needs. Their own conflicts about feelings of selfishness versus needing some self-focus can be very intense. You may be one of these people.

My goal here is not to increase a person's capacity to be self-centered. The goal is to help the practitioner, over decades of work, to be able to engage in caring for others and sharing his or her professional expertise in counseling, therapy, teaching, or health care. Maintaining oneself personally is necessary to function effectively in a professional role. By itself, this idea can help those in the caring fields feel less selfish when meeting the needs of the self.

There are many methods of personal renewal. In this chapter, I suggest some of them. You may have developed others.

Constant Investment in a Personal Renewal Process

Constant renewal is essential so that our "pond" does not become stagnant. Being fed by "springs" and "streams" is important so that we can continue to attach professionally as practitioners who assist others with emotional, educational, and physical needs. Self-care means finding ways to replenish the self. The result is more important than the method. The point here is to find ways to produce constant self-renewal.

A major goal for professional self-care could be described as adrenalin boosting. This means searching for and finding positive life experiences. By this, I am suggesting that personal self-care should focus in part on producing feelings of zest, peace, euphoria, excitement, happiness, and pleasure. These are adrenalin boosters.

Awareness of the Danger of One-Way Caring Relationships in One's Personal Life

Individuals in the caring professions are experts at one-way caring. Others are attracted to them because of their expertise and caring attitude. This can lead to interactions like when a doctor is asked to diagnose a mysterious ailment in the middle of a festive party. What to do? One therapist decided to shed two friendships that seemed like work to her; she was the giver in these one-way caring relationships. A teacher made sure that the caring was two-way by assertively telling the other his problems while also being a good, supportive listener. As an overall self-care strategy, practitioners must be careful about the number of one-way caring relationships in their personal lives.

Sometimes one's intimate partner cares for the professional nurturer in a different style. For example, female professional nurturers can miss the care expressed by male partners who are not counselors, therapists, teachers, or health professionals. The combination of the female versus male gender code and the Realistic versus Social[1] occupational personality code (Holland, 1985) can lead to a major gender cultural gap in expressions of caring. As a counselor, therapist, teacher, or health professional, she may express care directly by giving words (a card), gifts (flowers), touch (a hug), or food (chocolate). As a trades person, technician, or engineer, for example, he may express indirect caring by doing things (changing the oil), fixing things

---

[1]In this well-researched and accepted theory, *Realistic* refers to technical and skilled trade occupations; *Social* refers to counseling, teaching, and healing type occupations (Holland, 1985).

(faucet repair), making things (building a deck), or providing for things (working a second job). A female professional nurturer may easily sense caring from someone who gives flowers and an affectionate personal note. Does she feel the same caring from a partner who, for decades, works a boring second job to provide resources but seldom talks? Perhaps cultural differences of gender and personality explain why the first can feel like caring and the second like indifference. Hopefully, the counselor, therapist, teacher, or health professional can experience this personal caring even though it is a foreign expression across a major gender cultural gap.

Nurturing One's Self

One could describe the self as composed of parts, with each part needing nurturing by the counselor, therapist, teacher, or health professional. These parts of the self are labeled differently by personality theorists (e.g., Jourard & Landsman, 1980). Here, we describe the parts as the emotional self, the financial self, the humorous self, the loving self, the nutritious self, the physical self, the playful self, the priority-setting self, the recreational self, the relaxation–stress reduction self, the solitary self, and the spiritual or religious self. Each of these elements of the personal self can use nurturing by the counselor, therapist, teacher, or health professional for ongoing sustenance.

Nurturing the Emotional Self

> Problems do not go away. They must be worked through or else they remain, forever a barrier to the growth and development of the spirit.
>
> —PECK (1978, p. 30)

> When I do not know myself, I cannot know who my students are. I will see them through a glass darkly, in the shadows of my unexamined life—and when I cannot see them clearly, I cannot teach them well.... The work required to "know thyself" is neither selfish nor narcissistic. Whatever self-knowledge we attain as teachers will serve our students and our scholarship well. Good teaching requires self-knowledge; it is a secret hidden in plain sight.
>
> —PALMER (1998, p. 23)

We need to acknowledge that what is good for others is good for ourselves. Psychotherapists have led the way in emotional self-care through the concept of "therapy for the therapist." In a study by Pope and Tabachnick (1994), 476 psychologists described their own therapy. The vast majority of this group (85.7 percent) found it to be very or extremely helpful. The major focus of the therapy was to reduce distress emotions such as anxiety or depression or to help with difficult relationships. Many reported positive changes in self qualities such as awareness, understanding, esteem, and confidence. Because helping professionals often use the self as the work instrument, these positive changes are notable. More often than other helpers, teachers, and healers, psychotherapists also tend to seek out one-to-one professional supervision with a senior practitioner. They do so because supervision is a major focus of professional training and because of the strong self-care benefits. Perhaps psychotherapists, in their use of therapy and supervision for themselves, are setting a valuable self-care example for other helpers, teachers, and healers. Yet, it is even difficult for psychotherapists (the shoemaker has no shoes problem) according to senior practitioner E. Nightengale (personal communication, 1995) who said, "Too many therapists fail to take the 'medicine' they prescribe for others."

Nurturing the Financial Self

Culture can have a profound effect on the causes of happiness by influencing the goals people pursue as well as the resources available to attain goals...selecting compatible goals may be a critical aspect of achieving [subjective well-being].
—*E. DIENER, E. M. SUH, R. E. LUCUS, &*
H. L. SMITH (1999, p. 285)

For most of its inhabitants, the United States is a place of wealth. A rich country is a place where there is only one person in most cars. A rich country is a place like the United States where the percentage of consumption of the world's resources vastly exceeds the country's percentage of the world's population. Living, however, within a cultural bubble of unending messages to consume more means that most people do not feel wealthy. The unrelenting saturation of advertisements and pleas to buy are successful. See *The Overspent American* by Schor (1998) for a description of this reality. In America, people spend all that they make. The irony is that, in a rich country, "the personal savings rate is...zero. In the aggregate, Americans are spending every dollar they take home" (Cassidy, 1999, p. 88). A note to students: Beginners usually feel that, after school is over, they will have money and save. The record, however, is different. When they get money, they tend to spend all of it and more.

In days before the demise of communism, it was said that the Soviet Union controlled the behavior of its citizens. Yet, this behavior control did not extend to thoughts and feelings. American culture is also successful at control. Here, thoughts and feelings are controlled, and then behavior automatically follows. In the United States, consumption is the national religion, with religion being defined as the reality that most people believe to be sacred. Having lots of good, new stuff is the basic belief. Many are trying to keep up with the Joneses. Another way of saying this is that, when people have a chicken, they want to have a goose like their neighbor. This is the reality portrayed by commercials and believed by citizens.

Why, you may ask, do I speak strongly here about this issue? I do so be-cause the high touch occupations pay well but not in cash. The pay comes in the immense satisfaction and pleasure one gets from the work at the deeper level of human existence. The pay comes from making a significantly positive difference in the lives of many other people. It is the joys, rewards, and gifts of practice effect. A major practitioner stress factor comes from be-ing paid modestly yet living in a consumption-saturated culture. Controlling this dominant cultural voice is a key to sustaining the financial self.

Most jobs within human services, education, and health pay modestly. The starting salary gets the attention of most beginners. That number is often low, but it is not the really important statistic; salary range is. High-paying occupations can start low but have a large range. Low-paying occupations start low and have a narrow range. The range is more important because, in the high touch fields, the narrow range means a person will *never* be paid a lot. Of course, there are some exceptions, like psychotherapists for the wealthy, industrial psychologists to large corporations, professors with lucra-tive consulting contracts, and physicians in many specialties. These, however, are exceptions. Most counselors, therapists, teachers, and health profession-als work in jobs that start low and cap within a narrow range.

For practitioners, the key to developing the financial self is to spend less and invest more. It is impossible to do this if one is strongly influenced by the intense advertising propaganda in the culture. Almost all people living under any cultural bubble are strongly influenced by the dominant message.

Three factors can help mitigate this effect. Living in a developing country gets one out of the cultural bubble and makes it easier to really see the wealth in the developed world. Then one can see that the majority of those in the United States live "high on the hog." Knowing that one is already high on the hog makes for less motivation to live higher and higher on the hog. To aspire to higher consumption levels seems to make less sense. Because of the power of the cultural bubble, a person is usually encapsulated and feels that overcon-sumption is a worthy goal. Outside of the bubble, it seems less sensible.

A second factor is the literature, which shows that an individual's finan-cial health has a stronger association with modest spending and moderate risk investing than it does with income. It is common to think that one's in-come is the central determinant of financial prosperity. This focus is mis-guided. Some of the best academic research on this topic is described in *The Millionaire Next Door* (Stanley & Danko, 1996). The central finding of this ac-ademic study is a surprise because it violates two basic ideas of the Ameri-can ethos—that millionaires are very different from the rest of us and that buying a lot now and paying with credit is a reasonable thing to do. The cen-tral premise is that millionaires are people who could be living next door and are millionaires because they live well below their means and invest the difference.

A similar thrust comes from the simplicity movement. Dominguez and Robin (1992) argue in *Your Money or Your Life* that frantically living to pay for overspending, which they say is the basic American approach, is a very unwise use of time, which they call a person's most precious resource. Their book title spells out this option—chasing money to spend or having time for a life. Their answer is found in the charts they use, where they offer evidence for how low consumption and high savings can lead, at midlife, to living off one's investments. This, they suggest, dramatically reduces the time and energy one needs for work to pay the bills. Instead, they say, people can use their time for richly meaningful life activities.

One other factor is worth mentioning concerning the financial self of the counselor, therapist, teacher, or health professional. In these jobs, the pay is usually mediocre, but sometimes it is even more mediocre than necessary because the practitioner has poor assertiveness skills regarding money. Let me tell you a story. A friend of mine worked at a university on a nine-month contract. Usually he found work in the summer. One summer, it was especially important because his salary had to support two adults and four children. He was told that there would be summer work, but he was passive about the whole process. Then, a few weeks before summer was to begin, he was told that there was no summer money. It was a good lesson for him. He told himself that it would never happen again and that he had to be more active and assertive about financial needs. The point of this story is that financially unassertive practitioners in the low-paying human services, education, and health jobs can become very demoralized because of financial stress.

If a practitioner has poor money skills (a good example of poor money management is buying a new car, a depreciating asset, with a car loan, an undetectable loan; in time, the person owes more on the loan than the car is worth), is financially unassertive, and also has been seduced by the consumption culture, then the financial self can be highly stressed. In time, this can affect the practitioner so that he or she can no longer make the necessary emotional connections with clients, students, or patients. If that happens, competent work is no longer possible.

Nurturing the Humorous Self

Maintaining a sense of humor was the number one career sustaining behavior, endorsed by 82 percent of the sample in a study of psychotherapists' coping strategies (Kramen-Kahn & Hansen, 1998). Actively laughing, being playful, telling jokes, and being humorous are very positive activities for individuals whose work environment is often filled with serious human problems. How then does one laugh in a serious environment? It takes time to learn the "art and science of laughter" at work. Students in training often lose their humor because they worry that it will be perceived as unprofessional. In time, one's sense of humor often emerges from hiding, and gradually there is, in the best situations, a proper place for humor in the environment of the caring professions. Laughter sustains counselors, therapists, teachers, and health professionals. Learn how to be serious *and* have fun can help sustain the self.

Nurturing the Loving Self

This can be the most powerful source of professional vitality, enabling practitioners to sustain themselves amidst significant professional stress. For many people, this means a strong primary relationship with one other person who is loving, affectionate, nurturing, and fun to be with. It often means having and raising children. For many practitioners, a family is a very rich source of the best ingredients of self-care. For others, it takes a different form. The overall effect, however, is a sense of well-being that radiates from the practitioner's personal life.

Counselors, therapists, teachers, and health professionals are occupational experts at addressing the needs of others. Often, they have a long personal and professional history of successfully nurturing the mind, body, soul, and heart of others and getting praise for doing so. They may also have hopes, fantasies, and dreams of others anticipating and addressing their own needs. The nurturing dream often involves a sense of anticipation by the other and may sound like this: "The other will know what I want and gracefully—in timing, method, and style—care for me." The dream may end with a sense of frustration and resentment because no one seems to notice. Where is he or she or somebody or anybody for the professional nurturer? Too often, the dream ends with a disappointing reality.

The terms used earlier in Chapter 9, *altruistic egotism, holy selfishness,* and *self-attentiveness,* suggest that professional nurturers must learn how to do more than dream. One could call this "the nurturer has no nurturing" (the shoemaker has no shoes) problem. They can make shoes for others but not so easily for themselves. In moments of reflection, they realize that their feet are bare. Part of the conflict for counselors, therapists, teachers, and health professionals is their own ambivalence about putting their own needs versus the needs of others under the spotlight. Perhaps it is important to realize that, according to the attachment process described earlier as an *essential* element of practitioner success, care of the *self* is a *sacred* responsibility. Being loved by another, or others, is a wonderful method of self-care for those in the high touch fields. The personal life caring can be very sustaining and is often greatly appreciated by the practitioner.

Nurturing the Nutritious Self

Recently, psychologist and performance specialist Kate Hays (1999a) addressed practitioners at a "Taking Care of Yourself" symposium. There, she provided nine nutritional recommendations for high performance. The commentary under each one is mine.

1. *Happiness is a steady rhythm of blood glucose.* The steady idea speaks against skipping and binging patterns of eating such as "sugar hits" and supports regular eating. The idea of eating small meals combined with snacks (Schafer, 1996) is one way to maintain a steady glucose stream. Consultation with a dietician can be a valuable way to discover what foods provide each practitioner with a steady glucose stream.

2. *Provide yourself with a regular routine of eating.* Routine provides structure and stability and encourages planfulness. It helps us to avoid the impulsive eating that serves as admission to the "paved with good intentions" double lane, filled with traffic, road to hell.

3. *Breakfast is the one meal a day not to skip.* In a world of mixed, contradictory, and confusing messages about nutrition, this one is consistently recommended. Why? It seems that breakfast is used as gasoline to get the body going. Without food early in the day, the body runs out of gas late in the day and screams for food. It is a timing problem because food late in the day tends to go into storage, perhaps forever.

4. *Eat like a peasant to live like a king or queen.* Peasants eat the plant food around them because it is inexpensive, whereas kings and queens eat expensive dishes and desserts. In an income discrepancy twist of fate, inexpensive means low fat and calories and high vitamins and minerals. Expensive translates to high of the bad and low of the good. Perhaps we can call this "revenge of the vegetable."

5. *Your body needs water.* Back to the basics, as with number 4. Water, and lots of it, seems to be one of the top nutritional secrets. Because over 70 percent of the body is water, it makes sense that the hose should keep running. On this note, Balch and Balch (1997) state, "To keep the body functioning properly, it is essential to drink at least eight 8-ounce glasses of quality water each day" (p. 30). Products containing water, such as cola and coffee, are not part of the secret because the caffeine acts as a diuretic, stealing water from the body.

6. *Befriend food and be flexible.* Eating disorders are at war with food when they use and abuse food to serve other gods and goddesses. It is better to enjoy the friendship of food, just as one enjoys, but does not abuse, other friends. Flexibility speaks to the failure of fad diets whose inflexibility means that they desist rather than persist. Flexibility also means that small indulgence is a positive trait for long-term success.

7. *Learn how to distinguish true hunger signals from other bodily or emotional signals.* Earlier in my career, I worked with students with eating disorders at the University of Florida. The students there were experts at emotional eating, but they did not have a corner on the market. Bad feelings such as anxiety, loneliness, anger, fear, confusion, hurt, and sadness trigger eating for lots of people. The problem is that the person may not be hungry. Trouble!

8. *Learn for what your body is hungry and thirsty.* Self-awareness can be a valuable people skill. Listening to oneself can provide lots of important information. Knowing the language of hunger and thirst can lead to efficient responses to the message of the body rather than useless utterances in another language, which may be telling the person to eat unnecessary foods.

9. *Develop a long-term perspective with regard to eating habits.* Eating is forever, and for most people, that is a long time. This means that all kinds of short-term schemes (e.g., losing 20 pounds before the reunion) don't cut the mustard. Going from a bad relationship with food to a good one is more than adding a little veneer. Sometimes it's a major remodeling job. The payoff is that, after major remodeling, one has something.

Following the nine nutrition recommendations of Kate Hays gives the practitioner another attractive piece of fabric when making the "sustaining the personal self" quilt.

Nurturing the Physical Self

The vast majority of studies examining the role of exercise on psychological well-being and mood support the notion that exercise will improve well-being and mood states such as anxiety, stress, depression, tension, and fatigue.
—*T. G. PLANTE (1993, p. 362)*

The research that I have reviewed here provides consistent evidence that aerobic fitness plays an important role in determining the way in which humans respond to stress.... The breadth and consistency of these findings is impressive, but even more impressive is the magnitude of the findings.
—*D. S. HOLMES (1993, p. 59)*

Comparisons show a tremendous decline in physical activity with age...from 65% participation at ages 10–17 to 15% at ages 18–64.... Statistics about participants' adherence to various forms of physical activity in both normal and clinical settings are equally sobering...the dropout rate can be as high as 50% within the first 6 months of participation.
—*L. R. BRAWLEY & W. M. RODGERS (1993, p. 254)*

Over and over again, we hear that we are supposed to "get exercise!" Often, this is said as a way to improve general physical health; however, here I am bringing up this topic for a different reason. There is now strong evidence that vigorous physical exercise is beneficial in reducing the stress emotions of anxiety and depression (Holmes, 1993). It is only a short step to suggest that intense physical activity is an antidote for the emotional toxins in the practitioner's work life. Given the benefits of exercise, it is easy to speculate that, if it came in pill form, exercise would be *THE* most popular pill taken on a daily basis.

The work in the high touch caring professions is emotionally demanding and draining. Remember that the term *burnout* originated in these professions. For a reminder that practitioners' work is stressful, I ask you to look again at the content in earlier chapters: The Caring Cycle, The Elevated Stressors of the Novice Practitioner, and Hazards of Practice. These chapters, read together, present an overwhelmingly difficult view of the work. For example, there is the hazard of living in a world of distress emotions. One needs methods to combat the depression, anxiety, and pain that the practitioner feels when closeted with the distressed client, student, or patient. This is why helpers, teachers, and health professionals must seriously consider intense physical activity as a piece of the "sustaining the personal self" puzzle.

In addition to knowing that intense physical activity is good for us, we also know, as described by Brawley and Rodgers (1993), how hard it is to maintain a highly active physical life. Why is it so hard for practitioners? For one thing, competent practitioners in the caring fields tend to put the needs of others before their own. It is an occupational characteristic. A great example occurs in the practitioner's personal life when he or she is a parent. Of course, good parents do focus on the needs of their children; however, the result is a reality where the practitioner's needs get squeezed. Then, there is the time problem in modern life, or shall we call it the lack-of-time problem? Also, there is the way that we have starched out almost all physical activity from modern life. This happens in building design (the elevator is available, but where are the stairs?) and attitude (at the health club, people try to park close to the door).

It seems that one of the greatest self-care challenges for many practitioners is the challenge of creating and maintaining a highly active physical life. Research suggests that physical exercise can be highly effective in combating the emotionally stressful parts of the work. Unfortunately, it does not come in pill form. It does, however, come in another form. How can you swallow this form into your ongoing demanding, full life? Realizing that exercise adherence is difficult, Hays (1999b) offers a sophisticated approach to the topic.

Nurturing the Playful Self

Practitioners are serious people trying to do good work under stressful conditions. To have a long, happy career, there is an ironic prescription for these serious people. That prescription is play. Listen to these words: "The world of play favors exuberance, license, abandon. Shenanigans are allowed, strategies can be tried, selves can be revisited. In the self-enclosed world of play, there is no hunger. It is its own goal which it reaches in a richly satisfying way" (Ackerman, 1999, p. 6). The emotional world of the practitioner is filled with words like *earnest, hard, stressful, challenging,* and *serious* and more intense words like *sad, anxious, fearful,* and *angry.* The words of play are different. These words include *fun, zest, relish, delight, enjoyment, gusto, enthusiasm,* and *exuberance.* The world of play helps make the world of work possible.

In transactional analysis (TA), it is the child ego state that does the playing. One version of the child is the baby. So how does one nurture this part of the self? We call it babying oneself. What does it mean to baby the self? It usually means to attend to, to pamper, to be tender. Why is this important? Because it is the self of the counselor, therapist, teacher, and health professional that must work very hard. The professional self attaches to the client, student, or patient and makes human growth possible. As stated in Chapter 3, the attachment process is crucial for human development. So how can the practitioner baby the self? Lots of ways—bubble baths and chocolates for some, playing golf or watching a great basketball game for others. The choices are endless. Finding something that babies the self and doing it are the essentials.

In her book *Deep Play,* Ackerman (1999) describes it as an ecstatic form of play. She says that there is an unconscious engagement with the world and an exalted zone of transcendence. In the book, she travels through multiple examples: scuba diving, mountain climbing, wearing a mask, studying animals in the wild, and visiting exotic sites. Describing one form of deep play, she says, "While cycling, I tend to commune with nature, feel life's elements, and repeat a simple mantra of sensations that I experience separately: blue sky, white clouds, green trees, apple scent, bright sun, warm breeze" (p. 33).

Her discussion of the Grand Canyon reminded me of my own deep play nine-day rafting trip on the Colorado River through the Grand Canyon. At the time, I was very tired from my own high touch work. Every day, I sat on the raft and watched the beauty unfold all around me. Looking through this kaleidoscope of color, shape, and form brought pleasure and peace. I was transcending the reality of my work life and being renewed by my own playfulness.

May I invite you as a practitioner to inventory your play time. Perhaps it is there; perhaps it needs to be added.

Nurturing the Priority-Setting Self

Let's start with this premise: There is always too much to do. Or this one: It does not get easier (students hate to hear this one because the illusion of "better and easier later" keeps them going). Why is it so? Modern life is a decent answer, with information overload (it comes from the north and south, east and west, from everywhere), the disappearance of boundaries, and accessibility by cell phone and e-mail everywhere. The Berlin Wall of our lives has disappeared, a blessing and a curse.

We must make our own boundaries around our work and lives. What is the compass for this task? It is our own values, job and boss demands, and our personal lives. Set priorities for your time—an irreplaceable, precious commodity. Then, the chance improves that you will get to your primacy, your hot center of importance, and never have time for the flotsam of your life. This can be a good outcome.

Setting priorities and time management are, first of all, a recognition that there is always too much to do. Secondly, they are a realization that the locus of control for the person's agenda can be internal or external. As they say in Alcoholics Anonymous (AA), "Who is driving your bus?" The task is difficult for those in people occupations who readily want to assist the other. The struggle to stand upright and follow one's own compass gets hard on the slippery floor of trying to be there for the other. The bells and whistles of time management—put an A next to the important tasks for the day—are easily mastered when the bigger issue of setting priorities is directly faced and managed. Good luck.

Nurturing the Recreational Self

Hobbies can be great for self-care because they have so many elements of renewal. An element of this is what C. Wambach (personal communication, 1989), a college teacher of high-risk students, calls "positive significant distractions." We control the involvement and outcome, the domain is manageable, and the task is fun, interesting, and absorbing.

Being a collector, of whatever, captures so many of these positive elements, and it is CONCRETE—one can see and feel results! Is it any wonder that collecting is a popular activity in the stress-filled world of other-care practitioners? E. Nightengale (personal communication, 1995), a senior Veterans Administration hospital psychologist, responded to these comments by saying, "The value of a hobby, with concrete results, clear beginnings and finished 'products,' is important for the helping professional. The need for completion, for progress, and success can be channeled or 'found' by these kinds of activities." One of my friends, an other-care practitioner in a high-stress job, collects rocks. For her, it is a low maintenance, concrete hobby with no care or watering needed; even after a long Minnesota winter, the rocks left outside emerge from the receding snow undamaged. She can look at them, touch them, move them around, and add to her collection. No care is needed! The key is to be taken away from the focus on one's own professional work demands. The result can be a healthier perspective on work, the world, and oneself.

Nurturing the Relaxation–Stress Reduction Self

Do members of the helping, teaching, or health fields manage stress by using techniques developed from their own professions? Often, the answer is no. Many of us in these practitioner fields are familiar, through our professional work, with stress-management methods such as relaxation training, meditation, biofeedback, yoga, and self-hypnosis. Yet, we often do not personally practice these methods to reduce our own physical body response of overarousal, although we know that overarousal is the key to many current lifestyle-type physical problems and diseases.

There are many sources of stress that lead to overarousal. There is the constant need for practitioners to focus on the needs of the other. These may be emotional, intellectual, physical, or other needs. There are, of course, many other sources of stress, such as organizational politics and policies that may greatly affect the individual practitioner who often has little voice in major decisions. Another source of stress is internal in the practitioner's own thoughts and appraisal of self in a variety of contexts.

A century ago, overarousal was termed the "fight or flight response" by Cannon, a professor at Harvard. Cannon suggested that, in response to threat, the human body goes into an emergency mode to either attack the threatening object or escape from it. The attack mode produces physical changes in the body that can help in the attack or escape. Modern life produces the same physical reaction but within a different context, for example, a traffic jam. The long-term consequence is the onset of stress-related disease turning into a disease. These current diseases, which sometimes have a stress component, include heart disease, depression, cancer, arthritis, and gastrointestinal system disorders.

Nearly one hundred years after Cannon, another Harvard professor, Herbert Benson (1975), stated that the best antidote to overarousal is a simple procedure he called "the relaxation response." Benson (1999) believes that relaxation as an antidote to the chronic overarousal of modern life can be done through two simple steps. Within a context of quiet and comfort, the individual is to:

1. Repeat a word, sound, prayer, thought, phrase, or muscular activity.
2. Return to number one whenever other thoughts or activities intrude.

These two steps, along with slow, deep breathing, are the elements of the relaxation response. Benson (1999) states that increasing oxygen consumption is a powerful yet easy-to-add part of stress reduction. He also maintains that all of the world's major religions, over their hundreds of years of history, have incorporated these elements into their religious prayers, rituals, and practices. Benson says that use of the relaxation response is a major way to ward off illness.

Learning through practice and overpractice to reduce the stress response of overarousal can be of great value in the practitioner's personal and professional life. *The Relaxation and Stress Reduction Workbook* by Davis, Eshelman, and McKay (1995) is one of many sources of useful techniques. Some of the stress reduction methods they emphasize are body awareness, breathing, progressive relaxation, and visualization. They describe body awareness as a first self-assessment step regarding stress management and breathing as a central part of stress reduction. They say, "Improper breathing contributes to anxiety, panic attacks, depression, muscle tension, headache, and fatigue. ...Breathing awareness and good breathing habits will enhance your psychological and physical well-being, whether you practice them alone or in combination with other relaxation techniques" (p. 23). They emphasize the importance of deep abdominal, diaphragmatic breathing as opposed to shallow chest, thoracic breathing.

First developed by Jacobson in 1929, progressive relaxation is an old method of relaxing the body. It has been a central part of therapist-directed anxiety management for many years. It essentially consists of tightening and then relaxing different muscle groups in the body. The theory is that a person cannot be tense and relaxed at the same time. By relaxing, the person is teaching the body to respond differently during periods of overarousal.

Visualization is the practice of seeing something in the mind's eye. It is a way of using one's imagination and creativity to enhance one's life. Similar terms are *imagery* and *guided fantasy*. With others, I have described the use of visualization in career and life planning (Skovholt, Morgan, & Cunningham, 1989). In managing stress, Davis and colleagues (1995) say that guided visualization can be used by imagining a place where you can be very relaxed. For many people, this involves an outdoor scene such as the ocean, a lake, or the wilderness. The individual can develop this picture in the mind and then imagine it during high-stress times.

Let me suggest that your work as a practitioner can be immensely gratifying while also stressful. There is also the reality of membership in the rat race of modern life. So regarding stress reduction methods, let us all try to refrain from the reality of the shoemaker having no shoes.

Nurturing the Solitary Self

It is a difficult lesson to learn today—to leave one's friends and family and deliberately practice the art of solitude.... I feel a limb is being torn off, without which I shall be unable to function. And yet once it is done, I find there is a quality to being alone that is incredibly precious. Life rushes back into the void, richer, more vivid,

fuller than before. It is as if in parting one actually did lose an arm. And then, like the starfish, one grows it anew; one is whole again, complete and round—more whole ever than before, when the other people had pieces of one.
—*ANNE MORROW LINDBERGH (1975, p. 42)*

Solitude, an antidote to people intensity is important for professional givers of the self. Solitude can nurture in a profound way. Learning to enjoy solitude can be a difficult process for counselors, therapists, teachers, and health professionals. It means removing oneself from the known channel of life (intense contact with others in need) to an often unknown channel (silence, no human voices, aloneness). Those in the caring professions often have to fight through the disquieting elements of the quiet—the loneliness, the self-focus, an alienation from nature. They need to learn how to change loneliness into solitude. In time, however, the sounds of the natural world, the singing wilderness, can fill up the self in a way that refreshes. So too can just plain quiet. A negative byproduct of technology has been noise pollution; noise is everywhere. The beeper imprisons as much as it frees. The phone rings; cars drive by; people are talking all around. The life enhancing machinery around us, such as washing machines and lawn mowers, also are life nonenhancing because of noise. In solitude, silence is the gold. Spiritual and religious practices also offer a bed for solitude. One can meditate and pray alone with the focus often being the connection between the self and the eternity.

Usually those in the caring professions live a life of intense interaction with people who need something. Almost all of the time in the lives of helpers, teachers, and health workers is filled with people. For example, the typical K–12 teacher is exposed to overwhelming numbers of living, breathing, needing things called students every day, Monday through Friday.

Was it a genius who invented a professional teaching year of nine months? This permits a teacher to recover and be ready again after three months away from the people intensity. Maybe the 9 month : 3 month cycle of intensity and distance was created by a very wise student of professional development rather than from the agrarian pattern of early American life. I prefer to think that the calendar came from someone who knew decades ago that the caring cycle demands time away, that it demands solitude.

Of course, teachers do not go from work to three months of hermitlike existence. In fact, many take classes and work extra in the summer. However, at least the occupation is structurally set up to permit removal from the intense human contact at work. The 9 month : 3 month rhythm permits something else that is very valuable. It permits the felt separation phase of the caring cycle to occur within the structure of the occupation. Listen carefully to elementary teachers talk about their work. They often use the words "my children" when describing their students, and they often describe end-of-the-year rituals that they say are to help the children make the transition to summer. I hope that the rituals are also for the teachers to help them grieve the loss of their caring attachments, attachments that will change forever. Positive loss experiences permit a new round of attachments for teachers when August and September come again. With too many unresolved and painful losses, we cannot attach again in our personal lives. With too many unresolved and painful losses at work, we cannot attach in our professional lives.

Unlike K–12 teaching, most careers in the high touch fields do not have a very good intensity-distance structure built into the occupation. Let me remind you that I am talking about a 40-year career perspective. Anyone can go for a few years without adequate occupational nutrition. In time, the inadequacy catches up to the person. Solitude can help.

Nurturing the Spiritual or Religious Self

The mystery of life, cloaked so guilelessly in day and night, makes the search for God the enduring human drama. We know so little, we feel so much. We have only the shape of our lives, experienced in the cycle of light and dark, to guide us toward meaning. —HAMPL (1995, p. xxvi)

Several friends have told me that *The Denial of Death* by Ernest Becker (1973) is the most profound book, the one with the greatest depth, they have read. In the book, Becker describes death as the great human fear, a fear so great, he says, that people construct their whole lives to manage its intensity. Becker suggests that denial of death's reality is a central coping strategy for this intense fear.

It seems to me that the reality of death is a major motivation in the human quest for a spiritual or religious life. This quest is both cross-cultural and historic. Concerning which spiritual or religious path is the right one, I personally have difficulty believing that "all the marbles" are possessed by one narrow, highly dogmatic belief system. In houses of worship, I have celebrated the sacred and God's presence with Moslems in Turkey, Buddhists in Thailand, Catholics at the Vatican, Jews when my father was a resident of a Jewish nursing home, Chinese Baptists in Singapore, and Lutherans at my grandfather's church in Norway. I have also experienced the power of the Christian God in the beautiful wilderness of Minnesota's canoe country. I have come to believe that a spiritual or religious life is an important part of how one sustains the personal self. The exact form that this should take is something of which I am less sure. It is not my role or right to tell others what to believe.

For me, there are two reasons why being active spiritually or religiously is important. First, an active spiritual or religious life acknowledges the reality described by Becker. Death can be terrifying, and facing the reality directly through a spiritual or religious life is a reaction of more depth than the use of denial. Also, an active spiritual or religious quest addresses the central mysteries of life: What is the meaning of life? Is there an active divine presence? What is God's plan for my life? Are people basically good or evil? How does one achieve forgiveness, atonement, and peace? What moral rules should govern my life? Is there eternal life?

Second, workers in the high touch, caring professions, such as counselors, therapists, teachers, and health professionals, are actively present in the drama of human tragedy, disappointment, and pain. Examples include hearing as a counselor of betrayal of one person by another, seeing as a teacher a student try but fail, or watching as a nurse while a severely injured person struggles with intense pain. An active spiritual or religious life can help the practitioner search for meaning and understanding of these painful human realities seen at work on a daily basis. For example, it is important to ask questions such as: Why does God permit acute human pain and suffering? An active spiritual or religious life seems for many practitioners to be an important part of sustaining the personal self.

Summary: Keeping in Focus One's Own Need for Balanced Wellness—Physical, Spiritual, Emotional, and Social

Counselors, therapists, teachers, and health professionals need to be assertive about their own wellness. One way of conceptualizing this involves four dimensions of health and the balance between them (Figure 11.1).

The diamond and its four dimensions help one to see the need for a focus on the dynamic interplay between them. The diamond symbolizes the reality that the whole is greater than the sum of the parts. Yet, the whole is strong only by attending to each dimension.

Physical health

Emotional/social health   Intellectual health

Spiritual health

FIGURE 11.1   Four Dimensions of Health

12

Burnout Prevention and Self-Care Strategies of Expert Practitioners

Mary Mullenbach and Thomas Skovholt

This chapter focuses on the methods used by one group of practitioners, those in mental health, to maintain professional vitality. Hopefully the ideas presented here can be of use to a wide variety of practitioners across the rainbow of the high touch fields.

Mental health practitioners encounter stressors that originate from both internal and external sources (Freudenberger, 1990). Both have a direct effect on the practitioner. Burnout is especially prevalent in this group of helping professionals. Practitioners are expected to engage in an ongoing series of professional attachments and separations, as discussed in Chapter 3. The stress of attachment and separation is often intensified by a lack of client success, nonreciprocated giving within the counseling relationship, overwork, difficult client behaviors, discouragement as a result of the slow and uneven pace of the counseling process, the practitioner's existing personal issues that emerge in response to involvement in the counseling process, isolation, and administrative demands from agency and managed care organizations (Dupree & Day, 1995; Farber, 1990; Kassam-Adams, 1995). Burnout occurs when the practitioner is continuously depleted from this intense process of engagement.

The debilitating effects of the counseling role on the practitioner have long been recognized as an occupational hazard with far-reaching effects (Freudenberger & Robbins, 1979). Based on his research, Farber (1983) concluded that counseling work can have a substantial negative impact on practitioners' self-identity, behavior, and attitudes both within and outside of the work setting. Historically, studies in this area have primarily focused on identifying work-related stressors.

In 1996, a research program was started with 10 peer-nominated mental health practitioners. The purpose of the initial study was to identify the components of mastery among this group of expert practitioners. Since that time, the research program has been expanded. The current study[1] identified components relevant to wellness and professional resiliency in this group of practitioners. In this study, a qualitative design was utilized as a means of drawing a store of rich information from the sample group. Data were collected through the use of a semistructured interview format, with questions cultivated from existing research focused on stressors among mental health practitioners. The questions were designed to identify stressors and to access information pertaining to the emotional wellness and professional resiliency of these practitioners. The data analysis relied on an inductive approach that allowed for an in-depth exploration. Two interviews were completed with each of the participants. An analysis of a second data source obtained from a previous study with this same group of participants was used to supplement the findings. The selected findings presented in this chapter focus on high-level stressors and self-care strategies identified within this group of practitioners.

This chapter presents 20 themes within five categories that originated from the data analysis. The five categories are (1) professional stressors, (2) emergence of the expert practitioner, (3) creating a positive work structure, (4) protective factors, and (5) nurturing self through solitude and relationships. A summary of the information is in Table 12.1, Categories and Themes.

Category A. Professional Stressors

Category A contains four themes that identify stressor areas that are confronted by the participants in their work.

Theme 1. Participants are Stressed by Issues That Challenge Their Competency

Participants reported an array of issues and events that challenge to their sense of wellness. Sometimes, as in the case of a suicidal client, these experi-

[1]This chapter is drawn from Mullenbach, M.A. (2000). *Expert therapists: A study of professional resiliency and emotional wellness.* Unpublished doctoral dissertation, University of Minnesota, Minneapolis. Thomas Skovholt was the dissertation advisor.

TABLE 12.1   Categories and Themes

Category A. Professional Stressors

Participants are stressed by issues that challenge their competency.
A frozen therapy process is highly stressful for participants.
Breaches in peer relationships are stressful.
Intrapersonal crises negatively impact the professional role.

Category B. Emergence of the Expert Practitioner

Participants learned role limits and boundaries.
Over time, participants experienced less performance anxiety.
With experience, participants moved from theory to use of self.
Participants view attachment and separation as a natural process.
Participants understand human suffering at a profound level.

Category C. Creating a Positive Work Structure

Mentor and peer support was critical at the novice phase.
Participants have ongoing and enriching peer relationships.
Multiple roles are a protective factor.
Participants create health-promoting work environments.

Category D. Protective Factors

Participants directly engage highly stressful professional dilemmas.
Participants confront and resolve personal issues.
Highly engaged learning is a powerful source of renewal.

Category E. Nurturing Self Through Solitude and Relationships

Participants foster professional stability by nurturing a personal life.
Participants invest in a broad array of restorative activities.
Participants construct fortifying personal relationships.
Participants value an internal focus.

ences represented unpredicted critical incidents for the practitioners. Other, less intense events and issues were chronic in nature and occurred on an ongoing basis. Regardless of the specific experience, a commonality that ran through was the participants' experience of feeling "tapped-out" in regard to their level of competency or comfort. One participant discussed the emotional impact of a client who committed suicide during a hospitalization.[2]

> *I know that she ended up in the hospital; I arranged it.... So I took care of her safety, I felt. And I don't know what the heck they did; she was suicidal, and they weren't watching her, and she hung herself. And it was really hard; I just felt heartbroken, and I was so pissed at the psychiatrist.*

[2]Quotations have been edited with small changes that increase the clarity of the writing.

One participant discussed the ongoing stressors that are related to working with chronically ill clients who don't progress:

> ...depression that doesn't lift. All kinds of interventions; I mean, some people have had therapy for years before they get to me. Some of them have had shock treatment, some of them have had medication, and nothing seems to be helpful. You know, people who have been searching for a long while, and maybe you can help them make some inroads, but there are some people for whom it just feels like we don't have what's needed yet.

Other participants discussed their sense of feeling lost or depleted when working with specific client behaviors:

> And I'm realizing that, for example, I don't work well with addictives, people who are addictive. I find I get sucked into their dynamics, and I can't keep track that these people are also con people because they need to be.

> I've had a few men who have been very abusive...they're coming to me, and the allegation of physical or sexual abuse may be in the air, but they haven't dealt with it at all, or maybe it hasn't been in the air at all. But I find myself angry at the end of those sessions. Those are the people that I find myself, I feel used up rather than giving 100%; I feel like I've been stolen from; I feel like I've been taken from. It's totally unrewarding, like they don't give anything back.

Sometimes this sense of being tapped out resulted from the level of distress expressed by the client:

> I think it has more to do with when there's been a lot. So, for example, there are some weeks where it feels like you always thought you heard the worst that you could possibly hear and then someone comes in with something worse about what people are able to do to people that causes pain and distress.... And sometimes it's just in waves.

Theme 2. A Frozen Therapy Process Is Highly Stressful for Participants

Participants reported that they experienced a sense of boredom related to clients who were unmotivated or resistant to treatment. This experience of feeling bored within the therapeutic relationship was reported as a significant stressor. Participants stated:

For me the issues would be probably somebody is just really without any willingness whatsoever to reflect. It is always something outside of themselves, continuously so....mostly I think I lose interest.

I think what's challenging, frankly, are the boring clients, you know, where it's time after time and very little is happening.

In reflecting on his work with clients who were resistant, one participant spoke about the need to deal with his own defensive response:

Well, I find I don't mind their resistance; it's when I start getting resistant in the face of their resistance. I mean, they have the right; I expect them to get resistant. But then when they do their resistance in a way that engenders my resistance, then I don't like that.

Theme 3. Breaches in Peer Relationships Are Stressful

Participants consistently reported that they derived a beneficial sense of support from their peer relationships, both within the work environment and in the broader professional community. Not surprisingly, breaches in these relationships are especially stressful. One participant stated:

Some of the most stressful times have been when I've accidentally ended up working with colleagues that I didn't feel compatible with, to come to work every morning and greet a face that you're not happy to see. Someone you don't trust or respect who doesn't seem to trust or respect me, that's very hard, but it's not my situation now.

Another participant discussed his struggle to stay engaged with peers in the broader professional community when discussing issues relevant to professional practice and integrity:

[Stressful for me are] my own relationships and associations with colleagues where we hit points of important divergence. And my willingness to stay present to those, to stay in a relationship with those colleagues and to stay present to the divergence without favoring a tendency to want to split off or isolate or withdraw.

In a similar way, a participant spoke about her negative response to conflicts between separate divisions in the psychological community:

They're both really good groups, and I think it's good for our practices and the community and everything else, but there are elements of competition and resentment and politics, I guess is what you'd call it, but I really dislike it, and when I'm caught in the middle of one of those frays, I'm very unhappy.

Theme 4. Intrapersonal Crises Have a Negative Impact on the Professional Role

Participants reported that personal life crises and related problems presented challenging situations in their professional role. Although the participants had developed proactive methods for coping with these issues, they reported a strong sense of discomfort when initially faced with this type of challenge. One participant described the unease that he felt when personal issues created a sense of incongruence in his perception of self:

When I was experiencing a lot of tearing in relation to my own family, which I did some years ago, a long time ago. That was pretty difficult, and I think the difficulty was having to redo my conception of myself while I was continuing to practice. And you really can't take yourself off line and decide to redo your conception of yourself and come back because that's always so closely integrated to whatever you're doing every place else.

Another participant described the hardship that she encounters when she is in the process of resolving her own crises:

So then I feel very split in terms of what I need to attend to with clients, and yet knowing this other thing is playing in my own life that is not going to resolve today in a phone call and is not going to resolve in a week, and it's going to be with me for whatever period of time. And so those, frankly, are torture chambers for me.... When I'm sitting with clients and they're talking about anything that remotely is similar or identifies with or touches on, the anxiety just shoots up.... How do I manage that level of anxiety and at the same time try to be here for my clients?

Category B. Emergence of the Expert Practitioner

Category B contains five themes that highlight aspects of the participants' approaches to professional practice. These themes reflect attitudes and techniques that promote wellness and preserve professional vitality.

Theme 1. Participants Learned Role Limits and Boundaries

Over time, participants learned the value of establishing clear boundaries and limits in areas that included their role as a helper, the level of responsibility that they assumed, the structure of their practice, the makeup of their caseloads, and their relationships with clients. The establishment of these boundaries and limits enabled the practitioners to maintain a sense of well-ness and vitality, to cope more effectively with difficult client behaviors, and to manage their own continuous exposure to suffering. In discussing her evolving role, one participant stated:

> *I'm far more wise about all the things that I don't need to know about and don't need to fix, and I think when I started out, like most of us when we start out, feeling a need to have all the answers. My job was to fix this, be helpful. I think with experience and time in the field, you learn that our job is really to relax more and sit back and listen and hear better what it is that the person is trying to sort through.*

One participant discussed the establishment of limits and boundaries as a necessary ingredient in both practicing with integrity and fostering a sense of wellness and vitality:

> *It is up to me to do everything I can to maintain my own emotional health so that I can actually be available to my patients without needing them. I think one of the ways therapy goes awry is that the therapist starts to use the patient for their own emotional sustenance, regulation of the therapist's self-esteem, all those sorts of things. I think that to be a good therapist, you must be well fed and well loved. Basically, have a life out there that is working.*

Participants noted that limits and boundaries played a key role in struc-turing their actual work day. In discussing the framework of her schedule, one participant stated:

> *It's important for me to keep track of the hours I'm putting in because it's very easy to start going over a 40-hour week. And I start to know that something's wrong when I wake up in the morning and I'm not rested or when I'm dreading the day, or I'll find myself sleepy or bored, and this is not boring work, and I start to make mistakes, double schedule people, or there are just certain signs I recognize as that I'm working too hard.*

Regarding his ability to implement limits on client behaviors, one par-ticipant stated:

> *I'm more sure of myself…. I can set limits with, you know, the authority of a Dutch uncle, and it can have the subtleties of both nurturance and a stop sign.*

Another participant noted the importance of understanding her limita-tions as a practitioner:

Part of it has been to really advocate for clients where it feels like it's really important; part of it has been to make alternatives available, like sliding fees for people; some of it is just coming to grips with that there are certain agencies that can provide certain things, and that we can't provide everything for everybody. So part of it is accepting limitations.

Theme 2. Over Time, Participants Experienced Less Performance Anxiety

With time, participants became more comfortable in their professional role. With this change, they experienced a decrease in stress and an increase in confidence and ability to handle a variety of difficult therapeutic issues and client behaviors. This shift allowed them to be more open and genuine in their role as a helper. Three practitioners commented:

There's less of a need to prove yourself, and so you can be more open because you don't feel as much that you need to defend anything or protect anything. I think when you first start out sometimes, it feels like you're on the line, you know; no one knows who you are, how you're doing, and so I think there's much more a sense of protection around yourself; seems like as you grow older and more experienced, there's more of a sense of "We all don't know, and we're all learning," so you can be pretty open about hearing feedback, getting information.

I laugh a lot more, a lot more. I am old. That is one thing that helps. And…I am not forever wondering if I am good enough.

Comfort with coming to work each day and assuming that it would be okay. You know, I'd do all right somehow, or I'd be able to deal with whatever happened that day; I'm just guessing, but I'm thinking maybe 10 years into my practice, I started to have that kind of sense of equilibrium about it.

Theme 3. With Experience, Participants Moved from Theory to Use of Self

Participants noted that, as they accumulated experience, they moved from a reliance on specific techniques and approaches to being more open and genuine. This change occurred as they became increasingly aware of the therapeutic process and how to best use their own self within the relationship. For these participants, the shift from a reliance on specific approaches to the use of self required an element of risk and openness. Once achieved, it felt more like a comfortable professional "fit" that was conducive in creating intimate and intense interactions with clients that enhanced their work. When focusing on the intense and intimate nature of the therapeutic relationship with clients, participants stated:

In a sense it's a joy.... It's the fact of working with people and watching them grow and feeling that you have a part in that growth. It's fun.

Well, I get off on it. I mean, honest to God, contact is very exciting. I mean, when two boundaries meet, that's where the energy is.

Well, I think the one thing that has prevented me from burning out… is the fact that no two people look alike to me. The people who burn out begin to see everybody as alike; they see people as problems, and they see problems as the things they are working with.

Theme 4. Participants View Attachment and Separation as a Natural Process

Participants discussed their belief that attachments and separations in the therapeutic relationship followed a natural course, similar to those experienced in other relationships. This belief appears to fortify the participants through years of fostering attachments and facilitating separations with a multitude of clients. They are committed to engaging in that process, even through times of difficulty, and hold the belief that it is a mutually beneficial process. One participant discussed her belief that the therapeutic process of attachment and separation mimics life:

But it seems to me that all of life is about attachment and separation. You know, even with marriage, there are times when attachment is really important, but there's also times when separation is really important. Where you're individuals and you have different needs and different abilities to be present. So I think that's how I help myself with it, is that it feels part and parcel with just what's true in life… I think it's totally important that people are able to attach in order to work through some of what might not have happened for them. But I also think it's important to be able to separate and let go.

Participants also discussed their experience that relationships continue beyond the separation. This continuation may exist on an internal level or, in other cases, actually involves the client returning to therapy. In some cases, work that began with a client eventually extended to the client's children. This belief regarding the ongoing nature of relationships appeared to insulate the participants from the potential distress of repeated attachments and separations:

And then a number of people come back over the years, so I have more and more confidence, sort of like an object constancy, in me at least, that these people remain alive in my psyche. They're out there in the world, and I feel connected to them and believe that they'd return if the situation arose.

I think in a core way, attachment is an internal phenomena rather than ex-
ternal. You can see people for years every day and probably not have that
much attachment. So if you stop seeing people, there is some loss, but it
doesn't mean that, therefore, something got yanked out.

I feel like I really do give people something, part of myself, and when they
leave, I really have an investment. But these days, I almost never say a per-
manent goodbye to anybody. I'm always having old clients come back; I'm
even having the children who were playing on the floor coming in with
their spouses at this point.

Theme 5. Participants Understand Human Suffering at a Profound Level

Through their work, participants developed a profound understanding of
suffering. This includes an awareness of the painful elements and the potential for growth. The participants' comments reflected a profound awareness
of suffering and the healing process that is part of their role as a helper. Their
hopeful outlook toward how suffering can be transformed also seemed to
enhance their own lives. One participant talked about how his perspective
has been altered through continual exposure to suffering:

I think all in all, it leaves me with a certain kind of enthusiasm because I
see people go through extraordinary pain and come out the other side. And
so it makes me patient.

Another participant differentiated between the short-term stressors and
the long-term benefits continually confronting client suffering:

In visiting the intensity of the private world of several people who are your
clients, empathizing with the misery, and it can feel like, at the end of the
day, lonely to have been so intensely in all of those places, and nobody had
been in all of those places with me. And I couldn't tell anybody where I'd
been.... The loneliness of that is a big part of the burden, I think. But that's
more like the immediate at the end of the day kind of thing. What I think
I'm left with is more a sense of the humanity.... And I think I'm a lot more
comfortable with the topics of grief and sex and life crises. I just think that
I just have that settled sense of the humanity of it.

Category C. Creating a Positive Work Structure

Category C contains four themes that focus on how, over time, the participants created important support that enhanced their sense of wellness in the
work environment. The four positive work structure factors are a designed

private practice, multiple professional involvements, mentor and peer relationships, and health-promoting environments.

Theme 1. Mentor and Peer Support was Critical at the Novice Phase

Participants reported that positive mentor and peer relationships had a great impact on the novice phase of their careers. These relationships often developed during long-term first placements that were frequently described as challenging but not overwhelming. The novice setting provided enriching work environments full of learning opportunities and encouragement for responsible autonomy and risk-taking. While at these sites, a foundation was built for the participants' future practices. In reflecting on his first placement, one participant stated:

> *I remember those as good years. I'm sure they were stressful because a lot was new, but I felt very supported. I had resources about me, and I was valued and also I had a tremendous amount of independence.*

Another participant stated:

> *[It was] a time of working intensely with colleagues in relation to having lots of feedback, lots of inspection of one's practice. All of that, by and large, was very good. I certainly wouldn't trade those years.*

While discussing a supervisor at her first placement following graduate training, one participant stated:

> *At my first job, I was fortunate enough to have a really fine supervisor who literally I credit with the major amount of training and experience that I have. And that was totally geared to emotional self-awareness and use of self in ways in which I grew a hell of a lot, but I also learned never to ignore that part.... It opened all the doors for me, and it also made what I was doing very vital and real, and I feel real grateful for that.*

Another participant discussed her decision to join a group of seasoned clinicians who then became important mentors and teachers:

> *I think that I had either the good fortune or the good judgment to join a group of senior clinicians, all people 20 years older than I, very experienced, and I brought them something they needed which was the M.D. I could prescribe medications for their patients, and I could hospitalize their patients, which was fine. But they gave me the depth and breadth of clinical*

experience and an understanding of how the practice works, and it was very important to me.

Although the need for strong mentor relationships gradually diminished over time for many of the participants, the salience of these early relationships was highlighted in the reflections of one participant:

It's more in retrospect than I was aware at the time, that there were people along the way who believed in me and kind of engaged with me because they believed in me. And I really thrived on that, more than I knew, in the moment. I got so much from that in a way that if I hadn't gotten that, my life…would have taken a different path.

Theme 2. Participants Have Ongoing and Enriching Peer Relationships

Participants reported that they initiated and sustained relationships with a variety of peers and coworkers beyond the novice phase. These relationships served a critical role in supporting the participants. One participant described the value of combining ongoing experience with peer relationships in this way:

I don't think years of experience by itself does it, because…I might have the same year of experience 20 times, and so I need to put that together with good consultation and a good collegial system around you; that is a part of the therapist's well-being.

When discussing peer relationships specific to the work environment, one participant stated:

I think that it is actually kind of a unique and rare environment that offers a therapist that kind of support for continuing growth. One that says even if you've been in this business for a number of years, you are still allowed to not know, you're still allowed to be afraid of what's happening, you're still allowed to feel like a failure, or whatever the issue is.

Both formal and informal interactions were emphasized as being important components of peer relationships in the work environment. One participant described how she and her coworkers had strategically created a work environment that provided a variety of interactions:

We've made a coffee room so that we run into each other on purpose, and we meet once a week for lunch, and that's very helpful both for relaxation and socializing and for consulting. There's always somebody I can say, "Listen to this situation, tell me what you think," and without naming names, I can describe the problem and get feedback from somebody that I respect.

In reflecting on his peer relationships, one participant highlighted the value of friendship and of sharing life events along with professional concerns:

We sit down for our staff meeting, and before we do anything else, we just sit at the table, take a few minutes, and talk about our lives. It's sort of this is what's happening with my kids; this is what I did last weekend; by the way, I saw a great movie; and just that personal level, before we get into talking about [clients].

Often times, the intimate quality of peer and coworker relationships was an enriching factor in the participants' ability to deepen their level of self-awareness and, in turn, to invest more intensely in the therapeutic process with clients. Two participants described the importance of sustained, close relationships in the actual work environment:

Here, for example, we have a group of six, and some of us have been together for about 14 years, so you really have a chance to deepen the experience with one another and, therefore, I think also be able to deepen your work with clients, because you're better able to know about yourself in relationship to the work, and other people know you well enough to say, "Hey, look at this."

...we've been present here in this practice for going on 18 years, and we've always done weekly consultations and the kind that really gets at what might be stopping us, what might be blocking us, what we might be struggling with.

Diverse peer relationships in the broader professional community were also highlighted as vital sources of support. Participants tended to be actively involved in numerous professional activities, organizations, and community groups. One participant discussed the value of serving on a committee with a cross section of helping professionals:

To have all these people giving time and energy to thinking about what will make our work improve. It's just inspiring, and for me it's invigorating and energizing. Just helpful in that way.

Similarly, another participant stated:

> *I have a group of colleagues that are very important to me, have been for 10 years now, and we meet in the West Coast every year; we spend a week together; we rent a room together for a week. They're all existentialists, and they're my closest colleagues in terms of tradition, and I see them maybe two, three times a year in groups or individually.... And that has been very, very helpful over the years.*

Theme 3. Multiple Roles Are a Protective Factor

Participants reported that they structured their practices to include multiple tasks and professional involvements. They also exhibit a measure of freedom in choosing the type of clients they work with and how they do their billing. The ability to control the nature of their practice provided the participants with a stimulating balance of professional responsibilities while limiting the stressors that they encounter. In discussing her need for task diversity versus doing only clinical work, one participant stated:

> *If I did only this work, I would be bored out of my mind.... It has nothing to do with the people I see; it's about having to empty yourself out so constantly and regularly to do that work. And that wouldn't be healthy; it just wouldn't be healthy.*

Another participant discussed how involvement in diverse activities improved her professional and clinical work:

> *I think there is something really enriching about supervising and teaching. It keeps me interested in my work and feeling alive and motivated to read and to think from some point of view other than just inside my head.*

Participants reported that freedom to design one's caseload and control the billing also contributed positively to the professional experience. On client-related stressors, one participant stated:

> *I don't think of my clients as impacting me in ways that I would consider stressors;...there's been stuff obviously over the years...we'll be dealing with suicide or we'll be dealing with this or that.... I haven't had much of that for a long time, and it's partly this practice; I mean, it's set up in a way in which I'm not dealing with crisis. I mean I'm dealing with...wellness perspectives. So I'm also not in situations at this point that would push that.*

One participant discussed the way that she structured her caseload and completed billing:

> *I've been very fortunate in two ways. One is that I'm an old-timer, so I've developed my own reputation and my own referral. Most of my patients come referred by other patients. And many pay out of pocket, and I'm willing to make some adjustments; I'd rather give them the money than the insurance company actually in terms of discount.*

Theme 4. Participants Create Health-Promoting Work Environments

Participants said that their work environments were suited to meet specific needs of space, aesthetics, and personal comfort. Equally important, these environments were conducive to facilitating successful therapeutic relationships. One participant outlined the benefits of her work area:

> *I really like it here. I like my space. I like being here. I love being here when it's raining or snowing, and it's kind of a cocoon kind of feel to it. I think about the holding environment that helps therapy to work. That is part of what's here, and I like it, and I've heard clients talk about that it's nice to be here.*

Other participants also discussed the need to create a comfortable, therapeutic work area:

> *Space that allows for both enough distance to accommodate mine but also the other person's personal space requirements. And with clients, that varies actually. So I think sometimes I move forward or backward, depending on what I'm sensing, but also not so big that it feels like you're talking into a room rather than connect to people. I think something that feels, that gives the sense of privacy and safety. I think it has the sense of being protected but not trapped.*

> *You know, I'm really into friendly textures and colors, and the light is important; the quiet is important. We went to great lengths to soundproof all these offices. The building would think that it was adequately soundproof, but I could still hear what was going on next door. We just kept putting insulation in the walls until it was soundproof. I guess I have to feel generally safe. I know people who work in clinics and kind of dangerous parts of town, and I think that's not conducive to the comfort of therapist or patient.*

Category D. Protective Factors

Category D contains three themes identifying proactive strategies that participants employ to master stressors.

Theme 1. Participants Directly Engage Highly Stressful Professional Dilemmas

Participants are skilled in their ability to handle ongoing difficult situations and to manage crises in a proactive manner that serves to prevent future incidents. Their strategies reflect an ability to adapt to change and to "bounce" about unexpected or shifting events and issues. Participants tended to identify and frame challenges and issues in a hopeful light and to access appropriate resources. In confronting challenges and issues, participants discussed their need to remain receptive to possibilities and approaches on both internal and external levels:

> *And then I have to engage [the stressful issue] in myself because there's always the possibility that there's some piece of me working here that would rather not see this, would rather not own the power that I have; I'd rather see that I wasn't that important, diminish my own responsibility in that way, or minimize my responsibility to be a better attender to somebody else's experience.*

> *One of my most profound learning experiences was stimulated by, first of all, working with a couple of therapists who turned out to be highly unethical and abusing their patients, and I had a dear friend of mine exploited by a therapist, and I'm thinking, "I've got to understand this; something really went wrong here." I find myself somewhat of an expert on boundaries and boundary violations because it really challenged my whole self-concept as a therapist or challenged the whole idea of therapy as a healing process. So I wanted to go after that problem.*

An appropriate reliance on peer consultation was a critical resource that participants used in their process of exploring important issues and incidents:

> *I get lots of consultation, so I'm not by myself with the really hard cases. That's primary for me. If there's anything that feels really important, it's not to be by myself in really hard situations, that I have colleagues with me. So that I feel that kind of a sense that I'm not all alone in this. It's really important to me that I'm seeing things clearly, and I think it's hard some-*

times when you're all by yourself. And to have other eyes and ears looking at something with you. So that's one major way [to protect myself].

A key characteristic of the participants' reports was their willingness to remain open and to adapt. In discussing these traits, one participant stated:

I think sometimes it's caused me not to feel like I know what I know at times, but on the other hand, it also keeps me kind of fresh and open. I'm willing to entertain almost anything, and I'm willing to look at where I could be off base about almost anything.

Another participant described her daily clinical work and provided an example of her ability to adapt from one client to another:

I think I'm emotionally resilient in the sense of I can be with someone in their pain...but then I can in the next session be laughing with somebody about something or celebratory with somebody. So it feels like that's a way that I can move.

Theme 2. Participants Confront and Resolve Personal Issues

Participants reported that their own personal life crises and problems were a challenging area for them. They also believed that direct acknowledgment and resolution of these issues allowed for a congruence between the personal self and the professional self. One participant explained how her experience in dealing with the unexpected death of a family member challenged her at a profoundly personal level yet allowed her to be more attuned to clients:

Well, I think the suicide [in the family] made the work very challenging. And yet at the same time, I was fortunate in that I had a very fine therapist. And because I had that therapist, while the work was difficult, I constantly felt like I was being so tended to emotionally... I found myself taking from that experience and just automatically moving it into what I was doing with clients. So it's like as the therapist was willing to go with me where I needed to go and that opened up areas or that developed areas inside of me that I didn't even know were there. Then, automatically, I would hear those areas in clients. I would ask the questions because they were coming from where I'd been taken to.

Theme 3. Highly Engaged Learning is a Powerful Source of Renewal

Participants reported that they had histories of being open to new experiences, seeking out diverse avenues of learning, and synthesizing information from multiple sources. Their lives were marked by an insatiable curiosity, a deep comfort with ambiguity, and constant consumption of knowledge. This ongoing learning process helped them to maintain an energy level necessary to continually engage in the helper role. In discussing a draw toward learning and its effect on her, one participant stated:

> *Well, it provides constant energy for one thing, and I think what happens in our field is that we can get tired and exhausted, but I think that's one of the things that keeps me feeling high energy and a lot of interest and love for what we do, and it's exciting.*

Some participants described why a tolerance for ambiguity and an openness for learning were critical ingredients in their work:

> *I mean, we don't throw away what we know in favor of mystery, but to favor mystery is to prefer it above what we know.*

> *If nothing else, you want to work with these people from all walks of life with various occupations and various interests, and if you don't sustain at least some awareness or at least openness to learn from your patients about their work, then how can you be of any use to them if you stay on the outside? So one has to have the interest and curiosity and some fondness, I think, for the client. If you're not interested in joining them, then why would they trust you to come and open themselves up.*

> *If you can't work with the unknown and the uncertain, you can't last in this business.*

Another participant discussed her efforts to bring new information into her work:

> *When I read, I always know what I define as active learning, which is trying to take the new information and see how I can incorporate it into what's already there, which means that I'm always modifying existing information too. And adapting it to my needs and integrating what I already know. It can be a negative thing if you go with the approach that everything has to fit to some rigid fixed scheme set already in existence. But I don't think I do that. I think I really constantly modify my schemes by incorporating the new stuff, but it's probably the integration and incorporation that are really important.*

One participant discussed how she utilized peers to facilitate her own learning process:

> *I think being in a group practice has helped because it keeps you kind of interested and hungry for what's available and keeps you open, I think. I've done groups with co-therapists for years upon years. I've done co-therapy, marriage therapy. I think that also helps to stay open because you're constantly getting new information, getting new ways of thinking when working with someone. Getting input about your ways of working, so I think that also helps.*

Category E. Nurturing Self Through Solitude and Relationships

Participants clearly identified their need to maintain a strong sense of self. Category E contains four themes that focus on components important to the participants for this need. The themes reflect multiple approaches and a network of internal and external involvements that enable the participants to maintain a personal and professional congruency.

Theme 1. Participants Foster Professional Stability by Nurturing a Personal Life

Participants were aware of the importance of maintaining a balance between their personal and professional lives. They believe that their role as a helper is facilitated by a lifestyle that includes multiple involvements and connections apart from their professional life. One participant verbalized this sentiment when he stated:

> *What helps me do it well is to give a damn about what I'm doing, but…I've got to have a life out of here. This can't be everything. I can't be over-invested in it. There's an appropriate kind of investment in which I care very much about what happens here, and I'm willing to invest myself as fully as I can, and part of what helps me do that is the fact that I've got a very real existence in a lot of ways, not just this.*

Another participant succinctly stated:

> *There's [need for] some kind of larger balance. I don't think anybody could do this work just and not tip over in some way. The tendency to get off center is too great.*

One participant reported a very similar point of view and then elaborated on the hazards of not maintaining a life outside of her professional role:

> *It is up to me to do everything I can to maintain my own emotional health so that I can actually be available to my patients without needing them. I think one of the ways therapy goes awry is that the therapist starts to use the patient for their own emotional sustenance, regulation of the therapist's self-esteem, all those sorts of things. I think to be a good therapist you must be well fed and well loved. Basically, have a life out there that is working.*

Theme 2. Participants Invest in a Broad Array of Restorative Activities

Participants cultivate a collection of activities and leisure pursuits. Although the actual involvements are varied, a shared theme that runs through them is their function of providing a diversion from work-related stressors and an avenue for reconnecting with self and others. The function of these activities and pursuits was reflected in one participant's statement:

> *[Helpful is] doing things personally like physical kinds of things. When we talked about secondary post-trauma, there are some days when I just feel like I need to go out and kick something and just kind of biking real hard or walking real fast; doing things like that can be really helpful I think. I do a lot of going to plays, going to movies, getting together with friends, and just talking about plays we've seen, books we've read.*

A similar draw toward multiple involvements was reflected when this participant stated:

> *I love mystery stories and historical biography; that's where I learn my history, from historical novels. I like movies; I love sports; I'm an avid football fan; I knit; I do a lot of knitting and crocheting.*

Other participants discussed the pull that they feel to nature and other creative activities:

> *I think something happens for me spiritually when I'm doing stuff with flowers and plants. I've got plants all over the place in my home, and it's kind of a ritualistic piece about tending those. I have gardens here and at a cabin up north, and there's, again, sort of a ritualistic piece with tending*

those. I think that takes me to a place that is real deeply nourishing, and I can get lost in it in a whole different way. I love the creative so the book that I wrote and stuff that I do for school and the papers, I really try to approach those as creative endeavors.

I find that music is a way for me to ground myself in the larger experience of my life and life itself. I suppose that's true for a lot of people…but that's certainly true for me, and always has been. And one of the ways, when I find myself feeling deprived of being able to cry, it'll come through that way.

One participant discussed the critical function of travel:

It's very helpful for perspective purposes. Very helpful. The trick is to be gone long enough…so you recognize fully your entire replaceability. That you are absolutely replaceable. And there, you talked about freedom and re- lief; there is real freedom and relief in that.

Theme 3. Participants Construct Fortifying Personal Relationships

Participants are highly skilled relationship builders. They establish nurtur- ing and challenging connections with family, friends, and other social groups that are intimate and rich. Among other things, their relationships with others provide consistent, ongoing support and enable a realistic per- spective of self. Although these relationships are important on a day-to-day basis, they are especially critical in times of crisis. Some of the participants discussed how a network of supportive relationships fortified their lives and acted as an emotional safety net:

If you have good friends in your life, if you have a good support system, folks will let you know that you're feeling worn out or depleted or whatever and then will support you getting some help.

A lot of close friends and my children are best friends. And they keep me very well balanced and keep my perspective, don't let me get a big head. They're very good, a very supportive bunch.

Having your own family connection solid is, at least for me, pretty impor- tant. I think I have a lot of reliance on other people in my life or friends or my wife, catching me in areas where I don't catch myself.

Some participants spoke about the encouragement and comfort they de- rived from a relationship with a spouse or life partner:

I married the right lady; my wife has a master's level degree in child development. And so we can talk, and she understood what I did. She never worked after we got married because she started having kids right away. But we could communicate and understand each other. And she was always a nice balance when my head started getting too big. She would pop it.... And so that was very supportive, still is.

We met actually as classmates. And I'm sure that's probably the most important relationship personally, but also I think probably professionally in some ways. We do talk psychology with each other, have all these years. So I'm sure that's been very important.

One participant highlighted the essential function of children and family:

We do a lot with family celebrations. Socializing, having people over for dinner. My children, now they are out of the home, but when they were younger, I think we did some things that were really helpful. Taking time just to play some games together. Just do something completely separate from work.

Another participant also commented on the very significant role that her friends play:

What I would say is that there are a few close friends, and when I'm in trouble, when they're in trouble, the rules are we get access to each other whenever and however long we need it. And when the trouble's over, we go back to our lives. And those people are very in place, and I think I am for them too.

Participants also fostered an essential relationship with the world at large, and they usually spoke about this in terms of a spiritual awareness or seeking a greater sense of connection with others:

I have a sense of spirit. I have a sense of reverence. I have a sense of place in the universe even though I know it's just a speck; it's a place to participate. I believe that there's benevolence in all that. I believe that warm, gentle breezes blow my way besides the cold, bitter winds.

Theme 4. Participants Value an Internal Focus

Participants reported that they are aware of the significant role that their internal processes play in sustaining their own sense of wellness and in their ability to function effectively as practitioners. They are open to, and willingly engage in, their own personal therapy as a means of enhancing this process of introspection and self-examination. This commitment to understanding self represents an important self-care method that has a positive impact on their sense of resiliency and wellness in the helping role. Statements by the participants reflected the value of being continually self-aware. One said that it was important to attend to:

> ...*what's coming up in my world that needs me to understand what's going on or feel like I get it in terms of whatever's happening internally so that when I'm doing my work, I'm sort of cleared out, and it isn't that the stuff isn't in there, but I'm not obsessing about it; it's not taking me some other place than where I need to be in the room.*

Another stated:

> *To learn something about vulnerability yourself, I don't know that anybody can really do therapy well until they know vulnerability, unless they are aware of their woundedness.... And be able to work from there.*

One participant shared her belief that staying attuned to internal processes was, in part, an ethical responsibility:

> *I think that's where we need to build this self monitoring and be self-aware. If I become psychotic, then probably those around me would notice it, but outside of those extremes, if my work fluctuates on life events or whatever like physical health...I think to what extent one is ethical in their conduct [relates to] the kind of posture of self-reflection and self-monitoring and judgment.*

Other participants discussed their belief that personal therapy was an important vehicle in their quest for self-awareness. One participant stated:

> *The other thing I would say is it's important for every therapist to know when it's time to go back for some therapy of your own; personal anxieties or problems are either getting stirred up by the work or are intruding from the outside world.*

Conclusion

Several pertinent areas were highlighted in this chapter. Participants identified stressors connected to various therapeutic issues and client behaviors, breaches in peer relationships, and the impact of their own personal crises and life changes. The areas of stressors that were reflected in the participants' comments underscore the demanding nature of the helping role and reinforce the value of protective approaches and self-care strategies as a means of ensuring practitioner wellness and professional vitality.

Important protective factors were identified by the participants. These factors ranged from internal coping strategies to variables within the external environment. A commonality that existed among this group of participants was their commitment to self-care and their high-level skill in accessing valuable resources.

This group of practitioners has acute awareness of the internal landscape and maintains a watchful focus on their emotional selves. Their strong commitment to self-observation was frequently combined with a proactive style in directly confronting stressors that emerged both from their work and in their personal lives. When combined, these approaches allowed the participants to maintain a sense of personal congruence and an energy level that are critical components in professional wellness and burnout prevention.

This group of participants was nurtured through multiple avenues and relationships. The role that peers played in providing the participants with a realistic perspective and ongoing professional support was emphasized. While peer support was vital throughout the participants' careers, it played an especially key role during the participants' novice phase of development and also during times of unexpected crisis. In a similar way, participants also noted the importance of immersing themselves in enriching relationships and activities apart from their work environments. It appears that these diverse involvements were essential components to self-care plans that maintained a healthy sense of balance.

13

Epilogue

Helping others with significant concerns in their lives can be highly effective, satisfying, and meaningful. It can be great work. To do this well, however, we must constantly attach and separate successfully, over and over again, with person after person. We must experience ambiguous professional loss, normative failure, primary trauma, and vicarious traumatization. Yet, we must continually invest positively in others, and this means constant renewal of the self and an ongoing caring for others vs. caring for self balance.

Our work can be so valuable and so pleasurable. A 68 year-old psychologist said in reflecting on her work at that age:

> *With diminishing anxiety, I became less and less afraid of my clients and with that came an ease for me in using my own wide repertoire of skills and procedures. They became more available to me when I needed them. And during those moments it became remarkable to me that someone would have the willingness to share their private world with me and that my work with them would bring very positive results for them. This brought a sense of intense pleasure to me. (Skovholt & Rønnestad, 1995, p. 96)*

Let me suggest that you imagine, if you will, a favorite tree in front of you. See its beauty, vibrance, vitality, and strength. Now imagine yourself as the tree—beautiful, vibrant, vital, and strong. As a tree, you take in carbon dioxide and give off oxygen to those you help. Taking in carbon dioxide and giving off oxygen is literally giving life to those you serve! To do so, however, the tree must work hard, and to work hard, it must be healthy. That means it must have ample sunlight, plenty of rain, rich soil, and freedom from dangerous pests, both overt and subtle, that will eat its leaves. To grow, it must branch out and respond well to pruning. How then can you insure that you, as a helping professional, will keep away those excessive professional losses, those dangerous pests that might eat your leaves, and that you will have abundant soil, rain, and sunlight? And what for you comprises the sunlight, the rain, and the soil?

What ultimately is a better way to spend one's working days than giving off oxygen to those choking and gasping for air? What is more beautiful than a strong, healthy tree doing its work, or more tragic than a tree that is now dead and devoid of the capacity to give life? How will you remain as the healthy tree and never forget the constant need, over 30 to 40 years to avoid pests and always have rain, soil, and sunlight?

I wish you well.

14

Self-Care Action Plan

The intent of the first 13 chapters in this book is to engage you, the reader, in topics that are central to your work as a practitioner. In this chapter on a self-care action plan, the focus is on doing more than reading. Like with the Nike slogan of "Just Do It!", here the hope is that you will actively use the chapter. I urge you to employ this chapter in a practical way that can be directly applied to your life as a practitioner.

This chapter on self-care asks you to respond in writing to ideas in the text and also to additional inventories and charts. Then you are asked to make a self-care action plan for yourself. The chapter has three parts:

Part 1. You are asked to reflect on the relevant ideas in the book for *you*. You are to reflect about questions and then write reactions to them. It is a kind of journaling.

Part 2. You are to assess your own other-care–self-care balance while finding out what activities other practitioners choose for self-care.

Part 3. You are to decide if any changes in your behavior, thinking patterns, or feelings are necessary to achieve a healthy other-care–self-care balance. Last, you are asked to make concrete but realistic plans for any change that seems needed.

Part 1. Reflecting on Relevant Ideas in the Book

I will now review the chapters and ask you to consider issues of importance to you.

Chapter 1. Caring for Others versus Self Preservation: The Great Human Drama

In Chapter 1 I attempted to describe a major human theme: Should one's energies go toward the well-being of others or the self? Or a combination? Of what? When?

1. What kind of reaction did you have to the ideas of Chapter 1?

_____

_____

_____

_____

2. How accurate is the description in first pages of the chapter for you?

_____

_____

_____

_____

Chapter 2. Joys, Rewards, and Gifts of Practice

In this chapter, I described moments of intense satisfaction for practitioners. Nurses, teachers, and counselors were quoted about special times when their work seemed very helpful to others. This significant helping of others has been called the "psychic income" of the work. It can make it all worthwhile.

1. While preserving the privacy of clients, students, and patients, describe one to three specific joy-of-practice experiences (moments of intense work satisfaction) for you in your life as a practitioner. What was the specific positive impact on the other person? What did you find most joyful about this work? Write your response here:

_____

_____

_____

---

2. Perhaps one or more joy-of-practice experiences were powerful critical incidents, which are events that often serve as turning points in our professional lives. We suddenly see ourselves in a new way because the event leads us to view ourselves differently. Sometimes, critical incidents lead us to understand theory or practice with sudden insight. Here, describe a joy-of-practice critical incident. What happened? How was it so impactful in your life?

---

3. If you are a seasoned practitioner, address these questions. Do you judge situations as joy-of-practice experiences in a different way than you did in the past? If so, what has changed? Are you pleased or disappointed with the impact of time and experience on your satisfaction with the work?

---

4. It is important for those of us in the high touch fields to continually have joy-of-practice experiences. Most practitioners do not have them on a daily basis. However, on a random and intermittent basis, they can be very reinforcing for us. Write below in response to these questions: Is this happening for you now? If not, what is missing? What can you do to increase the ratio of positive experiences in your life as a practitioner?

_____

_____

_____

_____

_____

_____

Chapter 3. The Caring Cycle as the Practice Essential

I have described the three engagement phases within the caring cycle as empathic attachment, active involvement, and felt separation. I have also said that the most successful work in the high touch fields involves a connection with the practitioner's "underside of the turtle." Considering the cycle, let me ask you some questions.

1. Describe how you feel about your skill level at each of these engagement phases.

Empathic attachment: _____

_____

Active involvement: _____

_____

Felt separation: _____

_____

2. Which of the three engagement phases is most safisfying for you? most exhausting for you? Why is that?

_____

_____

_____

_____

_____

3. What is your rhythm like in connecting and then disconnecting with your clients, students, or patients? If you relate to others within groups (i.e., teaching), as well as with individuals, is one less draining emotionally?

_____

_____

_____

_____

_____

Chapter 4. The Long, Textured Path from Novice to Senior Practitioner

Much of this chapter consists of themes and stages of professional development.

1. Concerning your own professional development, what themes are illuminating for you?

_____

_____

_____

_____

_____

2. Concerning your own professional development, does one of the stages describe you?

_____

_____

_____

_____

_____

3. In reference to the development-versus-stagnation model and the supervision discussion, what kind of implications can be drawn from this chapter for your growth and development as a resilient practitioner?

_____

_____

_____

_____

_____

Chapter 5. The Elevated Stressors of the Novice Practitioner

As you read this material, you may be a beginning practitioner in counseling, therapy, teaching, or health care. Perhaps you are a student in a training program at the graduate or undergraduate level, or you may now be more experienced; but, like everyone, you were once a rookie.

1. Regardless of your experience level, how do you react to the description of the elevated stressors experienced by the novice? Do they ring true or not so true for you?

_____

_____

_____

_____

_____

2. Perhaps of more importance, what could be long-term implications of your novice experience on your capacity to be a resilient practitioner?

_____

_____

_____

_____

_____

Chapter 6. Hazards of Practice

In this chapter, I discussed many difficulties that can effect the work of the practitioner. I suggest that you review the chapter and then pick five from the list of 20 hazards. As a next step, fill out the following:

1. Hazard number _____ Name: _____

Why has this been a significant practice hazard for you? _____

_____

_____

_____

_____

_____

What methods have you tried to alleviate its impact? How successful have you been? _____

_____

_____

_____

_____

_____

2. Hazard number _____ Name: _____

Why has this been a significant practice hazard for you? _____

_____

_____

_____

_____

_____

What methods have you tried to alleviate its impact? How successful have you been? _____

_____

_____

_____

_____

_____

3. Hazard number _____ Name: _____

Why has this been a significant practice hazard for you? _____

_____

_____

_____

_____

_____

What methods have you tried to alleviate its impact? How successful have you been? _____

_____

_____

_____

_____

_____

4. Hazard number _____ Name: _____

Why has this been a significant practice hazard for you? _____

_____

_____

_____

_____

_____

What methods have you tried to alleviate its impact? How successful have you been?

_____

_____

_____

_____

_____

5. Hazard number _____ Name: _____

Why has this been a significant practice hazard for you?

_____

_____

_____

_____

_____

What methods have you tried to alleviate its impact? How successful have you been?

_____

_____

_____

_____

_____

Chapter 7. Burnout: A Hemorrhaging of the Self

First, consider all of the different meanings of burnout discussed in this chapter.

1. How would you define this now well-known term first described by Freudenberger in 1974?

_____

_____

_____

_____

2. Using your own definition as a base, how burned out are you at this time? Circle the number.

0	1	2	3	4	5	6	7	8	9	10
Not at all			*A little*		*Some*			*A lot*		*Totally*

Describe the key factors in your rating.

_____

_____

_____

_____

_____

Chapter 8. Codependency: An Idea That Illuminates or Clouds?

Does this chapter speak to you? Yes or no and in what way?

_____

_____

_____

_____

_____

Chapter 9. Balancing Caring for Others and Caring for Self

One of the themes of this short chapter and, in fact, the whole book is the need to both lose one's innocence about the grinding nature of the work and to actively practice burnout prevention. I use the term *innocence* to describe the belief by practitioners that they can escape either insidious and overt burnout effects without active prevention efforts. Let me ask you: How is your practitioner innocence quotient, your PIQ? Describe yourself, perhaps before and after reading this book.

_____

_____

_____

_____

_____

Chapter 10. Sustaining the Professional Self

A variety of ideas were mentioned in this chapter. They comprise a bag of "tricks of the trade." These tips come from seasoned practitioners and the literature on professional functioning.

1. Which of these ideas do you already use in your own work? Perhaps you have a refined and improved version of one of these ideas. If so, please describe it.

_____

_____

_____

_____

_____

2. Are there any new ideas in the chapter for you? If so, write about one or two that may offer something to you as a practitioner.

_____

_____

_____

_____

_____

Chapter 11. Sustaining the Personal Self

Here, versions of the personal self were considered. In terms of a self-care action plan for you, which parts of the personal self are in "good shape" in your life, which ones need a "tune up," and which ones need a "major overhaul"?

1. Parts of the personal self in good shape:

_____

_____

_____

_____

_____

2.   Parts of the personal self in need of a tune up:

_____

_____

_____

_____

_____

_____

3. Parts of the personal self in need of a major overhaul:

_____

_____

_____

_____

_____

Chapter 12. Burnout Prevention and Self-Care Strategies of Expert Practitioners

1. What impresses you most about the methods used by experts to maintain professionally vitality?

_____

_____

_____

_____

_____

2. What can the experts teach you for your own burnout prevention and self-care?

_____

_____

_____

_____

_____

Chapter 13. Epilogue

In the epilogue, I suggested that you think of a favorite tree and the way that a tree takes in carbon dioxide and gives off oxygen. Working with people who have emotional, intellectual, and physical needs, practitioners do the same thing. I also mentioned that a tree must get nourishment to be healthy and continue to give off oxygen while taking in carbon dioxide. A tree is nourished by clean water, rich soil, and plenty of sunlight. The pests, both large and small, must be kept away. Such a greenhouse effect produces growth. Apply this tree metaphor to your life as a counselor, therapist, teacher, or health professional.

1. What is your water, your sun, your soil? How adequate are they for you?

_____

_____

_____

_____

_____

2. What are the large pests that can potentially eat away at your vitality? What are the small, invisible and stealth-like, but dangerous pests?

_____

_____

_____

_____

3. What changes, if any, do you need to make to have a healthy tree that can serve others by taking in carbon dioxide and giving off oxygen?

_____

_____

_____

Summary of Part 1

The focus so far in the self-care action plan has been on the content of the book. The goal has been for you to use the book in a practical way for your own self-care and burnout prevention. Hopefully, the writing of answers to questions, this journaling, has been a valuable way for you to gauge yourself in self-care and burnout prevention.

Part 2. Assess Your Own Other-Care/Self-Care Balance

This part of the self-care action plan asks you to consider other questions and fill out inventories.

Step 1. Assessing the Stress Level of Your Work

A first step is to assess your job stress level. In stressful jobs, individuals often feel high demands and low control. For example, quadrant four in Figure 14.1 is often thought of as much more stressful than quadrant one. How would you assess the stress level of your job? The results are helpful in calibrating the other-care vs. self-care balance.

Next, fill out the short questionnaire in Figure 14.2 on page 204.

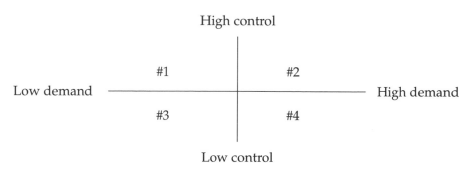

FIGURE 14.1   Elements of Job Stress

Source: Karasek, R., & Theorell, T. (1992). Healthy work: Stress productivity and the restructuring of working life. New York: Basic Books.

How stressful is your job?

This test can give you a rough indication of how much stress you're under at work. The test was adapted for us by researcher Robert Karasek, Ph.D., of the University of Massachusetts at Lowell, based on a longer questionnaire of his. Answer yes or no:

Demand	Yes	No
I have to work very hard	____	____
I am not asked to do an excessive amount of work*	____	____
I have enough time to get my work done*	____	____

Control		
I have to do a lot of repetitive work*	____	____
I have to be creative	____	____
I have to learn new things	____	____
I have a lot of say about what happens	____	____
I have very little freedom to decide how I do my work*	____	____

Social support		
I work with helpful people	____	____
I work with people who take a personal interest in me	____	____
My supervisor is helpful	____	____
My supervisor is concerned about my welfare	____	____

Scoring: Calculate a separate score for each of the three parts—demand, control, and social support. In each part, give yourself one point for every "yes" answer to the questions that don't have an asterisk(*). For those that do have an asterisk, give yourself one point if you answered "no." Jot down your three scores in the spaces below. Then write in the word that describes each of those scores.

Demand score: ☐
   My job demands are _____ .
   (Write "low" if your score was 0 or 1; "high" if your score was 2 or 3.)

Control score: ☐
   My control at work is _____ .
   (Write "low" if you scored 0 to 2; "high" if you scored 3 to 5.)

Social-support score: ☐
   My social support at work is _____ .
   (Write "low" if you scored 0 or 1; "moderate" if 2; "high" if 3 or 4.)

Interpretation: High demand, low control, and low social support all tend to increase job stress. The more of those factors that you face at work—and the more extreme your score on each factor—the greater your stress. Jobs where you experience all three tension-producing features are generally very stressful, while jobs with two such features generate moderately high stress. Those with only one stressful factor may be moderate or moderately low in stress, depending on how much the other two scores offset that factor. The least stressful jobs combine high control and high social support with low demand.

FIGURE 14.2

Source: Consumer Reports on Health (1996). Used by permission of Robert Karasek.

Using the four quadrant chart and the inventory, describe the stress level of your job.

_____

_____

_____

_____

Step 2. Assessing Your Other-Care/Self-Care Balance

Another step is to assess your other-care/self-care balance. Choose your type in Figure 14.3 below, and indicate the other-care/self-care balance score. Is it 50–50, 10–90, 90–10, 70–30, or 30–70?

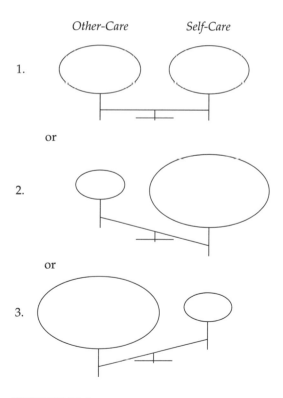

FIGURE 14.3

What is your other-care–self-care balance score? _____ – _____

Often, other-care practitioners are more oriented to other-care than self-care. Some imbalance can be fine, but when is this direction excessive for you?

_____

_____

_____

_____

_____

Step 3. Assessing Your Professional Self-Care

In Chapter 10, 16 factors are presented to sustain the professional self. For each factor, what are you doing to sustain your professional self? How well are you sustaining your professional self?

1. In the second column of the following table, list example activities that you are doing to sustain your professional self.

2. Assess how well you are sustaining your professional self regarding each factor, and indicate the assessment score of 0 to 6 in the third column.

0	1	2	3	4	5	6
Not at all						*Very Well*

Factors	Example Activities	Assessment
Avoiding the grandiosity impulse		
Thinking long-term		
Creating and sustaining an active, individual development method		

Factors	Example Activities	Assessment
Professional self-understanding		
Creating a professional greenhouse at work		
Leadership that promotes balance between caring for others and self		
Professional social support from peers		
Receiving support from mentors, supervisors, or bosses		
Being nurtured from your work as mentors, supervisors, or managers		
Learning how to be professional and playful		
Using professional venting to release distress emotions		
Being a "good enough practitioner"		
Understanding the reality of pervasive early professional anxiety		
Increasing excitement and decreasing boredom by reinventing yourself		
Minimizing ambiguous professional loss		
Learning to say no to unreasonable requests		

From the preceeding assessment, list your three strongest professional self-care areas and your three weakest areas.

Strongest professional self-care areas:

1. _____

2. _____

3. _____

Weakest professional self-care areas:

1. _____

2. _____

3. _____

Step 4. Assessing Your Personal Self-Care

In Chapter 11, parts of the personal self are presented. What are you doing to nurture each part of yourself? How well are you nurturing each part of your self?

1. In the second column of the following table, list specific activities to nurture each part of your self.
2. Assess how well you are nurturing each part of your self, and indicate the assessment score of 0 to 6 in the third column.

0	1	2	3	4	5	6
Not at all					→	*Very Well*

Part of Your Self	Specific Activities to Nurture This Part of Your Self	Assessment
Emotional self		
Financial self		
Humorous self		

Part of Your Self	Specific Activities to Nurture This Part of Your Self	Assessment
Loving self		
Nutritious self		
Physical self		
Playful self		
Priority-setting self		
Recreational self		
Relaxation and stress reduction self		
Solitary self		
Spiritual or religious self		

From the preceeding assessment, list your three strongest personal self-care areas and your three weakest areas.

Strongest personal self-care areas:

1. _____

2. _____

3. _____

Weakest personal self-care areas:

1. _____

2. _____

3. _____

Step 5. Review the Poor Self-Care Deadly Dozen below and the Positive Strategies Used by Psychologists and other practitioners in Tables 14.1 and 14.2.

The Poor Self-Care Deadly Dozen

1. Toxic supervisor and colleague support
2. Little fun (e.g., playfulness, humor, laughing) in life or work
3. Only a fuzzy and unarticulated understanding of one's own needs
4. No professional development process that turns experience into more competence and less anxiety
5. No energy-giving personal life
6. An inability to say no to unreasonable requests
7. Vicarious traumatization that takes an accumulated toll
8. Personal relationships that are predominantly one-way caring relationships with self as giver
9. Constant perfectionism in work tasks
10. Continual unresolved ambiguous professional losses
11. A strong need to be needed
12. Professional success defined solely by client, student, or patient positive change or appreciation (Data from workshops by Skovholt in 1998)

Step 6. Assessing Self-Care Strengths and Weaknesses

Using information gathered from Steps 1 to 5, write an assessment of your self-care strengths and weaknesses. As has been noted throughout the preceding chapters, there are joys in the work but also hazards, plenty of them. The constant giving of the self, a necessity in optimal work by counselors, therapists, teachers, and health professionals means that practitioners must assertively nurture the wellness of the professional and personal selves. How are you doing with nurturing your own wellness?

_____

_____

_____

_____

_____

TABLE 14.1 Three Studies of Psychologists' Self-Care Activities

Study 1. Top 10 Helpful Activities[1]	Study 2. 10 Important Themes from Interviews with 6 Well-Functioning Psychologists[2]	Study 3. 234 Well-Functioning Psychologists' Top 10 Activities Contributing to Well Functioning[3]
Taking vacation	Peer support	Self-awareness and self-monitoring
Social activities	Stable personal relationships	Personal values
Emotional support from colleagues	Supervision	Preserving balance between personal and professional lives
Pleasure reading	A balanced life	Relationship with spouse, partner, or family
Seeking consultation on difficult cases	Affiliation with a graduate training program	Personal therapy
Reading relevant professional literature	Personal psychotherapy	Relationship with friends
Taking breaks during workday	Continuing education	Vacations
Emotional support from friends or family	Family of origin as a source of personal values	Professional identity
Spending time with children	The negative costs of professional impairment	Informal peer support
Listening to music	Positive coping mechanisms (vacations, rest, relaxation, exercise, evening with friends, spirituality)	Mentor

[1]Gamble, S. J., Pearlman, L. A., Lucca, A. M., & Allen, G. J. (1995). Vicarious traumatization and burnout among Connecticut psychologists: Empirical findings. Cited by Pearlman, 1995.
[2]Coster, J. J., & Schwebel, M. (1997). Well-functioning in professional psychologists. *Professional Psychology: Research and Practice, 28*, 5–13.
[3]Coster, J. J., & Schwebel, M. (1997). Well-functioning in professional psychologists. *Professional Psychology: Research and Practice, 28*, 5–13.

TABLE 14.2   Self-Care Methods of Practitioners

Trauma Therapists' Top 10 Helpful Activities[1]	Counselors', Teachers', and Health Professionals' 10 Commonly Described Activities (in alphabetical order)[2]
Discussing cases with colleagues	Being with family
Attending workshops	Education for job skills
Spending time with family or friends	Fun hobby
Travel, vacations, hobbies, movies	Physical activity
Talking with colleagues between sessions	Reading
	Receiving consultation or supervision
Socializing	Social activity at work
Exercise	Time alone
Limiting case load	Time with friends, partner, spouse
Developing spiritual life	Vacation
Receiving general supervision	

[1]Pearlman, L. A., & MacIan, P. J. (1995). Vicarious traumatizations: An empirical study of the effects of trauma work on trauma therapists. *Professional Psychology: Research & Practice, 26,* 558–565.
[2]Data from workshops by T. M. Skovholt in 1996.

Part 3. Action Plan for Change

Step 7. Action Plan

Now, develop an action plan to work on one or two self-care weaknesses. Remember that slower behavioral change usually works best. I suggest that you be modest in your goals and build on attainable change with reinforcement to maintain the change.

Your general action plan:

Specific Goal 1:

_____

_____

_____

Method for achieving Goal 1:

_____

_____

_____

Reinforcement to maintain new behavior:

_____

_____

_____

Specific Goal 2:

_____

_____

_____

Method for achieving Goal 2:

_____

_____

_____

Reinforcement to maintain new behavior:

References

Ackerley, G. D., Burnell, J., Holder, D. C., & Kurdek, L. A. (1988). Burnout among licensed psychologists. *Professional Psychology: Research and Practice, 19*, 624–631.

Ackerman, D. (1999). *Deep play.* New York: Random House.

Adams, H. (1918). *The education of Henry Adams.* New York: Houghton Mifflin.

Adolson, M. J. (1995). Clinical supervision of therapists with difficult-to-treat patients. *Bulletin of the Menninger Clinic, 59*, 32–52.

Ambrose, S. E. (1996). *Undaunted courage.* New York: Touchstone.

Anonymous (Ed.). (1982). *Each day a new beginning.* San Francisco: HarperCollins.

Asay, T. P., & Lambert, M. J. (1999). The empirical case for the common factors in therapy: Quantitative findings. In M. A. Hubble, B. L. Duncan, & S. D. Miller (Eds.), *The heart and soul of change: What works in therapy* (pp. 23–55). Washington, DC: American Psychological Association.

Ayers, W. (1993). *To teach: The journey of a teacher.* New York: Teachers College Press.

Bachelor, A., & Horvath, A. (1999). The therapeutic relationship. In M. A. Hubble, B. L. Duncan, & S. D. Miller (Eds.), *The heart and soul of change: What works in therapy* (pp. 133–178). Washington, DC: American Psychological Association.

Balch, J. F., & Balch, P. A. (1997). *Prescription for nutritional healing.* Garden City Park, NY: Avery Publishing Group.

Baltes, P. B., & Smith, J. (1990). Toward a psychology of wisdom and its ontogenesis. In R. E. Sternberg (Ed.), *Wisdom: Its origins and development.* Cambridge, England: Cambridge University Press.

Bandhauer, B. (1997). Waiting for wisdom to arrive. In J. Kottler (Ed.), *Finding your way as a counselor* (pp. 7–9). Alexandria, VA: American Counseling Association.

Beattie, M. (1986). *Codependent no more.* Center City, MN: Hazelden Foundation.

Becker, E. (1973). *The denial of death.* New York: Free Press.

Beckett, S. (1997). *Waiting for Godot.* New York: Grove Press.

Belenky, M., Clinchy, B., Goldberger, N., & Tarule, J. (1986). *Women's ways of knowing.* New York: Basic Books.

Benner, P. (1982). From novice to expert. *American Journal of Nursing, 82*, 402–407.

Benner, P., & Wrubel, J. (1982). Skilled clinical knowledge: The value of perceptual awareness, part 2. *Journal of Nursing Administration, 12,* 28–33.

Bennet, J. (1997, January 19). I see 'em! We'll fight 'em! Profiles in courage beyond the call. *New York Times,* p. E7.

Benson, H. (1975). *The relaxation response.* New York: Morrow.

Benson, H. (1999, August). *Power and biology of belief.* Presented at the annual convention of the American Psychological Association, Boston.

Bergin, A. E., & Garfield, S. L. (1994). Overview, trends, and future issues. In A. E. Bergin, & S. L. Garfield (Eds.), *Handbook of psychotherapy and behavior change* (pp. 821–830). New York: John Wiley and Sons.

Bernard, J. M., & Goodyear, R. K. (1998). *Fundamentals of clinical supervision.* Boston: Allyn & Bacon.

Berry, C. R. (1988). *When helping you is hurting me: Escaping the messiah trap.* New York: Harper and Row.

Block, G., & Drucker, M. (1992). *Rescuers: Portraits of moral courage in the Holocaust.* New York: Holmes and Meier Publishers.

Borders, L. D. (1989). A pragmatic agenda for developmental supervision research. *Counselor Education and Supervision, 29,* 16–24.

Borders, L. D. (1992). Learning to think like a supervisor. *Clinical Supervisor, 10,* 135–148.

Boss, P. (1999). *Ambiguous loss: Learning to live with unresolved grief.* Cambridge, MA: Harvard University Press.

Boss, P., Caron, W., Horbal, J., & Mortimer, J. (1990). Predictors of depression in caregivers of dementia patients: Boundary ambiguity and mastery. *Family Process, 29,* 245–254.

Bowlby, J. (1969). *Attachment.* New York: Basic Books.

Bowlby, J. (1973). *Separation: Anxiety and anger.* New York: Basic Books.

Bowlby, J. (1980). *Loss: Sadness and depression.* New York: Basic Books.

Bowlby, J. (1988). *A secure base: Parent–child attachment and healthy human development.* New York: Basic Books.

Brawley, L. R., & Rodgers, W. M. (1993). Social-psychological aspects of fitness promotion. In P. Seraganian (Ed.), *Exercise psychology: The influence of physical exercise on psychological processes* (pp. 254–298). New York: John Wiley & Sons.

Brinson, J. (1997). Reach out and touch someone. In J. Kottler (Ed.), *Finding your way as a counselor* (pp. 165–167). Alexandria, VA: American Counseling Association.

By a general practitioner. (1985). Hope is the key. In V. Rippere & R. Williams (Eds.), *Wounded healers: Mental health workers' experiences of depression.* Chichester, England: John Wiley & Sons.

Campbell, D. (1994). *Career interest and skill survey.* Minneapolis, MN: National Computer Systems.

Carkhuff, R. (1969). *Helping and human relations.* New York: Holt, Rinehart and Winston.

Cassidy, J. (1999). No satisfaction: The trial of a shopping nation. *The New Yorker, 129*(43), 88–92.

Cedoline, A. J. (1982). *Job burnout in public education.* New York: Teachers College Press.

Cerney, M. S. (1985). Traumatized by the traumatized: The experience of secondary trauma. In C. Figley (Ed.), *Trauma and its wake.* New York: Brunner/Mazel.

Cherniss, C. (1980). *Staff burnout: Job stress in the human services.* Thousand Oaks, CA: Sage.

Cherniss, C. (1995). *Beyond burnout.* New York: Routledge.

Chi, M. T. H., Glaser, R., & Farr, M. J. (Eds.). (1988). *The nature of expertise.* Hillsdale, NJ: Erlbaum.

Chodorow, N. (1978). *The reproduction of mothering.* Berkeley: University of California Press.

Collins, B. G. (1993). Reconstructing codependency using self-in-relation theory: A feminist perspective. *Social Work, 38,* 470–476.

Copeland, W. T., Birmingham, C., De La Cruz, E., & Lewin, B. (1993). The reflective practitioner in teaching: Toward a research agenda. *Teaching and Teacher Education, 9,* 347–359.

Corey, M. S., & Corey, G. (1989). *Becoming a helper.* Pacific Grove, CA: Brooks/Cole.

Corsini, R. J., & Wedding, D. (1989). *Current psychotherapies.* Itaska, IL: F. E. Peacock.

Coster, J. S., & Schwebel, M. (1997). Well-functioning in professional psychologists. *Professional Psychology: Research and Practice, 28,* 5–13.

Cousins, N. (1979). *Anatomy of an illness as perceived by the patient.* New York: Norton.

Danby, H. (Trans.). (1933). *The Mishnah, Talmud.* London: Oxford University Press.

Davis, M., Eshelman, E. R., & McKay, M. (1995). *The relaxation and stress reduction workbook* (4th ed.). Oakland, CA: New Harbinger Publications.

Dawes, R. M. (1994). *House of cards: Psychology and psychotherapy built on myth.* New York: Free Press.

Demographic yearbook. (1993). New York: United Nations.

Diener, E., Suh, E. M., Lucas, R. E., & Smith, H. L. (1999). Subjective well-being: Three decades of progress. *Psychological Bulletin, 125,* 276–302.

Dodge, K. A., & Feldman, E. (1990). Issues in social cognition and sociometric status. In S. R. Asher, & J. D. Coie (Eds.), *Peer rejection in childhood* (pp. 119–155). New York: Cambridge.

Doehrman, M. J. (1976). Parallel processes in supervision and psychotherapy. *Bulletin of the Menninger Clinic, 40,* 1–104.

Dominguez, J., & Robin, V. (1992). *Your money or your life.* New York: Penguin Books.

Donne, J. (1975). *Devotions: Upon emergent occasions* (A. Raspa, Ed.). Montreal: McGill-Queen's University Press.

Dreyfus, H. L., & Dreyfus, S. E. (1986). *Mind over machine: The power of human intuition and expertise in the era of the computer.* New York: Free Press.

Dupree, P. I., & Day, H. D. (1995). Psychotherapists' job satisfaction and job burnout as a function of work setting and percentage of managed care clients. *Psychotherapy in Private Practice, 14*(2), 77–93.

D'Zurilla, T. J., & Nezu, A. (1982). Social problem solving in adults. In P. C. Kendall (Ed.), *Advances in cognitive-behavioral research and therapy,* Vol. 1 (pp. 201–274). Toronto: Academic Press.

Eison, J. A. (1985, August). *Coming of age in academe: From teaching assistant to faculty member.* Presented at the annual convention of the American Psychological Association, Los Angeles.

Eliot, G. (1956). *Middlemarch* (G. S. Haight, Ed.). Boston: Houghton Mifflin.

Ellwein, M. C., Grace, M. E., & Comfort, R. E. (1990). Talking about instruction: Student teachers' reflections on success and failure in the classroom. *Journal of Teacher Education, 41*(4), 3–14.

Erikson, E. (1968). *Identity, youth and crisis.* New York: Norton.

Etringer, B. D., Hillerbrand, E., & Claiborn, C. D. (1995). The transition from novice to expert counselor. *Counselor Education and Supervision, 35,* 4–17.

Farber, B. (1983). The effects of psychotherapeutic practice upon the psychotherapists. *Psychotherapy: Theory, Research, and Practice, 20*(2), 174–182.

Farber, B. (1990). Burnout in psychotherapists: Incidence, types, and trends. *Psychology in Private Practice, 8*(1), 35–44.

Farber, B. A., & Heifetz, L. J. (1981). The satisfactions and stresses of psychotherapeutic work: A factor analytic study. *Professional Psychology: Research and Practice, 12,* 621–630.

Firestone, R. W., & Catlett, J. (1999). *Fear of intimacy.* Washington, DC: American Psychological Association.

Fisher, B. L. (1989). Differences between supervision of beginning and advanced therapists: Hogan's hypothesis revisited. *The Clinical Supervisor, 7,* 57–74.

Foa, V. G. (1971). Interpersonal and economic resources. *Science, 171,* 345–351.

Frank, J. D. (1974). Psychotherapy: The restoration of morale. *American Journal of Psychiatry, 131,* 271–274.

Frank, J. D., & Frank, J. B. (1991). *Persuasion and healing* (3rd ed.). Baltimore: Johns Hopkins University Press.

Frankl, V. (1963). *Man's search for meaning.* Boston: Beacon Press.

Freudenberger, H. (1974). Staff burnout. *Journal of Social Work, 30,* 159–165.

Freudenberger, H. J. (1990). Hazards of psychotherapeutic practice. *Psychotherapy in Private Practice, 8*(1), 31–34.

Freudenberger, H. J., & Robbins, A. (1979). The hazards of being a psychoanalyst. *The Psychoanalytic Review, 66*(2), 275–295.

Galluzzo, G. R., & Kacer, B. A. (1991). *The best and worst of high school student teaching.* Paper presented at the annual meeting of the American Educational Research Association, Chicago.

Garfield, C. (1995). *Sometimes my heart goes numb.* San Francisco: Jossey-Bass.

Garfunkel, G. (1995). Lifeline. In M. R. Sussman (Ed.), *A perilous calling: The hazards of psychotherapy practice* (pp. 148–159). New York: John Wiley & Sons.

Gilligan, C. (1982). *In a different voice.* Cambridge, MA: Harvard University Press.

Glaser, R., & Chi, M. T. H. (1988). Overview. In M. T. H. Chi, R. Glaser, & M. J. Farr (Eds.), *The nature of expertise.* Hillsdale, NJ: Erlbaum.

Golden, A. (1997). *Memories of a geisha.* New York: Vintage.

Goldfried, M. R. (1980). Toward the delineation of therapeutic change principles. *American Psychologist, 35,* 991–999.

Goodyear, R. (1981). Termination as a loss experience for the counselor. *Personnel and Guidance Journal, 59,* 347–350.

Grosch, W. N., & Olsen, D. C. (1994). *When helping starts to hurt: A new look at burnout among psychotherapists.* New York: Norton.

Guy, J. (1987). *The personal life of the psychotherapist.* New York: John Wiley & Sons.

Guy, J., Brown, K., & Poelstra, P. (1990). Who gets attacked? A national survey of patient violence directed at psychologists in clinical practice. *Professional Psychology: Research and Practice, 21,* 493–495.

Guy, J., Brown, K., & Poelstra, P. (1992). Safety concerns and protective measures used by psychotherapists. *Professional Psychology: Research and Practice, 23,* 421–423.

Gysbers, N. C., & Henderson, P. (1994). *Developing and managing your school guidance program.* Alexandria, VA: American Counseling Association.

Hagstrom, S. J., Skovholt, T. M., & Rivers, D. A. (1997). The advanced undecided college student: A qualitative study. *NACADA Journal, 17*(2), 23–30.

Hampl, P. (1995). *Burning bright: An anthology of sacred poetry.* New York: Ballantine Books.

Hays, K. F. (1999a, August). Nutrition and exercise: Key components of taking care of yourself. In L. T. Pantano (Chair), *Taking care of yourself: The continuing quest.* Symposium conducted at the annual convention of the American Psychological Association, Boston.

Hays, K. F. (1999b). *Working it out: Using exercise in psychotherapy.* Washington, DC: American Psychological Association.

Heitzmann, D. (1988). Role players. *Journal of Counseling and Development, 67,* 76.

Help for helpers: Daily meditations for counselors. (1989). Center City, MN: Hazelden Foundation.

Heppner, P. P. (1989). Chance and choices in becoming a therapist. In W. Dryden & L. Spurling (Eds.), *On becoming a therapist* (pp. 69–86). New York: Routledge.

Heppner, P. P., & Roehlke, H. J. (1984). Differences among supervisees at different levels of training: Implications for a developmental model of supervision. *Journal of Counseling Psychology, 30,* 252–262.

Hill, L. (1988). From chaos to organization. *Journal of Counseling and Development, 67,* 105.

Holland, J. L. (1985). *Making vocational choices: A theory of vocational personalities and work environments* (2nd ed.). Englewood Cliffs, NJ: Prentice Hall.

Holmes, D. S. (1993). Aerobic fitness and the response to psychological stress. In P. Seraganian (Ed.), *Exercise psychology: The influence of physical exercise on psychological processes* (pp. 39–63). New York: John Wiley & Sons.

Hoshmand, L. T. (1994). *Orientation to inquiry in a reflective professional psychology.* Albany, NY: State University of New York Press.

Internship and Postdoctoral Programs in Professional Psychology. (1994). Washington, DC: Association of Psychology Postdoctoral and Internship Centers.

Jacobson, E. (1929). *Progressive relaxation.* Chicago: University of Chicago Press.

Johnson, N. (1994). *My professional development.* Unpublished, University of Minnesota, Minneapolis.

Johnson, T. H., & Ward, T. (Eds.). (1958). *The letters of Emily Dickinson* (Vol. 2). Cambridge, MA: Belknop Press of Harvard University.

Jourard, S. M., & Landsman, T. (1980). *Healthy personality.* New York: Macmillan.

Karasek, R., & Theorell, T. (1992). *Healthy work: Stress, productivity and the restructuring of working life.* New York: Basic Books.

Kassam-Adams, N. (1995). The risks of treating sexual trauma: Stress and secondary trauma in psychotherapists. In B. H. Stamm (Ed.), *Secondary traumatic stress: Self-care issues for clinicians, researchers, and educators* (pp. 37–48). Lutherville, MD: Sidran Press.

Kendrick, R., Chandler, J., & Hatcher, W. (1994). Job demands, stressors and the school counselor. *The School Counselor, 41,* 365–369.

Kiecolt-Glaser, J. K., & Glaser, R. (1989). Caregiving, mental health and immune function. In E. Light & B. D. Lebowitz (Eds.), *Alzheimer's disease and family stress* (pp. 245–266). Washington, DC: U.S. Department of Health and Human Services.

Kinnetz, P. L. (1988). Saving myself vs. serving clients. *Journal of Counseling and Development, 67,* 87.

Kohlberg, L. (1979). *Measuring moral judgment.* Worcester, MA: Clark University Press.

Kokotovic, A. M., & Tracey, T. J. (1990). Working alliance in the early phase of counseling. *Journal of Counseling Psychology, 37,* 16–21.

Kram, K. (1985). *Mentoring at work: Developmental relationships in organizational life.* Glenville, IL: Scott, Foresman.

Kramen-Kahn, B., & Hansen, N. D. (1998). Rafting the rapids: Occupational hazards, rewards and coping strategies of psychotherapists. *Professional Psychology: Research and Practice, 29,* 130–134.

Kushner, H. S. (1996). *How good do we have to be? A new understanding of guilt and forgiveness.* Boston: Little, Brown & Co.

Ladany, N., Hill, C. E., Corbett, M. M., & Nutt, E. A. (1996). Nature, extent, and importance of what psychotherapy trainees do not disclose to their supervisors. *Journal of Counseling Psychology, 43*(1), 10–24.

Lange, S. (1988). Critical incidents aren't accidents. *Journal of Counseling and Development, 67,* 109.

Larson, D. G. (1993). *The helper's journey.* Champaign, IL: Research Press.

Lasch, C. (1978). *The culture of narcissism.* New York: Norton.

Levinson, D., Darrow, D., Klein, E., Levinson, M., & McKee, R. (1978). *The seasons of a man's life.* New York: Ballantine Books.

Lieberman, M. A., Yalom, I. D., & Miles, M. B. (1973). *Encounter groups: First facts.* New York: Basic Books.

Lief, H. I., & Fox, R. C. (1963). Training for "detached concern" in medical students. In H. I. Lief, V. I. Lief, & N. R. Lief (Eds.), *The psychological basis of medical practice.* New York: Harper and Row.

Lindbergh, A. M. (1975). *Gift from the sea.* New York: Pantheon Books.

Linville, M. (1988). The long afternoon. *Journal of Counseling and Development, 67,* 101.

Lisle, L. (1987). *Portrait of an artist: A biography of Georgia O'Keeffe.* Albuquerque, NM: University of New Mexico Press.

Luborsky, L., Crits-Christoph, P., Mintz, J., & Auerbach, A. (1988). *Who will benefit from psychotherapy? Predicting therapeutic outcomes.* New York: Basic Books.

Luborsky, L., McLellan, A. T., Woody, G. E., O'Brien, C. P., & Auerbach, A. (1985). Therapist success and its determinants. *Archives of General Psychiatry, 42,* 602–611.

Lynch, J. J. (1979). *The broken heart: The medical consequences of loneliness.* New York: Basic Books.

Maclay, E. (1977). *Green winter: Celebrations of later life.* New York: Readers Digest Press.

Maggio, R. (1997). *Quotations from women on life.* Paramus, NJ: Prentice-Hall.

Mahoney, M. J. (1997). Psychotherapists' personal problems and self-care patterns. *Professional Psychology: Research and Practice, 28*(1), 14–16.

Majeski, T. (1996, August 6). Hospital turns a corner. *St. Paul Pioneer Press*, pp. 1A, 5A.

Mallinckrodt, B. (1991). Clients' representations of childhood emotional bonds with parents, social support and formation of the working alliance. *Journal of Counseling Psychology, 38*, 401–409.

Mallinckrodt, B. (1992). Childhood emotional bonds with parents, development of adult social competencies, and availability of social support. *Journal of Counseling Psychology, 39*, 453–461.

Mallinckrodt, B., & Bennett, J. (1992). Social support and the impact of job loss in dislocated blue-collar workers. *Journal of Counseling Psychology, 39*, 482–489.

Martin, J., Slemon, A. G., Hiebert, B., Halberg, E. T., & Cummings, A. L. (1989). Conceptualizations of novice and experienced counselors. *Journal of Counseling Psychology, 36*, 395–400.

Maslach, C. (1982). *Burnout: The cost of caring.* Englewood Cliffs, NJ: Prentice-Hall.

Maslach, C., & Jackson, S. E. (1981). *The Maslach Burnout Inventory.* Palo Alto, CA: Consulting Psychologists Press.

Maslach, C., & Leiter, M. P. (1997). *The truth about burnout.* San Francisco: Jossey-Bass.

Maslow, A. H. (1968). *Toward a psychology of being.* New York: Van Nostrand Reinhold.

May, R. (1969). *Love and will.* New York: Norton.

Mayeroff, M. (1990). *On caring.* New York: Harper Perennial.

McCann, L., & Pearlman, L. A. (1990). Vicarious traumatization: A theoretical framework for understanding the psychological effects of working with victims. *Journal of Traumatic Stress, 3*, 131–149.

McCarthy, P., Kulakowski, D., & Kenfield, J. A. (1994). Clinical supervision practices of licensed psychologists. *Professional Psychology: Research and Practice, 25*(2), 177–181.

McConnell, E. A. (Ed.). (1982). *Burnout in the nursing profession.* St. Louis: Mosby.

Mead, G. H. (1934). *Mind, self and society* (C. W. Morris, Ed.). Chicago: University of Chicago Press.

Milbouer, S. (1999, August 21). Social worker slain outside client's home. *Boston Globe*, pp. B1–B2.

Mitchell, K. R., & Anderson, H. (1983). *All our losses, all our griefs: Resources for pastoral care.* Louisville, KY: Westminster, John Knox.

Molassiotis, A., & Haberman, M. (1996). Evaluation of burnout and job satisfaction in marrow and transplant nurses. *Cancer Nursing, 19*, 360–367.

Monsour, T. (1996, April 20). Teacher's award carries her to White House. *St. Paul Pioneer Press*, pp. 1A, 3A.

Montagu, A. (1974). *The natural superiority of women.* New York: Collier Books.

Moreland, L. (1993). Learning cycle. *Family Therapy Networker*, May/June, 13.

Morton, L. L., Vesco, R., Williams, N. H., & Awender, M. A. (1997). Student teacher anxieties related to class management, pedagogy, evaluation and staff relations. *British Journal of Educational Psychology, 67*, 69–89.

Naisbitt, J. (1984). *Megatrends: Ten new directions transforming our lives.* New York: Warner Books.

Neufeldt, S. A. (1999). *Supervision strategies for the first practicum* (2nd ed.). Alexandria, VA: American Counseling Association.

Neufeldt, S. A., Karno, M. P., & Nelson, M. L. (1996). A qualitative study of experts' conceptualization of supervisee reflectivity. *Journal of Counseling Psychology, 43*(1), 3–9.

Neusner, J. (Trans.). (1984). *Torah from our sages.* Dallas: Rossel Books. (Original work approximately 900 A.D.)

Newman, J. L., & Fuqua, D. R. (1988). A comparative study of positive and negative modeling in counselor training. *Counselor Education and Supervision, 28,* 121–129.

Norcross, J. C., & Freedheim, D. K. (1992). Into the future: Retrospect and prospect in psychotherapy. In D. K. Freedheim (Ed.), *History of psychotherapy: A century of change.* Washington, DC: American Psychological Association.

Olson, D. H. (2000). Circumplex model of marital and family functioning. *Journal of Family Therapy, 22*(2), 144–167.

Otto, R. K., & Schmidt, W. C. (1991). Malpractice in verbal psychotherapy: Problems and potential solutions. *Forensic Reports, 4,* 309–339.

Palmer, P. J. (1998). *The courage to teach: Exploring the inner landscape of a teacher's life.* San Francisco: Jossey-Bass.

Pearlman, L. A. (1995). Self-care for trauma therapists: Ameliorating vicarious traumatization. In B. H. Stamm (Ed.), *Secondary traumatic stress: Self-care issues for clinicians, researchers, and educators* (pp. 51–64). Lutherville, MD: Sidran Press.

Pearlman, L. A., & MacIan, P. S. (1995). Vicarious traumatization: An empirical study of the effects of trauma work on trauma therapists. *Professional Psychology: Research and Practice, 26,* 558–565.

Peck, M. S. (1978). *The road less traveled: A new psychology of love, traditional values and spiritual growth.* New York: Simon & Schuster.

Perry, W. G. (1981). Cognitive and ethical growth: The making of meaning. In W. Chickering & Associates (Eds.), *The modern American college* (pp. 76–116). San Francisco: Jossey-Bass.

Piaget, J. (1972). Intellectual evolution from adolescence to adulthood. *Human Development, 15,* 1–12.

Pica, M. (1998). The ambiguous nature of clinical training and its impact on the development of student clinicians. *Psychotherapy, 35,* 361–365.

Pilpay. (1872). *The fables of Pilpay.* New York: Hurd and Houghton.

Pincus, S. (1997). Recognizing your emotional vulnerabilities. In J. Kottler (Ed.), *Finding your way as a counselor* (pp. 59–61). Alexandria, VA: American Counseling Association.

Pines, A., & Aronson, E. (1988). *Career burnout: Cause and cures.* New York: Free Press.

Pistole, C. (1999). Caregiving in attachment relationships: A perspective for counselors. *Journal of Counseling and Development, 77,* 437–446.

Plante, T. G. (1993). Aerobic exercise in prevention and treatment of psychopathology. In P. Seraganian (Ed.), *Exercise psychology: The influence of physical exercise on psychological processes* (pp. 358–379). New York: John Wiley & Sons.

Pohl, M., Kay, D., & Toft, D. (1990). *The caregiver's journey.* Center City, MN: Hazelden Foundation.

Pollack, S. K. (1988). Grieving and growing. *Journal of Counseling and Development, 67,* 117.

Pope, K. S., & Tabachnick, B. G. (1994). Therapists as patients: A national survey of psychologists' experiences, problems and beliefs. *Professional Psychology: Research and Practice, 25,* 247–258.

Pope, K., & Vasquez, M. (1991). *Ethics in psychotherapy and counseling*. San Francisco: Jossey-Bass.

Prochaska, J. O. (1999). How do people change, and how can we change to help more people? In M. A. Hubble, B. A. Duncan, & S. M. Miller (Eds.), *The heart and soul of change: What works in therapy* (pp. 227–255). Washington, DC: American Psychological Association.

Prochaska, J. O., DiClemente, C. C., & Norcross, J. C. (1992). In search of how people change: Applications to addictive behavior. *American Psychologist, 47*(9), 1102–1114.

Radeke, J. T., & Mahoney, M. J. (2000). Comparing the personal lives of psychotherapists and research psychologists. *Professional Psychology: Research and Practice, 31*, 82–84.

Raimy, V. C. (Ed.). (1950). *Training in clinical psychology*. Upper Saddle River, NJ: Prentice Hall.

Readings book. (n.d.). Minneapolis: Voyageur Outward Bound School (P.O. Box 450, Ely, MN 55731).

Reissman, F. (1965). The "helper" therapy principle. *Social Work, 10*, 27–32.

Rittner, C., & Myers, S. (Eds.). (1986). *The courage to care*. New York: New York University Press.

Roberts, C. A. (1986). Burnout: Psychobabble, or a valuable concept? *British Journal of Hospital Medicine, 36*, 194–197.

Robiner, W. N., Fuhrman, M., & Ristvedt, S. (1993). Evaluation difficulties in supervising psychology interns. *Clinical Psychologist, 46,* 3–13.

Robinson, B. E. (1992). *Overdoing it: How to slow down and take care of yourself*. Deerfield Beach, FL: Health Communications.

Rodolfa, E. R., Kraft, W. A., & Reilley, R. R. (1988). Stressors of professionals and trainees at APA-approved counseling and V. A. Medical Center internship sites. *Professional Psychology: Research and Practice, 19*, 43–49.

Rogers, C. (1961). *On becoming a person*. Boston: Houghton Mifflin.

Rogers, C. R. (1995). *A way of being*. Boston: Houghton Mifflin.

Rønnestad, M. H. (1977). The effect of modeling, feedback, and experiential methods on counselor empathy. *Counselor Education and Supervision, 17*, 194–201.

Rønnestad, M. H., & Skovholt, T. M. (1991). En modell for profesjonell utvikling og stagnasjon hos terapeuter og radgivere [A model of the professional development and stagnation of therapists and counselors]. *Tidsskrift for Norsk Psykologforening [Journal of the Norwegian Psychological Association], 28*, 555–567. (In Norwegian)

Rønnestad, M. H., & Skovholt, T. M. (1993). Supervision of beginning and advanced graduate students in counseling and psychotherapy. *Journal of Counseling and Development, 71*, 396–405.

Rønnestad, M. H., & Skovholt, T. M. (1997). Die professionelle entwicklund und supervision von psychotherapeuten/psychotherapeutinnen [Professional development and supervision of psychotherapists]. *Der Psychotherapeut, 42*, 299–306. (In German)

Rønnestad, M. H., & Skovholt, T. M. (1999). Om terapeuters profesjonelle utvikling og psykoterapiveiledning I et utviklingspersopektiv [Psychotherapists' professional development and psychotherapy supervision in a developmental perspective]. In M. H. Rønnestad & S. Reichelt (Eds.), *Psykoterapiveiledning [Psychotherapy supervision]* (pp. 71–102). Oslo: Tano Aschehoug. (In Norwegian)

Rønnestad, M. H., & Skovholt, T. M. (2000). *Learning arenas for professional development: Retrospective accounts of senior psychotherapists.* Submitted to *Professional Psychology: Research & Practice.*

Ruddick, S. (1989). *Maternal thinking: Toward a politics of peace.* Boston: Beacon Press.

Rupp, J. (1994). *Little pieces of light.* Mahwah, NJ: Paulist Press.

Saakvitne, K. W. (1999, August). *Therapists at risk: How psychotherapy threatens your well-being.* Presented at the annual convention of the American Psychological Association, Boston.

Sammons, M. T., & Gravitz, M. A. (1990). Theoretical orientation of professional psychologists and their former professors. *Professional Psychology: Research and Practice, 21,* 131–134.

Samples, P. (1991). *Self-care for caregivers.* Center City, MN: Hazelden Foundation.

Schafer, W. (1996). *Stress management for wellness.* Fort Worth: Harcourt Brace College Publishers.

Schelske, M. T., & Romano, J. L. (1994). Coping skills and classroom management training for student teachers. *The Teacher Educator, 29,* 21–33.

Schoefield, W. (1974). *Psychotherapy: The purchase of friendship.* Englewood Cliffs, NJ: Prentice-Hall.

Schön, D. A. (1983). *The reflective practitioner.* New York: Basic Books.

Schön, D. A. (1987). *Educating the reflective practitioner.* San Francisco: Jossey-Bass.

Schor, J. (1998). *The overspent American.* New York: Basic Books.

Schorr, M. (1997). On being a wounded healer. In J. Kottler (Ed.), *Finding your way as a counselor* (pp. 55–58). Alexandria, VA: American Counseling Association.

Schulz, R., Biegel, D., Morycz, R., & Visintainer, P. (1989). Psychological paradigms for understanding caregiving. In E. Light & B. D. Lebowitz (Eds.), *Alzheimer's disease and family stress* (pp. 106–121). Washington, DC: U.S. Department of Health and Human Services.

Schweitzer, A. (1975). In Readers Digest Treasury of Modern Quotations. NY: Readers Digest Press.

Selye, H. (1974). *Stress without distress.* New York: Signet.

Sexton, T. L., & Whiston, S. C. (1994). The status of the counseling relationship: An empirical review, theoretical implications, and research directions. *The Counseling Psychologist, 22(1),* 6–78.

Skinner, B. F. (1953). *Science and human behavior.* New York: Macmillan.

Skovholt, T. M. (1974). The client as helper: A means to promote personal growth. *The Counseling Psychologist, 4(3),* 56–64.

Skovholt, T. M. (1986, Spring). Learning to teach. In *Focus: On teaching and learning.* Minneapolis, MN: Office of Educational Development, University of Minnesota.

Skovholt, T. M. (1988). Searching for reality. *The Counseling Psychologist, 16,* 282–287.

Skovholt, T. M., & D'Rozario, V. (2000). Portraits of outstanding and inadequate teachers in Singapore: The impact of emotional intelligence. *Teaching & Learning, 40(1),* 9–17.

Skovholt, T. M., & McCarthy, P. R. (Eds.). (1988). Critical incidents in counselor development [special issue]. *Journal of Counseling and Development, 67,* 69–135.

Skovholt, T. M., Morgan, J., & Cunningham, H. N. (1989). Mental imagery in career counseling and life planning: A review of research and intervention methods. *Journal of Counseling and Development, 67,* 287–291.

Skovholt, T. M., & Rønnestad, M. H. (1995). *The evolving professional self: Stages and themes in therapist and counselor development.* New York: John Wiley & Sons.

Skovholt, T. M., Rønnestad, M. H., & Jennings, L. (1997). Searching for expertise in counseling, psychotherapy, and professional psychology. *Educational Psychology Review, 9*(4), 361–369.

Slater, P. (1980). *The pursuit of loneliness.* Boston: Beacon Press.

Smetanka, M. J. (1992, November 6). Burnout vaccine: Institute gives teachers a shot of enthusiasm. *Minneapolis Star Tribune,* p. 1B.

Smiley, J. (1991). *A thousand acres.* New York: Ivy Books.

Smyth, J. M., Stone, A. A., & Itenewitz, A. N. (1999). Effects of writing about stressful experiences on symptom reduction in patients with asthma or Rheumatoid Arthritis. *JAMA, 281*(14), 1304–1309.

Söderfeldt, M., Söderfeldt, B., & Warg, L. E. (1995). Burnout in social work. *Social Work, 40,* 638–646.

Stamm, B. H. (1995). Preface. In B. H. Stamm (Ed.), *Secondary traumatic stress: Self-care issues for clinicians, researchers, and educators* (pp. ix–xii). Lutherville, MD: Sidran Press.

Stanley, T. J., & Danko, W. D. (1996). *The millionaire next door.* New York: Pocket Books.

Stone, G. L. (1988). The heroic syndrome. *Journal of Counseling and Development, 67,* 108.

Strupp, H. H., & Hadley, S. W. (1978). Specific vs. non-specific factors in psychotherapy: A controlled study of outcomes. *Archives of General Psychiatry, 36,* 1125–1136.

Sussman, M. B. (Ed.). (1995). *A perilous calling: The hazards of psychotherapy practice.* New York: John Wiley & Sons.

Tarasoff v. Regents of the University of California. 118 Cal. Rptr. 129, 529 P 2d 533 (1974)

Thorson, T. (1994). *Reflections on practice.* Unpublished manuscript, Minneapolis, MN.

Torrence, P. (1996). The culture and mentoring series. In A. M. Soliman, *Mentoring relationships in the Arab culture.* Athens, GA: Georgia Studies of Creative Behavior.

van Merriënboer, J. J. G., Jelsma, O., & Paas, F. G. W. C. (1992). Training for reflective expertise: A four-component instructional design model for complex cognitive skills. *Educational Technology Research and Development, 40,* 23–43.

Viorst, J. (1998). *Necessary losses: The loves, illusions, dependencies, and impossible expectations that all of us have to give up in order to grow.* New York: Fireside.

Walsh, D. (1988). To publish or not to publish: That is the question. *Journal of Counseling and Development, 67,* 88.

Wampold, B. E., Mondin, G. W., Moody, M., & Stich, F. (1997). A meta-analysis of outcome studies comparing bona fide psychotherapies: Empirically "all must have prizes." *Psychological Bulletin, 122,* 203–215.

Warner, C. (1992). Chinese Proverb. *Dictionary of Women's Quotations.* Englewood Cliffs, NJ: Prentice Hall.

Ward, C. C., & House, R. M. (1998). Counseling supervision: A reflective model. *Counselor Education and Supervision, 38,* 23–33.

Wells, M., Glickauf-Hughes, C., & Bruss, K. (1998). The relationship of co-dependency to enduring personality characteristics. *Journal of College Student Psychotherapy, 12*(3), 25–38.

Wentzel, K. R. (1997). Student motivation in middle school: The role of perceived pedagogical caring. *Journal of Educational Psychology, 87,* 411–419.

Wesley, T. (1979). *Oxford Dictionary of Quotations.* Oxford, England (p. 568).

Wessells, D. T., Kutscher, A. H., Seeland, I. B., Selder, F. E., Cherico, D. J., & Clark, E. J. (Eds.). (1989). *Professional burnout in medicine and the helping professions.* New York: Haworth Press.

Williamson, C. (1975). Waterfall. On *the changer and the changed* [Record]. Oakland, CA: Olivia Records, Inc.

Winnicott, D. W. (1965). *The maturational processes and the facilitating environment.* New York: International Universities Press.

Woolf, V. (1990). *A moment's liberty: The short diary* (A. O. Bell, Ed.). San Diego: Harcourt Brace Jovanovich.

Worthen, V., & McNeill, B. W. (1996). A phenomenological investigation of "good" supervision events. *Journal of Counseling Psychology, 43*(1), 25–34.

Yalom, I. D. (1985). *The theory and practice of group psychotherapy* (3rd ed.). New York: Basic Books.

Young, M. E. (1997). How to avoid becoming a zombie. In J. Kottler (Ed.), *Finding your way as a counselor* (pp. 45–48). Alexandria, VA: American Counseling Association.

Zeh, J. B. (1988). Counseling behind closed doors: How safe? *Journal of Counseling and Development, 67,* 89.

Zeigler, J. N., Kanas, N., Strull, W. M., & Bennet, N. E. (1984). A stress discussion group for medical interns. *Journal of Medical Education, 59,* 205–207.

Index